THE END OF THE PARTY

How Fianna Fáil Lost its Grip on Power

BRUCE ARNOLD
AND JASON O'TOOLE ∾

Gill & Macmillan

Gill & Macmillan
Hume Avenue, Park West, Dublin 12
with associated companies throughout the world
www.gillmacmillan.ie

© Bruce Arnold and Jason O'Toole 2011
978 07171 5064 9

Typography design by Make Communication
Print origination by O'K Graphic Design, Dublin
Printed by ScandBook AB, Sweden

This book is typeset in 12/15 pt Minion

The paper used in this book is made from the wood
pulp of managed forests. For every tree felled, at least
one tree is planted, thereby renewing natural resources.

A CIP catalogue record for this book is available from
the British Library.

5 4 3 2 1

CONTENTS

ACKNOWLEDGMENTS

The authors would like to thank our editor, Tess Tattersall, for her invaluable input into the book; Gill & Macmillan and our publisher, Fergal Tobin, for his enthusiasm for the project. We thank our literary agent, Jonathan Williams, for his all hard efforts with this, our first book together. As working journalists we have had help from colleagues and would like to thank in particular Eddie Cunningham and the *Irish Independent* News Analysis team, John Drennan, Paul Drury and Senan Moloney. Many others have given help who have asked to remain anonymous. Without their help it would not have been possible to complete the book.

Jason O'Toole would like to thank his editor Eric Bailey, editor in chief Eric Bell, editor of the *Irish Daily Mail* Conor O'Donnell and editor of the *Irish Mail on Sunday* Sebastian Hamilton for their help and encouragement; Frank McGarry, Darren Kinsella and Noel Taylor for their help. And finally he would also like to say a big thank you to his wife Agnieszka and daughter Marianne for their support.

Bruce Arnold would like to thank his family and friends for support and encouragement.

PROLOGUE

Fianna Fáil was dominant in Irish politics for the greater part of the 20th century and governed Ireland throughout the first decade of the 21st century. Founded in 1926, the party first came to power in 1932 under Eamon de Valera and formed successive governments for a 16-year period until 1948. There were two cross-party administrations, led by Fine Gael, from 1948 to 1951, and again from 1954 to 1957, both headed by a compromise figure, John A. Costello. Then Fianna Fáil returned to power, again for a 16-year period, under the unbroken sequential leadership of Eamon de Valera, Seán Lemass and Jack Lynch. During this 40-year period, from 1932 until 1973, whether in office or in Opposition, Fianna Fáil remained the central force in Irish political life, its leaders powerful and respected figures who shaped the State in most of its essentials.

Fianna Fáil was the principal legatee party of the Irish national independence revolution and this shaped its thinking and its policies. This was not exclusively beneficial. There was an authoritarian narrowness in the outlook and the national vision the party dispensed. But to a majority of people throughout most of these years, the party was a product of the central and fundamental achievement of representing the revolutionary dream and the reality of independence after being governed for centuries by Britain. In this it paralleled other legatee national independence parties, such as the Congress Party of India. Fianna Fáil's hold on power was underpinned by supposedly bedrock principles, such as the restoration of the Irish language and the reunification of the country. Again, it has to be assumed these were supported by a largely stable 50 per cent of the population who maintained the party's hold on power.

This predominant position allowed Fianna Fáil to create and sustain the rivalry that became a firm but puzzling political reality, that of two right-wing political movements—Fianna Fáil and Fine Gael—that never sat down together to consider a possibly closer relationship. Instead, they went forward in politics without any sustained or deep attempt to move on social reform and the development of a more equal and forward-looking legislative programme. This was a product of a 'Third Force' in Ireland's political life, the Roman Catholic Church.

Both movements recognised, accepted and then became subservient to the power held and often remorselessly exercised by this organisation. The Church held its own version of power virtually until the end of the 20th century. It had always been a political movement, increasingly so in the 19th century when it became allied to the revolutionary view of politics aimed at independence from Britain. This gave it great political strength in the life of the country, binding other political organisations to its extreme conservatism. While most European countries where the dominant faith was Catholic moved on to the secularisation of power, Ireland managed to sustain the central role of the Church in social, health and sexual affairs to a degree that invaded human rights and shaped legislation. The rigidity between the two main political groupings, both of them in subservience to the Church on important matters, severely held back change and reform. That the Church played no serious part in the narrative of this book resulted from its widespread disgrace and shaming over child abuse, rendering it a marginal force for the first time in its history. Other political parties tended to be on the fringes of political life, enjoying brief periods in power as partners or supporters of Fine Gael.

Fianna Fáil as the party of industrial progress drew strength from its programme of national industrial development in the 1930s. Before Independence, the Westminster Government policy had not financed industrial development on the scale achieved for example in Northern Ireland. Seeking to obtain full political independence was, in Fianna Fáil thinking under de Valera, reinforced by his economic and industrial strategies and greatly aided by Lemass's brand of economic pragmatism. The idea of independence being framed by a modernising programme of economic activity was made more real still by his nationalist determination to remove the insignia of the Crown, the oath of allegiance and the post of Governor General. A positive alternative inspired the adoption of de Valera's 1937 Constitution. This was debated for a year and then passed into law by referendum, thereby asserting the sovereignty of the Irish people as the basis of that law. Fianna Fáil was also the party that kept Ireland out of World War II, supported by the vast majority of citizens at the time. All this made the loss of sovereignty here recorded, as the European Union took over control of the economy, even more astonishing in that it was surrendered by the party that had created it and made it strong.

Already dominated by threads of social and moral conservatism, it was hardly surprising that Ireland also became economically more conservative and, in due course, its exploitation of wealth and the control of business enterprise and capital investment moved into the hands of a small number of entrepreneurs and businessmen who found a natural alliance with the Fianna Fáil party. This was later encouraged by the new generation of politicians who succeeded Seán Lemass, including his son-in-law, Charles Haughey, and like-minded figures in the party such as Donogh O'Malley. The ethos created in the decade of the 1960s gave birth to Taca, a semi-secret fund-raising body of Irish businessmen essentially sympathetic to Fianna Fáil.

It was only a matter of time before this approach degenerated into a morally and administratively questionable alliance between the party and a small and select new class of wealthy people. The step from this to the Fianna Fáil party becoming a mass patronage machine, involved in planning, development and the brown-envelope culture of more recent years, was a relatively short one. The privileged became the guests of the Fianna Fáil party tent at the Galway Races in July.

The break point for this change in the life of Fianna Fáil came when Charles Haughey succeeded Jack Lynch in 1979. Far from his takeover being the success story his succession was meant to bring to the fortunes of the party, assuring further electoral victories after the Lynch landslide of 1977, it produced an indifferent series of electoral catastrophes for Haughey, paralleled by failure to act on economic difficulties. He lost his first election. He achieved a brief and unstable administration on the backs of former revolutionaries. After a full term of Fine Gael and Labour in power under Garret FitzGerald, Haughey regained power in a minority administration dependent on a mixed bag of supporters. He then called an unnecessary election that led to a formal coalition with the party's greatest critic, Desmond O'Malley, who had formed a new political party, the Progressive Democrats. During his entire political career Haughey's great wealth was never explained. After his career ended, his life was blighted by revelations of entirely improper receipt of large sums of money and by his acts of perjury about this. His public ruin was great and humiliating.

Bertie Ahern, his loyal political lieutenant throughout his periods in office and in Opposition, did not immediately succeed him. Albert Reynolds did. When Ahern took over in 1994, he became the party's most notable success story, achieving three successive terms in power, unprecedented apart from de Valera's electoral record. Ahern rode on the tide of prosperity and on the commitment he made to eradicate from political life the kind of errors of judgment that Haughey had been accused of in the tribunal of investigation under Mr Justice Brian McCracken, a model for all tribunals, though followed by none. The events in this book begin at this point, as Bertie Ahern became enmeshed in shabby dealings that were revealed by the Mahon Tribunal, and was ousted by the man he had 'anointed' as his successor, Brian Cowen. Brian Cowen faced a sea of problems for which he was ill-equipped and ill-prepared. This book is really the Cowen story; it tells of how he failed, leading the party into political oblivion.

He was leading an 'all-class' party representing the economic interests of Ireland's manufacturing and business class, sections of the new professional class (especially public servants), the bulk of small farmers, as well as many employees and some members of the working class. Brian Lenihan Snr once said: 'We are the Labour Party of Ireland,' a view later expressed by Bertie Ahern, who declared himself to be the only socialist in the Dáil. How Fianna Fáil lost all these political relationships is also part of the story.

Significantly, however, pain and damage came from outside and from a reckless and irresponsible interpretation by Fianna Fáil of its rights and responsibilities within the changed circumstances of being part of the Eurozone and subject to the enhanced powers of the EU and the European Central Bank (ECB). Further to this and as a direct result of Ireland's capacities to influence and threaten the stability of the wider Eurozone, the international concerns of the International

Monetary Fund and of other global organisations became a growing encroachment on Ireland's political and economic life. The country had benefited hugely from European funding in the early days of membership, firstly of the EEC, then of the European Community and later the EU, at a time when the Union was small and Ireland occupied a favoured place, needing and deserving subventions. This changed radically with enlargement. However, the change failed to exercise or even introduce the restraints that the economy needed and the days of the Celtic Tiger saw Ireland running out of control.

Fianna Fáil was quite out of character in its totally uncritical adoption of ultra-Europeanism. What de Valera had created, in terms of national independence and a certain European isolationism, was abandoned in a carefree and irresponsible manner. There remained the partial exception of a pretended concern for 'Irish neutrality'. This was no more than a tattered rag, designed to keep its more traditionally inclined members and voters happy. It was valid so long as Brussels was a source of easy money and more patronage, through the Common Agricultural Policy, the EU Regional Fund, the Social Fund and other sources of 'free' money. Albert Reynolds won for Ireland undreamed of EU millions at the 1992 Edinburgh Summit. This bought from us espousal of, and loyalty to, the Maastricht Treaty on European Union and what was to follow, its plan for a euro currency. This was greeted by Fianna Fáil with foolish and irresponsible support for joining the euro. Ireland was not obliged to join then. It could have waited, along with Britain, to see whether they would participate, which the State's closest neighbour and largest trading partner wisely decided not to do. No one, of course, could have predicted it, but this besotted espousal of a currency change that did not serve Irish trading interests contained the seeds for the catastrophic collapse in its judgment within Fianna Fáil, leading to a precipitate loss of power.

The crisis in the advanced economies from 2007/8 onwards did not cause a complete collapse, but has led to a major recession in the more developed economies, which threatened—and still threatens—to turn into a lengthy depression. The recession arose from the bursting of big asset bubbles in the USA and the Eurozone, bubbles that had been blown up by unsuitably low interest rates in the years before.

The response to the impending crisis has been to throw public money at the banks in the USA, and in the EU for the private bank debts to be imposed on taxpayers. In the USA lots of private banks have been let go bust, beginning with Lehmans. In the EU only two banks have gone bust so far, and they are small ones outside the Eurozone. There has been no bank failure in the Eurozone area to date—a truly extraordinary fact, because ECB policy opposes that.

Fianna Fáil—and Ireland—have suffered by joining the Eurozone. Ireland has done three foolish things: adopted the currency of an area with which the country does only one-third of its trade, exports and imports combined; adopted an interest rate regime that suited the big countries but did not suit Ireland; and put the country under the control of the ECB—from which the blanket Bank Guarantee of September 2008 and the enforced bailout of November 2010 both stemmed.

In the early 2000s Fianna Fáil behaved as if there would be cheap money for ever. This cheap money was provided by foreign EU banks that lent to Irish ones in order for them to help in the buying of Irish property. The Fianna Fáil party did not realise that the true logic of a monetary union with Germany was that the Irish should behave like Germans. Instead, Irish men and women behaved with prodigal extravagance and no concern for the morrow.

The story outlined in the following pages covers the blanket Bank Guarantee given by Brian Cowen and Brian Lenihan on the night of 28/29 September 2008. This was carried out within the ECB's policy guidelines and was guided by direct intervention by the bank's leader. The State could not have given that guarantee without ECB approval. It was fair and sensible in the circumstances to guarantee depositors in the banks up to a limit. The horrendous error was to guarantee bank creditors/bondholders, especially in Anglo Irish Bank. These were mainly the foreign banks. They had lent hugely to the Irish banks during the boom, for on-lending to the Irish property market.

The nation became a pawn at this stage and Fianna Fáil was blown by the harsh international winds of chance, their force and direction dictated from Brussels, Washington, Frankfurt. The American and world dimension of Ireland's eccentric economic path, which went beyond the relatively comfortable ECB's zone of control, should not be overlooked. Under Democratic administrations, the Americans are much more EU-oriented than when the Republicans are in charge. This has been so from the beginning of the transition through the European Economic Community, the European Community and finally the European Union. This has been especially the case since the euro currency was established. Wall Street was never happy with the euro, and it has especially distrusted the pretensions of the Eurocrats that the euro would become an international reserve currency comparable to the US dollar and might actually displace the latter in time. The Americans have also been worried about the budget deficit and bank crisis in the EU PIIGS (Portugal, Ireland, Italy, Greece, Spain) States. This is because American banks were also engaged in lending to Eurozone banks during the property bubble, but more importantly because the Credit Default Swaps (CDSS) that are normally taken out by investors and bondholders in EU banks as insurance against default are substantially underwritten by US companies like AIG (American International Group). If EU banks go bust, these CDSS will be called in by the burned bondholders and American banks and insurance companies that have insured those bonds will be badly hit.

In spring 2010 when the Greek crisis led to the first EU bailout, with the establishment of the three-year temporary EU Stabilisation Facility to rescue Greece, Barack Obama was reported as having phoned Angela Merkel to express concern that EU banks would be hit unless something like this was done, and American banks would indirectly suffer as a consequence. According to economist Morgan Kelly—and no one has denied it—US Treasury Secretary Tim Geithner vetoed any 'haircut' being imposed on bondholders who had lent to the Irish banks, even though Ajai Chopra and the IMF negotiators were sympathetic to this idea. As Kelly put it in his *Irish Times* piece on 7 May 2011: 'At a conference call with the G7 finance ministers, the haircut was vetoed by Timothy Geithner, who, as his payment of $13 billion from government-owned AIG to Goldman Sachs showed, believes that bankers take priority over taxpayers.'

It may be worth noting that when the IMF, as international lender of last resort, is asked for a loan by some desperate country, its prescriptions normally are three-fold: to cut public spending, to raise taxes and to devalue the currency. This last is in order to establish economic competitiveness, encourage exports and thereby earn foreign exchange with which to pay off public debts. The last-mentioned is of course precluded as regards the Eurozone unless the IMF was to say that the Eurozone member countries, or just the PIIGS, should re-establish their national currencies. Dominique Strauss-Kahn was certainly not going to advocate the latter course, as an aspiring president of France. In 2010, when the IMF agreed to help out with the first EU bailout for Greece, Strauss-Kahn virtually imposed this policy on his own. He was strongly criticised for doing so by some of his fellow directors on the IMF board. To ensure that the IMF played ball with the ECB as regards the EU bailout money is the reason why the EU bureaucrats were so anxious to have Christine Lagarde as the new IMF boss. That is why Michael Portillo expressed surprise that her first public statement on hearing she had got her new job was that the IMF must help out the euro and the Eurozone. This is not of course the function of a body that has 150 or so members. But it accords with current US Government policy, which is why the Americans backed Lagarde for her new job. She would not have got it if the Americans had been against her. It is questionable whether the Irish Government ever grasped these subtleties or openly developed them as adjuncts of public policy.

During the period we cover, Fianna Fáil engaged in a love affair with the public sector trade unions through the 'social partnership' arrangements. These prevailed from 1987 onwards. Unfortunately, the trade union movement in Ireland and internationally has become ever more concentrated on the public sectors, which are overwhelmingly unionised—only a quarter or so of Irish private sector workers are. This had led to highly privileged and well-paid public sector workers, especially in the public service, notably teachers, policemen, health workers. The public sector pension situation is a principal embodiment of this. One can link this aspect of things to the patronage-oriented corporatist-club instincts of the modern Fianna Fáil party. They have been shared and followed by the Labour Party. Most workers and employees, however, have, until this election, traditionally voted Fianna Fáil. By February 2011 all this had changed. Where will they go in future? That is an important question.

On the night of the infamous blanket guarantee, Brian Lenihan, then newly appointed as Finance Minister and, as a lawyer, not well-versed in economics, was confronted by two of his principal seniors at the Irish Bar—both sympathetic to the banks: Dermot Gleeson as chairman of AIB and Paul Gallagher SC as Fianna Fáil Attorney General.

Gallagher would have told the two Brians, Cowen and Lenihan, that it was wrong in Irish law to draw any distinction between bank depositors and bank creditors and bondholders. This meant that they all should be bailed out. This happy legal fiction suited powerful interests and accorded with ECB policy. The same Gallagher advised the Fianna Fáil Government that there was no need for an Irish referendum on the proposed amendment to the EU Treaties permitting the establishment of the permanent European Stability Fund, coming into force from 2013. The same will probably apply to the EMS Treaty to be ratified by the end of 2012. Paul Gallagher, now no longer Attorney General, is regarded as an arch-Euro-fanatic. However, his influence on Brian Lenihan, at the time when crucial prescriptive decisions were being made, would have been huge.

If Anglo Irish Bank had been let go bust, which would have been the proper course, German, British and French banks would have lost €30 billion. There could have been 'contagion' to other banks across the Eurozone. If AIB and Bank of Ireland, the 'systemic' banks, had been restricted in the extent of their coverage by the 'blanket' of the guarantee, Fianna Fáil might just have gone on as the traditional 'safe hands' in charge of Ireland. But the hands were not safe. They were flapping in panic and the Irish people became first-hand witnesses to a very public collapse. That is the story we tell here.

Chapter 1 ∾

| BEGINNING AT THE END

On Saturday, 6 November 2010 the *Irish Daily Mail* and the *Irish Independent* both carried stories about Brian Cowen's knowledge of the crisis faced by Anglo Irish Bank well before the Bank Guarantee of 28 September 2008. Up to the time of the publication of these stories, Cowen had consistently claimed that he had first heard of the problems in Anglo Irish Bank at the end of September 2008. Though this seemed highly doubtful, it had not previously been the subject of investigation or challenge. The stories alleged that Cowen first knew that the fiscal roof was falling in on the bank when he was Minister for Finance, and that he became actively involved at least as early as April 2008. He was Minister for Finance from July 2004 until 7 May 2008, when he replaced Bertie Ahern as Taoiseach. This was nearly five months before the Bank Guarantee.

The probability that he knew of the bank's problems as Minister for Finance was argued in both stories, which alleged that Brian Cowen knew the end was nigh for Anglo Irish Bank in late 2007, and that he involved himself then in the bank's growing crisis. In April 2008 he attended a dinner with the Anglo Irish Board in Heritage House on St Stephen's Green, the bank's headquarters, but his involvement and knowledge, according to both articles, pre-dated this event. The source for the stories claimed that 'it was a dinner for Brian Cowen. Brian sat there, one of the gang.' At this stage, while he was still Minister for Finance, he knew in some detail the state of the crisis the bank was facing. The actions he took were defensive and uncertain. He did not know what to do but sustained his knowledge through direct meetings, either in the bank or elsewhere, at which he was told about the impending disaster. It would be later claimed by Anglo director David

Drumm that Cowen, when Finance Minister, had set up a 'kitchen cabinet' that contained several people connected with Anglo Irish Bank, such as Seán FitzPatrick. Surely they would have advised him on the detail and provided him with at least some inside information about the bank's circumstances which, during 2008, were becoming perilous? However, it's also easy to imagine that such information was probably being fed to Cowen on a need-to-know basis. Despite these close connections, it's hard to imagine FitzPatrick having revealed to Cowen a full account of the bank's precarious state and what would later emerge as illegal practices.

Cowen claimed that he first heard of the problems in Anglo Irish in late September 2008. In the debate on the introduction of the blanket Bank Guarantee by Minister for Finance Brian Lenihan, Labour Party leader Eamon Gilmore asked Brian Cowen whether he knew that Anglo Irish Bank was facing insolvency. Cowen replied: 'No, I did not.'

The stories alleged that he was at an Anglo Irish board dinner in April of that year where the discussion was exclusively about the problems faced by the bank. Cowen, who had acknowledged earlier that he was at the April meeting, had insisted that the bank's internal problems had not been discussed. The unnamed source for these 6 November stories claimed that the discussion was 'openly and deliberately' focused on the bank's difficulties.

Seán Quinn, of Quinn Insurance, had seriously aggravated the problems faced by the bank through heavy gambling at the time with 'Contracts for Difference' (CFD)—a means of entering the market without buying the bank's shares and without being subject to stamp duty—the net effect of his investment was to threaten the survival of Anglo Irish Bank. These ultimately came to represent a quarter of Anglo Irish Bank shares, but Anglo continued to haemorrhage, leaving Quinn with a €2.5 billion shortfall. On St Patrick's Day, 17 March 2008, a month before the dinner referred to above, Anglo Irish Bank shares had been 'attacked' by speculators while the Dublin Stock Exchange was closed. Hedge funds had been selling the stock down. Anglo Irish Bank had responded by claiming it as cynical speculation against 'an Irish success story'. In fact, the Seán Quinn involvement had leaked out and the bank was characterised as ludicrously over-exposed and wide open to share speculation.

Anglo director David Drumm said:

These guys [stockbrokers] don't care about Seán Quinn, they care about hedge funds. They would have been fed the information and then taken the short position and kill [sic] the bank.

We had a mini-run on the bank. Quinn shot himself in the foot and shot the bank while he was doing it. With Quinn, our worst fear we had seen the monster [*sic*]. We had seen a run on the bank, most people don't. The run didn't take off completely. In March '08, we just about survived. But we literally had to go into the vault and get ready to lock the doors, you know? We talked about Armageddon. The world was at the end of the line.

Quinn owned a quarter of the company. Twenty-five per cent was not on our mindset at all. Twenty-five per cent was just nuclear. We could be dead already. A drop in the share price, the way that was read on the street was the market is telling us there is a problem with that bank, i.e., a credit problem. 'Get us out.' When the share price drops, money goes out the door.

The bank desperately put together a group of business people known as the 'Maple Ten' to take on 40 per cent of Quinn's shares, so that the former billionaire would not have to sell a significant chunk of his enormous savings. But the efforts were in vain and Anglo's share price continued to drop from a peak of 30 to a staggering low of 21 cent.

'Nobody in the bank—but maybe we were [distracted by] everything else going on—ever foresaw the immense damage that would do. The shock heard around the world actually killed us. The loan is probably immaterial. What was wrong with the bank is that the bank ran out of money,' said Drumm.

This knowledge of an impending disaster was recognised and discussed by the board as early as 11 September 2007. Sensitive information was leaking from Anglo Irish Bank on a number of issues, including Seán Quinn's speculations. One of the sources for these leaks was identified as Seán FitzPatrick, by now quite close to Brian Cowen. At one meeting Patrick Neary, the Financial Regulator, told a member of the bank's board that Seán FitzPatrick was talking too much and too openly about the Quinn stake, which shows how up to their neck in it

Neary's office was before the placing. According to David Drumm, 'a member of the Central Bank board had overheard Seanie at some party spouting on about Quinn and brought it back into the Central Bank board room'. Drumm was told to tell him to 'shut his mouth'. It was alleged that if it got out, 'there could be [a] run on the system'. Unfortunately, and despite the extraordinary fact of it being discussed at the Central Bank, leading to the instruction to shut him up, Seán FitzPatrick continued to enjoy political protection, as did Seán Quinn.

A further example of Brian Cowen's direct involvement in the bank's affairs was contained in the claim by the unnamed source for the 6 November stories that Cowen promised intervention with the National Treasury Management Agency (NTMA). The bank asked him to get the NTMA to put deposits with Anglo Irish Bank. Cowen knew this was necessary but, despite his claim that he had told them to step in, the NTMA failed to follow this course. Thus, though Cowen consented to the request to seek NTMA support for Anglo Irish Bank, it was not forthcoming.

The truth was that a negative decision had already been made. According to Brendan McDonagh, the former Director of Finance and Risk at the NTMA, the decision had been taken to stop placing deposits with the bank 'because they [the Agency] didn't understand the business model at Anglo'. McDonagh was asked whether this decision and the reasons for it were communicated to the Government. McDonagh could not answer the question. He said that such reporting was a matter for Dr Michael Somers, head of the NTMA. When questioned, Dr Somers said: 'I didn't know enough to say anything to anybody, and if I had, they would have said, "Would you ever go and mind your own business? This [the Bank] is a very successful institution—what are you on about?" It would not have mattered if I had said something to Cowen. What could he have done?' This was true. Nevertheless, following a Department meeting with Dr Somers on 21 May 2008, two weeks after Cowen had become Taoiseach and had appointed Brian Lenihan as his successor at the Department of Finance, a memorandum marked 'strictly confidential' was prepared and circulated with the following purpose:

The key message we would wish to see communicated is that the

NTMA and NPRF [National Pensions Reserve Fund] should continue its [*sic*] welcome engagement with the Department of Finance, Central Bank and Irish banks to help sustain financial stability.

In a context note opening the memorandum, Brian Cowen was identified, as of course he must have been, writing to Dr Somers the previous December (2007) to the effect that the two institutions 'in view of their financial resources and commercial mandate' needed to indicate the role they might play. The Department stressed that 'the NTMA/NPRF can play a very important role in helping to meeting [*sic*] the funding needs of the Irish banks in stressed financial market conditions'. There was no exclusion of Anglo Irish Bank from these views at this stage. The memorandum emphasised the openness of the State agencies to 'discuss commercial proposals for support from the Irish banks and [the Department] has had a number of meetings with various financial institutions on this basis'. NTMA funds had already been deposited with the main banks and, though 'relatively small', these were 'an important signal to the banks of support from public authorities', the role of the NTMA being seen as ready to 'intervene to seek to pre-empt what might otherwise lead to a major funding crisis in an Irish bank'.

The two stories also presented a different view of the Financial Regulator, Patrick Neary. Widely characterised in the media as having been asleep at the wheel, Neary was in fact in close contact with the bank and knew what had to be done. This is also confirmed by the memorandum, which underlines the fact that the Financial Services Authority of Ireland, which includes the Financial Regulator's office with its extensive personnel, had participated in the discussions about financial stability and the planning required to sustain it.

The Financial Regulator, the Department of Finance, Anglo Irish Bank and Morgan Stanley (through which Quinn invested in CFDs and which later advised Anglo on the Quinn situation) all knew that the CFDs spelt death for the bank and the Regulator should have picked up on them, an essential part of regulation. This was not done. Instead, the Financial Regulator, the Central Bank and the Department of Finance, with Cowen's knowledge, were allowing Seán Quinn to take money from his insurance company and gamble it through the bank.

The treatments given in the two newspapers of this story were quite different but the message was the same. The *Irish Daily Mail* splashed it on page one with the headline 'Cowen "did know about Anglo debts"' and went on to claim that he had been 'less than truthful'. The *Irish Independent* published a report and analysis inside the paper but made the same points.

Bruce Arnold's political judgment in the *Irish Independent* was scathing in the following terms:

> These reported events, encounters and arguments represented the most blatant and most damaging example in recent Irish economic history of the State's interests being placed second to a corrupt, internal, private involvement of politicians and of servants of the State. In the light of it, the idea of them remaining in office any longer is repulsive and objectionable to all right-thinking Irish men and women. They must go. When they do the State must be reinvested with men and women who speak the truth and act exclusively in the interests of the people.

The stories were immediately recognised as of crucial importance to Cowen's position and his integrity, threatening his continued leadership of the Government. Questioned by journalists on the day the stories appeared, his spokesperson said: 'We don't respond to comment from "anonymous sources".' Cowen maintained his silence despite serious, if restrained, media analysis. This spelt out the implications of what Cowen's refusal indicated. True, the original stories were based on an unnamed director of Anglo Irish Bank. But he was identified in the stories that were published on the following day, Sunday, 7 November, as David Drumm, the former CEO of the bank, who was now living in Boston. He had filed for bankruptcy there and was the subject of ongoing legal investigation. What was more compelling was the detail, the coherence and the fitting together of circumstantial evidence.

The original stories reported a number of allegations clearly showing a serious and documented conflict between what Cowen had done at the time and his later claim that he did not know until the end of September 2008 the state of affairs in Anglo Irish Bank. The version published in the two 6 November articles said that Brian Cowen, in late 2007, had involved himself directly in the crisis at Anglo Irish Bank and had done so in response to board members, including the chairman of the bank, Seán FitzPatrick.

If true in general terms, then Cowen had taken office as Taoiseach, on 7 May 2008, already seriously compromised. This was in respect of the country's economy and its finances through his ministerial responsibility for the Department of Finance and for other institutions involved in what happened at Anglo Irish Bank. He must have known that the banking system was in danger of loss of liquidity and credibility. Cowen himself was in the shadow of a flawed and largely disgraced predecessor, Bertie Ahern, whom he had served in the increasingly sensitive position of Minister for Finance. He was also compromised, much more seriously, by his commitment to protecting the Fianna Fáil party at the country's expense.

Both as Minister for Finance and then as Taoiseach, Cowen gave a consistently upbeat account of the economy, including the country's banking system. He claimed more than once that the influence of the EU project had been pervasive across every aspect of Irish life. There was a growing irony in almost everything he said.

Cowen's refusal to respond to questions because they emanated from 'anonymous' sources was simply putting off his ultimate confrontation with the truth. But in the short term it worked. The stories had considerable media impact and went one step further with calls from the Opposition Leader, Enda Kenny, for an exact explanation of when Cowen had first learned of the enormous financial problems faced by Anglo Irish Bank. Specifically it was pointed out to him that the 'Government told the Dáil this was a problem of liquidity as opposed to insolvency, so, arising from that report, if it's to be confirmed, the Taoiseach should clarify the matter again'.

John McGuinness, a Fianna Fáil Carlow-Kilkenny deputy and long-time critic of Cowen's leadership, said the Government 'must have known more than they admitted. I think that an awful lot of people involved, including the Department of Finance—so you can extend that to include Brian Cowen—must have known … what was going on in relation to the banking system.'

Brian Cowen managed to deal with these challenges and to ignore the central questions raised by the David Drumm allegations in the two articles of 6 November. But he was running out of time and room to manoeuvre.

Then came a curious intervention from two quite different journalists, Tom Lyons and Brian Carey, who had been covering the Anglo Irish Bank story (for the *Sunday Times*) since the crisis began in 2007. Tom Lyons, a business reporter, met Seán FitzPatrick in May 2009 and began taping interviews with him, which were published in *The FitzPatrick Tapes*. According to Penguin, which published the book, FitzPatrick 'talked at length and in detail about his banking experiences and philosophy, his colleagues and clients, his investments, his public disgrace, his arrest and his bankruptcy'. Adding to these details 'their many sources within Anglo, the state and the business community', the two reporters wrote the story, 'a tale of toothless regulators, hopeless accountants, politicians and civil servants out of their depth, and businessmen in denial about the crash'. To the surprise of the authors of this book, very little was confirmed of their discoveries in respect of Brian Cowen's involvement with Anglo Irish Bank. However, there was a great deal of other confirmation, expanded from the tapes and other researches to considerable length, and giving a vivid portrait of such characters as Seán Quinn.

The hands of all the principal participants holding power and having a role in Ireland's economic collapse seem to have been stayed by the sustained protection of Seán Quinn. His contribution to the collapse of confidence in Anglo Irish Bank—and his extraordinary gambling in the bank's shares—plays a huge and almost totally distorted part in *The FitzPatrick Tapes*. So much is said of his role and so little of that of other people, notably Brian Cowen, that one has to search for hidden reasons. One of these is the fact that Fianna Fáil, including Cowen, according to David Drumm, lobbied for Quinn and thereby helped to protect him. They must have done so on account of Quinn having made a huge contribution to the party—part of the business world's backing for Fianna Fáil, and in the end the source of its collapse—which was a recognised component of the earlier invincibility of Fianna Fáil. It explains why the Financial Regulator, who knew that Quinn was taking money from his insurance company—picked up by the bank's auditors, PricewaterhouseCoopers (PWC) of Belfast—and that this was illegal on two counts, did not act as he should have done. Quinn, effectively, was 'untouchable'.

If we pursue the fact that what is offered in *The FitzPatrick Tapes* on Quinn is not balanced with the negligible detail on Cowen's knowledge, a story emerges that is totally at odds with the version given by David Drumm and confirms the concealment or misrepresentation by Seán FitzPatrick of what was happening in Anglo Irish Bank or between himself and Brian Cowen. These were things not to be told.

In respect of Cowen, *The FitzPatrick Tapes* contains two episodes highlighted in the Penguin Ireland publicity leaflet. The first of these was that Cowen had taken a call in March 2008, while on a trip to Malaysia, from Seán FitzPatrick. The Anglo Irish chairman was reporting on the so-called 'St Patrick's Day Massacre' of Anglo shares on the London Stock Exchange.

Given the discussions that had gone on in all the major financial institutions in Ireland, as well as in the Department of Finance, involving the Minister himself—at the time Brian Cowen—FitzPatrick's account of his contact with the Taoiseach, two weeks after Cowen took up the premiership, simply does not make sense. FitzPatrick rang Cowen on his mobile. Cowen was staying in Kuala Lumpur at the Shangri-La Hotel. He says that he spoke about 'rumours going round about the bank that were unfounded'. Cowen had little to say. In the circumstances this is not credible and the absence of any questioning of it, as a response by the head of the Irish Government, who had been involved also as Minister for Finance during the whole period in which Quinn had invested in CFDs a figure that rose from €653 million in 2006 to €790 million in 2007, was significantly worse than the extraordinary performance by the bank's chairman, which FitzPatrick's 'explanation' to Cowen represented.

The second episode, equally unbelievable, was the occasion when Seán FitzPatrick spent an entire day with Brian Cowen in July 2008, playing golf at Druids Glen, having lunch and dinner, but at no stage discussing the growing crisis faced by the bank or the potential further damage of Seán Quinn's involvement. Their seven-hour interlude, according to FitzPatrick, included discussion of 'the world, Ireland, the economy'. It did not cover Seán Quinn, Anglo Irish Bank 'or anything like that'! What else could have been like that? One supposes the answer is: wholesale CFDs on all sides. Quinn was special, a funding backer of Fianna Fáil to a huge extent and therefore not to be touched. Luckily (relatively speaking) no one else was so favoured, so flawed and so fatal. 'Uncharacteristically', according to the authors of *The FitzPatrick Tapes*, FitzPatrick refused to be drawn further!

It was not difficult for Cowen to concur later with this version. By the time he did so, however, the difficulty he faced was that of being believed. Further details emerged. One was the presence, during the golf outing, of Gary McCann and Fintan Drury, two of the bank's directors, fuelling greater disbelief in the idea that the fortunes of Anglo Irish had not been discussed. The other was the presence in the hotel of Caoimhghín Ó Caoláin, of Sinn Féin, who was at a wedding reception and spoke to Cowen. On foot of these slight references, Cowen was later confronted with a new set of questions about what he knew and when. He was able to say that no crisis was discussed and no one could assert the opposite. The confrontation on this in the Dáil by Opposition Party leaders followed. Cowen came out of it superficially unscathed but in fact irreversibly wounded. It seemed to the authors of the present book that *The FitzPatrick Tapes* had all the appearance of a tailor-made script for Brian Cowen, giving him events where he could easily answer in the negative and sustain his denial about the quite different Drumm allegations.

Six days later we published the full facts, naming our source, who had already been widely named and exposed by other newspapers. David Drumm did not participate any further. We confirmed that he was frustrated by the way the media were distorting all stories related to him and portraying him simply as the only villain who had wrecked Anglo Irish Bank.

The sensational defence, by the court trustee in David Drumm's bankruptcy hearing in Boston, in November 2010, centred on the fact that Anglo made €7.65 million available to Drumm for fraudulent purposes. The trustee was challenging that Anglo's change of loan documentation from 'non-recourse' to 'recourse' was a 'fraudulent transfer'. It removed value from David Drumm's 'estate' that would otherwise be available to creditors. Lawyers appointed by the Irish State as part of its investigation of the affairs of Anglo were involved, according to Drumm, in order to challenge the bank in respect of the loan documentation. They were legally impeded in this by the bankruptcy proceedings.

Drumm acted honourably in the face of incorrect loan documentation. The first documents would have released him from paying back the loans. Instead, he signed new documents in return for the bank agreeing that it would not sue him, or possess his family home, and would give him long-term repayment schedules, since the shares and his income had disappeared.

Anglo reneged on this, dragging Drumm into court in November 2009, just in time for the Budget. He fought the case and tried to settle, which Anglo did not want. It 'preferred', seemingly for image purposes, the 'hot pursuit of bankers'.

Drumm offered all his assets and his pension fund voluntarily. This was ignored. Instead, assets were to be force-sold, but minus huge bankruptcy costs swollen by the quite unnecessary legal pursuit. Drumm's wife agreed to transfer their house in Malahide back to him in order for it to be surrendered. The bank's response was to object in court and seek an injunction against the attempt to put the house back into joint names, which would have allowed it to be surrendered!

A letter to Drumm of 10 January 2008 spelt out that the loan was to buy Anglo shares. It detailed strict security charges. The Boston hearing made it unlikely that Anglo would achieve anything like Drumm's offer to the bank because of the claim by bankruptcy trustee Kathleen Dwyer that these claims undermined the bank.

Drumm was scathing about what was being done:

> The 'arm of the FF Junta' that is Anglo Irish Bank let it be known they were going to 'oust' the Court appointed trustee in my case. I had no choice in this Trustee and she operates totally on the directions of the Court. The mandarins are trying to keep up the image of 'following bankers/developers to the ends of the earth'. What they have done here is not only stupid, it is reckless, wasteful, cynical and worse.

The Boston hearing was widely covered—two pages in the *Irish Independent*. RTÉ gave the story 18 seconds. On the main evening news Eileen Dunne told taxpayers: 'A trustee in the case of the bankruptcy of the former chief executive of Anglo Irish Bank, David Drumm, has claimed that Anglo Irish Bank's entire claim on Mr Drumm is based on a fraudulent premise. The Boston attorneys say Anglo Irish gave Mr Drumm the money to buy shares in his own company and, as this was illegal, it negates their claim on Mr Drumm.' Big story, small coverage. RTÉ reported, the next day, that the trustee had decided to counter-sue Anglo Irish Bank, which was seeking to have her dismissed. RTÉ conceded: 'this is rapidly becoming a complex and surprising court case'.

Making scapegoats to bear the blame for Ireland spiralling down into huge debt had been the response of the Cowen Government essentially because of his own mismanagement of public affairs. The response was not otherwise directed at bankers, who were central to the economic collapse, but it was singularly virile against David Drumm. There was also a dogged pursuit of developers through the National Asset Management Agency (NAMA). They again had become the victims of slack management and were now faced with the wholesale confiscation of their assets. The bank bailout, the austerity Budget and the IMF loan left ordinary Irish men and women with a huge clear-up operation and a load of debt. In addition, it seems evident from the extensive treatment of Seán Quinn by Seán FitzPatrick, in a chapter entitled 'The Mighty Quinn' in *The FitzPatrick Tapes*, that he also was a suitable person to be sacrificed.

As a result of the publication of *The FitzPatrick Tapes*, the reappearance of the David Drumm arguments and recollections took on a quite new and powerful significance. Brian Cowen's troubles deepened by the hour. He made a lengthy statement to the Dáil on 13 January 2011 concealing more than he conceded. *The FitzPatrick Tapes* had provided Cowen with three events that he could easily answer, by way of denial, though nothing was easy about the answers he gave: the St Patrick's Day phone call, the Anglo Irish Bank board dinner and the game of golf. Whatever one may think about the truthfulness or otherwise of the Taoiseach's account, it cannot be challenged further without forensic investigation and testimony on oath.

Many people in Ireland today would like to see that kind of investigation replacing the shambles in the Dáil as Cowen, more or less successfully, indulged in political rhetoric, insults and jibes. He managed to put over the claim that, on all occasions summarised above, nothing was said about the crisis facing Anglo Irish Bank. Drumm has stated:

> He [Cowen] was acutely aware of our problems. The conversation at that dinner was interesting. The big man has been less than truthful about it.
>
> I spoke with him one to one for quite a while about the NTMA and the other issues we were facing [at the dinner].... Every board member will confirm—the conversation was dominated by funding problems and the image of Ireland abroad and the need to send out the right messages to the international investor community.
>
> This was back in early 2008. He was acutely aware of our funding problems back then—how can he now claim he only realised the problems in September 2008?

The claim that Cowen did involve himself from an early stage—and while still Minister for Finance—in the Anglo Irish Bank crisis at that time had become irrefutable. Cowen's claim that he first heard of the problems in Anglo Irish in September 2008 looked more and more ridiculous. His position was fundamentally changed when it became clear that the source for the information was known to be David Drumm. The comparison between *The FitzPatrick Tapes* version of events and the version from David Drumm was starkly convincing in favour of Drumm. His words ring as true as they did then, with the added advantage of his name being behind them.

Drumm claimed that Cowen promised intervention with the NTMA in order to get the agency to put deposits with Anglo. 'We requested it to Brian Cowen through Fintan [Drury],' Drumm said. He knew this was necessary. No one saw it otherwise. It had become necessary after St Patrick's Day 2008. The NTMA, quite properly, failed to follow this course. It was too late. The damage was done. Only a year prior to this request, the NTMA had stopped putting substantial amounts of State money into Anglo after assessing it as an unacceptable risk, even though it offered the highest interest rate available. It would have been seriously improper if it had done otherwise.

But despite this astute move, Drumm claims that Cowen nevertheless 'intervened with the NTMA to get them to deposit with Anglo'. Drumm says he was 'not surprised at all' that Cowen agreed to help because 'Seán was in there'. There was even greater impropriety for the Minister for Finance—knowing what he knew then of the vulnerable state of Anglo Irish Bank—in taking the unprecedented step (now denied) of applying to the NTMA. The full truth about this would clarify the hopelessly compromised way in which we do public business in this country.

The fact that the anonymous source was David Drumm was revealed in the *Irish Daily Mail* on 14 January 2011. The occasion was the publication of the fullest possible text on Cowen's involvement and knowledge. This had been far from the case with *The FitzPatrick Tapes*. In contrast with that book and with the previous day's Dáil performance by the Taoiseach, the Drumm information—as opposed to *The FitzPatrick Tapes*—rings true in its general detail and in the specifics on what Cowen knew and when he knew it.

The full text on the part played by Drumm, now in the public domain, confirms the close-knit kitchen cabinet set up by Fintan Drury, the facilitator for Cowen who needed close and frequent contact with Seán FitzPatrick, who was—according to Drumm—sharp, able and well-advised. He said: 'He [Fintan] didn't sit on the right hand of God [Seán FitzPatrick] because that was me, but he sat on the left hand of God. Probably Fintan considered he was doing both a favour. Brian Cowen, by helping him, and by doing Seán a favour getting him plugged into the future Taoiseach.'

Drumm claimed that other kitchen cabinet members included Indecon Economic Consulting Group's managing partner Alan Gray and its former chairman for an Advisory Board of Directors, Paddy Mullarkey. But in November 2010 both men denied when asked by a newspaper if they were on Cowen's so-called kitchen cabinet. However, in January 2011, Alan Gray admitted that he'd been at the infamous golf outing in July 2008 to brief Cowen on the economy. Cowen would later admit in the Dáil that both men attended lunch with FitzPatrick.

When he was Finance Minister, Cowen appointed Gray as Director of the Central Bank and Financial Services Authority of Ireland and also as a member of the Irish Financial Services Regulatory Authority (IFSRA). Mullarkey is a former Secretary General at the Department of Finance and was an NTMA adviser.

In late 2010, Indecon contacted the website forum politics.ie to ask them to 'point out that despite what's been posted here and alluded to, Indecon have never acted for Anglo Irish Bank in any capacity'.

Only days prior to the banks' bailout, Drumm says he and FitzPatrick met with Gray as a 'go-between' between Anglo and the Department of Finance. He says the intervention was needed because Finance 'wouldn't tell us what way they were thinking'.

According to Drumm, calls were made to Alan Gray. He was asked: 'What should be done? What are they thinking? Are we doing the right things? Are we doing the *wrong* things? There could be no direct communication with the Department of Finance.' At meetings there attended by Drumm and FitzPatrick, the officials would sit and listen and look. In the end no one was any the wiser. According to Drumm, 'They wouldn't tell them what to do. They wouldn't help us.'

Their kitchen-cabinet meetings were, roughly speaking, on a weekly basis and took place in Government Buildings, Drumm claims.

On that much-noted dinner that Anglo Irish Bank directors had with Brian Cowen in Heritage House, Drumm stated: 'The dinner was for Brian Cowen. We put the dinner together for him. It would be really unusual to bring somebody with him. Brian sat there, one of the gang, right beside me.' At the dinner, Drumm asked Cowen if he had done anything about this essential deposit. Cowen did not say he told Dr Michael Somers.

We had a long conversation about our Budget worries and that not only would Anglo like the money, but that it would help to send out the right signal to the market—that the Government was supportive of the bank because 'right now the market know [*sic*] that you may have a problem with Anglo'.

It was to combat the negativity in the market. We had to shout. We could work a little bit harder and shout it out, 'Put your money in Ireland'—whereas the Government was allowing this negative wave to flow over.

This is an Irish bank, Irish money and the Germans have 200 million—why can't we get more from our own country? So, when I asked had anything happened with it, he [Cowen] looked (or feigned) surprised and said, I quote, 'I told those fuckers'.

It's only now that I know that they [NTMA] had some issue with us, that they didn't like us. They never came to us. They never crossed-examined our numbers. They never asked to see our loan book.

With the 'bank on the verge of collapse', our whistleblower, Drumm, says the Regulator worked 'hand in hand' with Anglo in an effort to get an investor on board.

When it became a problem [auditors PWC Belfast picked it up in the 2007 audit] the Regulator tried to get Anglo to lend money to fix the problem—i.e cover their ass.

They hounded Anglo to place the Quinn stake—daily phone calls and regular meetings. They were 100 per cent involved in the placing and were fully briefed on ALL aspects of it by the Bank and by Morgan Stanley....

I find it hard to be critical of the Regulator from the place that we were in. The global financial system had completely collapsed. There had been a major meltdown. The Central Bank and the Regulator were trying to survive the global meltdown. They were doing things as if they were in [a] battlefield. Say with the Quinn stock, the Regulator knew about it. Not only did he know about it, he was organising things and at one point I'd say harassing the bank to get it done. The Regulator was hand in hand with us and, I'm not exaggerating, through all attempts.

The impact on our daily cash balances [was that they] were literally melting while this was going on. The issue was, 'How much money went out today?' If the balance sheet wasn't changing at all, we could have ignored it. So, we had to do something.

Morgan Stanley put together a 'firm list' of potential investors.

[They] would make a phone call and say, 'There's a Western European bank of a certain size—are you interested [in that] type of thing?'

We ran to the Regulator and told them what we were going to do. They were thrilled. The main thing was, can you get it done? 'Yeah, we think we can get it done?' We felt we would be handpicking the client who would have the financial wherewithal to handle that kind of exposure.

Drumm flew out to the Middle East in an effort to get Saudi investors and the Regulator would constantly phone him. 'The Regulator would be on to me non-stop asking "How did you get on in the meeting today? Have you got another meeting tonight?"' said Drumm.

Drumm thought the meetings were 'actually going well, but then they didn't go ahead'. Anglo also had two meetings with the Dutch Rabo Bank, but unfortunately 'that didn't work either'. Drumm believes the bank would have found an investor and probably survived if Lehman Brothers hadn't crashed.

Drumm is highly critical of the Financial Regulator, Pat Neary, for denying prior knowledge about the Quinn disaster, adding that it's 'unquestionable that they fucking knew'. He says the Regulator should have stepped in sooner. He also believes that 'shouting it out loud would have been the better thing to do' when they first learned about the Quinn situation in September 2007, which they internally described as 'our own September 11'.

He believes that Fianna Fáil protected Quinn.

There is no question, there never has been in my mind, that Quinn was protected. Quinn is still protected. Quinn should be investigated. Quinn speculated with a credit institution. Corporate gambling. Really he got away with it.

If Quinn wasn't a regulator entity, they then could have concentrated on the effect on Anglo. Quinn was a regulator entity; so there you had one regulator entity breaking the law, taking money out of the insurance company, buying stock, gambling the stock in the bank. It's illegal.

Buying the stock wasn't illegal, but because he was a regulator entity, it didn't matter that it wasn't illegal, the Regulator could have forced him to [stop it].

But they [Regulator's office] didn't do it. They knew that he was taking the money out. And rather than say, 'stop and put the money back', he [Neary] worked with Quinn, he worked with the bank in the same mode—trying to save the bank at the same time.

The primary focus of the board and the regulator and the bank and the Department of Finance and everybody else was the Quinn thing. This wasn't [a case of us] being quiet until we arrived into the Regulator saying it.

Cowen later denied that he knew in March 2008 about the crisis facing Anglo Irish Bank. And yet Quinn was not fined by the Irish Financial Services Regulatory Authority for using customer insurance premia to build up his stake in Anglo until seven months after this event, in October 2008. Why was there such a delay? Could there have been a stalling tactic to resolve the issue before it became public knowledge? But the most damning thing of all from Cowen's perspective is his insistence that when he became aware that Anglo's market value had been substantially increased by Quinn's crazy gambling instincts, his only response was to pass on the information to the Central Bank. It all sounds implausible and has the whiff of a cover-up. Could Quinn—a man who once boasted that he had every mobile phone number for the Cabinet—have been, as Drumm suggests, protected by Fianna Fáil?

In our not inexperienced political judgment, this further publication of detail and of facts was as close as we could get to the truth at that time. David Drumm was prepared and happy 'to join everybody on the one stage—Brian Cowen and all the rest. I'd be happy to admit all my mistakes. But the problem is they want me to do it all on my own.'

This shabby episode—still not fully explored or explained—was a blatant and damaging example of the State's interests being placed second to a 'corrupt, internal, private involvement of politicians and of servants of the State' in misdoings of a frightening kind that have now led us into gigantic and improperly imposed debt.

Changing Cowen would not change the culture that bred this pus-filled carbuncle of iniquity. Changing the Government would help, but would still leave us with a huge burden of reparation. We needed to reinvest the State with men and women who speak the truth and act exclusively in the interests of the people. How this was achieved, over a period of four years, is the subject of the following pages.

| BERTIE TRIUMPHANT

fter he retired as Taoiseach, Bertie Ahern made ridiculous claims that he was in no way responsible for the worst recession to hit the State since its foundation. The country, according to him, was fine when he left office. But the meltdown of both country and Fianna Fáil can be traced back to his tenure.

Bertie Ahern was first elected to the Dáil in 1977 in the Fianna Fáil landslide victory led by Jack Lynch. Lynch had decided he would not contest another general election and resigned just over two years later, on 5 December 1979. In the leadership battle that followed, between Charles Haughey and George Colley, Ahern supported Haughey, who won. From then on he stuck closely to his new leader, learning about politics and never wavering in his attention. He could have chosen better, in terms of political capacities, but he did choose a determined man who remained for 12 years the head of the Fianna Fáil organisation.

Ahern and others in the party who had supported Haughey on the grounds that he stood the best chance of continuing to lead Fianna Fáil effectively in power were in for a rude awakening. Haughey botched his first general election in 1981, came back with the support of independents and three Workers' Party deputies early in 1982, an inherently unstable situation that did not last. Nevertheless, Ahern remained close to his leader and political mentor. After the formation of Haughey's first Government, Ahern became in 1980 Assistant Government Whip. Haughey then lost power in the summer of 1981. Ahern was Whip in Opposition and resumed the job as a Minister of State from March to December 1982 when he was also Junior Minister with responsibilities in the departments of Defence and the Taoiseach.

In the late summer of 1982 Charles Haughey's prospects of survival were again looking bleak, his wafer-thin majority crumbling. Charlie McCreevy—no friend of Haughey and critical above all of his lack of courage in handling the economy—tabled a no confidence motion in his leader. This unprecedented move, followed by the death of Clare TD Bill Loughnane, Carlow-Kilkenny TD Jim Gibbons's illness and the defection of the essential support of independents, brought about the second 1982 election, with Haughey again going out of power, this time with the added shame of the phone-tapping revelations. It was a move that infuriated Des O'Malley, who was out of the country when word of the no-confidence motion reached him. He thought McCreevy acted too quickly and, if the heave had been timed better, Haughey would have been forced out of office. In retrospect, O'Malley believes Haughey's hand was considerably strengthened by the botched heave. O'Malley remembers McCreevy simply shrugging it off when he told him it had been an unwise move.

Bertie Ahern remained loyal throughout this period. Haughey's inherent instability continued thereafter. He never won an overall majority. He never on his own faced up to the challenges of economic planning and policy, was permanently scarred as far as Northern Ireland was concerned because of his involvement in the attempted importation of arms in 1969 and was perpetually handicapped by his unexplained wealth.

Ahern watched the sustained failure in subsequent elections, the persistent failure to win a majority, the deals and the first enforced coalition with the Progressive Democrats in 1989. He learned a great deal from these events. He studied with much attention shifts in Government policy and style, the introduction of private advisers, the creation of dual methods of exercising power through early quangos. He was learning lessons that were important for him 15 years later.

He served as Minister for Labour on Haughey's return to power in 1987, displaying the negotiating ability that became his strong Cabinet skill, particularly effective in working out the relationship with the Progressive Democrats that became essential after Haughey made the bad mistake of going to the country in 1989 when the party lost seats. Ahern remained in the Department of Labour until November 1991 when Haughey appointed him Minister for Finance.

Charles Haughey was eventually removed as party leader and Taoiseach in 1992, the circumstances again being related to phone-tapping, of the journalists Geraldine Kennedy and Bruce Arnold. He was replaced by Albert Reynolds. Ahern held on to the Finance post under Albert Reynolds until that ill-fated administration collapsed in 1994 and Fianna Fáil went out of power.

Ahern replaced Reynolds as leader and came to be Taoiseach by default, and it was a rough passage. He did not win the June 1997 election; the Rainbow Coalition lost it. They did so in circumstances that still make one fume at the stupidity of their general approach to the most far-reaching political decisions that any political leader makes. John Bruton's timing, in going to the country when he did, was ill-judged, premature, wrongly motivated and crass. He led his own party, which at the time was in high good spirits and contemplating a further extension of its impact, into a dismal situation where the failure of its principal partner, Labour, brought about defeat.

In no sense could Ahern be credited with a victory. He threw himself into the election with demonic energy. He covered the country at a fierce rate, displaying impressive evidence of his desire for power, but in the end recording an overall vote that was disappointing, despite a well-constructed electoral campaign. The damage was mitigated by an effective voting strategy. Even so, Bertie Ahern became Taoiseach in a cobbled up deal, reflecting little merit on anyone.

His next major electoral test presented a similar picture. He outsmarted Dick Spring in choosing Mary McAleese as Fianna Fáil candidate after the minority nomination of Adi Roche. Ahern quickly terminated the presidential aspirations of Albert Reynolds. No new Fianna Fáil leader back in power wants any brooding presence at his elbow. But Ms McAleese's victory, giving a much-needed boost to Fianna Fáil, could as easily have been a defeat had Fine Gael been less amateur in its approach to the contest, and if Spring had chosen a more popular candidate. John Bruton never treated the presidential election seriously. At one point, it is said, he contemplated Fine Gael simply backing the Labour Party choice, so confident was everyone that Dick Spring could repeat the miraculous success of his 1990 choice.

John Bruton's deputy leader, Nora Owen, did try to treat the election seriously, but the co-ordination went wrong, and the planning and execution of the campaign was second-rate.

So in two important respects Bertie Ahern was helped in the confirmation of his position in power by the ineptitude of the Opposition parties. His leadership, over three years prior to being elected to Government, required the prompting and assistance of colleagues in the Fianna Fáil party, and displayed uncertainty, even prevarication, as general characteristics.

Ahern's other important test was the Raphael Burke affair, which he handled indecisively, but very much in character with his political personality as it developed over the next few years. Burke was first elected in 1973 and served under Charles Haughey, Albert Reynolds and Bertie Ahern in several important ministries, including Justice. He was found guilty of corruptly receiving money and was gaoled, one of two politicians who went to prison at this time for action while serving as public representatives; the other was Liam Lawlor. Allegations were made against Lawlor that he had received £80,000 from a property developer. He denied the allegations but resigned from the Cabinet and from the Dáil on 7 October 1997, after just four months in office. This allegation led to the setting up of the Planning Tribunal chaired by Mr Justice Fergus Flood. In an interim report of the subsequent Flood Tribunal, Flood judged Burke to be 'corrupt'. In July 2004 Burke pleaded guilty to making false tax returns and was sentenced to six months in jail. He was the most senior politician in the country's history to serve time in jail.

Having got the job and won a period in power, the question was: could Ahern do it and how well? His ministerial experience was limited enough, with two senior portfolios, first Labour and then Finance, performing better in the first than in the second, but capable in both. His Opposition tasks were numerous, while his closeness to Charles Haughey carried with it all the sulphurous odours associated with that man. It would have been encouraging for Ahern if it could have been claimed that this was all history, but it was not so. Representing a further test on unfinished business were the outstanding investigations of the questions from the McCracken Tribunal. Mr Justice Brian McCracken's 'Tribunal of Inquiry (Dunne's Payments)', set up by the Dáil on 6 February 1997 when John Bruton was Taoiseach, reported to Bertie Ahern on 25 August 1997. It was the briefest and best of all such public inquiries. Succinct, relevant and economic, it was notable for two important achievements: it demolished the integrity of Charles Haughey, finding him out in concealment and lies, and it laid down brief criteria on politicians receiving money from private individuals in a memorable statement that would later haunt Bertie Ahern.

In addition to all this, Ahern had to disembarrass himself from the character-reference given him by his former boss, when Haughey declared, after Ahern had saved his position as leader in the autumn of 1991: 'He's the man, he's the best, the most skilful, the most devious and the most cunning.'

'I don't think Bertie likes the expression my father used: "The most ruthless, the most devious, the most cunning of them all". But I think a lot of people think it was a very insightful observation,' stated Seán Haughey.

In the strangely exaggerated media climate of the time, the lingering Haughey portrait evoked wild claims on Bertie Ahern's behalf, as a potentially historic new leader for Fianna Fáil, destined to rectify its dismal ratings in the eyes of the Irish public. But, as it transpires, none of it was true.

What Ahern needed to do was restore to the Fianna Fáil party something of the integrity and trust that it had enjoyed when he was first elected. However, he had no intentions of doing anything like that. Despite the historically large majority that Jack Lynch obtained in June 1977 against the Liam Cosgrave-led administration, his Government style had been restrained and responsible, and he was trusted in dealing with the Northern Ireland question, and with the post-oil crisis circumstances in the country. Ahern, unfortunately, was indissolubly linked with the regimes led by Charles Haughey, responsible for the loss of much in Fianna Fáil that would remain lost. Secondly, despite the apparent flood-tide of support for the Sinn Féin peace-process approach to the future of Northern Ireland, Ahern should have adopted a more guarded attitude in the expectation that the debate was going to be undramatic and limited. By adopting a high-profile, hands-on approach, he exposed his flank more than he should have. Getting on with Gerry Adams and with David Trimble was not going to be the end of the story. A settlement, bringing real and lasting peace, was still a long way off.

Over 20 years in active politics, some of those years the most turbulent and dramatic Ireland has witnessed, Bertie Ahern seemed all too often to have been blown by the winds of chance. Despite all this, he settled down during the following two years, becoming more assured, though trailing behind him a working-class coat and uttering non-sequiturs and verbal infelicities that became by-words and made him often a figure of mirth. Nevertheless, he was politically shrewd and his appointment of Charlie McCreevy as Minister for Finance was astute.

Bertie Ahern's handling of power remained uncertain, indecisive, and at times incoherent. He was never in clear control of Raphael Burke, Liam Lawlor, Ned O'Keeffe, Willie O'Dea and others. He demonstrated no judgment, no approval or disapproval, virtually no action at all in the face of crisis. He allowed events to dictate decision-making, public approval to be part of Government policy, and the intervention of powerful sectors, such as the trade unions, to shape decisions in a way that confirmed the incoherence of policy. Having given way where he should have stood firm, Bertie Ahern stood firm on mistakes and wrong-doing that simply could not be sustained. A good example was the inexcusable patronage offered to the Supreme Court judge Hugh O'Flaherty, over the Sheehy case. At times these did immediate and extensive damage. Remarkably, he and the Government generally seemed to recover. It left the distinct impression that the political culture that had caused so much grief during the Charles Haughey era—a culture of disproportionate favouritism and political graft—was being given rebirth. It was done in the teeth of public anger over evidence of corruption that flowed from two Tribunals in particular, Flood and Moriarty, of which more later.

It was not inaccurate, then and later, as indeed it had been before, to draw a line between Fianna Fáil and the other parties. This designated Fianna Fáil as the party of patronage—which is how Fianna Fáil has come to operate under its recent leaders—Fine Gael and Labour as the parties of public service governance. The designation was not as prescriptive as it might have seemed. There was a degree of moral superiority but the difference of approach derived also from an inbuilt reliance on broadly balanced coalition governments. This sharing of power was a general, though not complete, disincentive to the abuse of that power in favour of cronyism. The Fianna Fáil approach, much more cautious under Jack Lynch, Seán Lemass and Eamon de Valera, nevertheless grew out of the corporatism espoused and developed by the party's founder, who consciously developed a special relationship with the Catholic Church, designed to gain its political support in exchange for legislative conformity with its teachings.

This divide, when put side by side with the popularity ratings of individual parties and their leaders, and with the periodic changes of power from one style of politics to the other, clearly indicated an ambivalent public. The Irish people were uncertain always of which choice to make. Long-term Fianna Fáil supporters benefited, at every level of public life, from their party association and did not want to part from it. Favouring a fair, open and honest approach to government, without an inbuilt culture of personal patronage and a management of the State that reflected at all times the law and the Constitution, was not necessarily appealing.

As well as Charlie McCreevy in Finance, Bertie Ahern's first Cabinet included Brian Cowen, the central figure in this book, who had been close to Albert Reynolds and was already an established member of the 'Country and Western' faction in the party where he had served under Reynolds, first as Minister for Labour and then as Minister for Transport, Energy and Communications. Ahern appointed him to Health and Children and Micheál Martin to Education. Brian Lenihan, elected to the Dáil only the previous year, taking his father's seat in a by-election after the death of Brian Lenihan Snr, was nowhere in sight. This was because, early in his political career, an inebriated Lenihan had metaphorically shot himself in the foot when one night at a Fianna Fáil event he bemoaned to colleagues that he felt his career was being held back by that 'fucker' Ahern, or colourful words to that effect. Unfortunately for an oblivious Lenihan, Ahern was in earshot. It's believed that Ahern never forgave Lenihan for such an insolent remark. He was to wait until 2007 before getting a Cabinet appointment as Minister for Justice. Justine McCarthy, writing in her *Sunday Times* column on 19 June 2011, after his death, tells of Lenihan's encounter in a bookshop with a friend of hers who noticed that he was buying books about Irish politics and current affairs. The friend thought he should buy Ahern's autobiography and they looked at it together. In one part

Ahern wrote of not getting Lenihan's support over the Mahon Tribunal and referred to him as one of those whom he had 'brought on and promoted through the ranks'. Brian's response was to reject this: 'The lying so-and-so! He kept me on the backbenches for ten years!' This was true and has never been adequately explained. It may have derived from Ahern's fear of Lenihan, as Cowen also feared him. It certainly put a damaging brake on Lenihan's political development.

After a three-year spell in Health, Brian Cowen was appointed Minister for Foreign Affairs in January 2000. It was the most difficult brief in the Government. Newly appointed, he presided over a crumbling Peace Process, and revived it by changing its direction. He had to work closely with Bertie Ahern, who himself played a major role in Northern Ireland affairs.

Cowen's task meant, among other things, replacing old myths with new ones. It also meant rewriting recent history. In the realm of myth-making, the Minister for Foreign Affairs began, in a radio interview in March 2000, the overdue business of dismantling the myths that surrounded George Mitchell. The US Senator, for all his calm and judicious analysis, and his painstaking chairmanship of immensely difficult negotiations, had failed in the tasks that were set him and was therefore responsible for the shaky foundations on which Ireland was then moving forward. His was the instability on which, eventually, the Northern Ireland executive was established, and on which it then foundered. Mitchell's Six Principles were the bedrock of what should have been agreed policy but no one signed up to them. Mitchell was unable, then or subsequently, to get agreement to them or to any genuine and irreversible peace moves. Mitchell's role was part of a 'twin-track' approach: he would deal with getting agreement to an exclusively democratic approach while the politicians engaged in all-party negotiations. Without the one, the other was hollow. And so it proved, despite Mitchell's subsequent returns to the North to try new and modified forms of persuasion and argument. Recognition of the failure was universally denied, with the exception of the Unionists, who were increasingly anxious that nothing concrete was being done about decommissioning.

If the Minister for Foreign Affairs had recognised this failure, it might have been helpful. But Brian Cowen was doing something rather different. This was to set aside Mitchell as 'too narrow' and move on to 'broader aspects' of the Belfast Agreement. Setting aside Mitchell meant setting aside decommissioning and finding a new formula. And both Brian Cowen and the Taoiseach were engaged in that. What was needed, he said, was for everyone 'to have the same idea' about what decommissioning meant.

Cowen himself later said that his time in the Department of Foreign Affairs (until September 2004) had been the best years of his career, an understandable posture later, though at the time he was persistently overshadowed by Ahern, doing much of the groundwork but seeing the major moves forward orchestrated by his leader. It was during this period that Cowen—thanks to his tough stance when dealing with both Republicans and Loyalists—emerged as a formidable, no-nonsense style politician whom backbenchers started to believe could one day lead the party. Unfortunately, he failed to translate this confidence from Foreign Affairs into the Taoiseach's office.

During this period, it was Charlie McCreevy who enjoyed the limelight. Confident, cheerful, quite outspoken, he was—as he had always been—that which is difficult in the Fianna Fáil party's subjection of its membership to the leader: 'his own man'. On one occasion, early in his political career, Gay Byrne said to him: 'You're an honest man and you'll not get far in politics.' For many years Byrne's prophecy seemed correct. First elected in 1977, with support for his candidacy in Kildare North from Jack Lynch, McCreevy turned critical of his leader in the light of the economic expansionism pursued by Martin O'Donoghue and George Colley, and became a late 1970s rebel.

This meant that he supported Charles Haughey. He did so in the belief—totally mistaken—that Haughey would control public finances, cutting public expenditure and allowing individuals more say over their money through reduced taxation. Haughey blew the whole concept of being tough and courageous, and blew a whole lot else as well. He was a coward over financial rectitude, and McCreevy despised him for that and openly turned against him. McCreevy had the refreshing characteristic that he spoke out in no uncertain terms. He was supported in this characteristic by constituents and was a poll-topper in Kildare North. He attracted a covert kind of admiration within the Fianna Fáil organisation, which worked to his advantage. Charlie McCreevy was always an enigmatic figure, despite his confident, extrovert nature. He was not then in any sense a contender for the leadership of his party and would have been reluctant even if handed it on a plate.

I never wanted to be leader of the party. I think I mightn't have been a bad Taoiseach for so long as it didn't mean having to lead the Fianna Fáil party. People would say over the years that I was very arrogant—maybe that's true; I don't know, that's for other people to judge. . . . I might have the skills necessary to be Taoiseach of the country. . . . I would be fairly efficient as Taoiseach. I thought I was fairly efficient as a minister. I know I don't have the personal or political skills to lead the party. I don't have the temperament. I wouldn't have the patience. A few colleagues of mine—there's no point in going into who they were at the time—when I was Minister for Finance would have liked me to become leader and I always said, 'Look, I'll never do that!' I would like to think I was a good Finance Minister. People mightn't like some of my policies—because that's the only job I was interested in doing. I wasn't trying to be popular with my colleagues because I wasn't looking for their support—support for me to be Taoiseach. I just wanted to do the job. So, it was easy for me. And it was easy for Bertie as well because he knew that I was never going to be a threat to him because I didn't want that job.

Three years into the job, McCreevy's Budget in December 2000 was constructed to make as many people as possible feel good about themselves. It had a central objective: to do this in respect of the social partners, bringing off a renewed and rewritten Programme for Prosperity and Fairness (PPF). But its remit was much wider. In many ways it reached out beyond the social partners to the other political parties, meeting many of their demands, and reducing the scope for criticism and for optional strategies.

McCreevy had a difficult time with the Budget of December 2001. He was confronted by a range of bad economic indicators. These included the maiming of the Celtic Tiger, the decline in tax resources, the rise in unemployment, the damage done to trade and especially tourism by the foot and mouth threat and the Twin Towers attack.

Chastened but unfazed by this, McCreevy reinforced his sense of long-term confidence by what Brendan Walsh described as 'a clever compromise', suggesting also, however, that the Minister had 'dropped the baton'. Thus the economist spoke. But, in this Budget before the 2002 general election, the baton became much more political. McCreevy, who always weighed carefully in the balance political as against economic matters, and party against country, had to construct a Budget that implied the temporary nature of the dip in national fortunes. He stated:

> There was a period of time when the economy went down to maybe zero and we had to take some appropriate measures, which were very, very controversial and very, very tough. I reduced spending considerably. But I've always said, 'You must do what you have to do!' And you must make up your mind what you think is the best thing. That's what the Government must do and then you must go about doing it.

That 2001 Budget, combined with the prudence with which he handled the previous Budgets, had to be the strategy for fighting the election on the economic front. And it was a sound one, with no better exponent of its essentials than McCreevy himself. His party, in the Budget, was given something that McCreevy always was—an electoral asset. The opinion poll findings of January 2001 in the *Irish Times* endorsed the Government's economic strategy in terms of public support, and gave to Charlie McCreevy's policies widespread approval. With the benefit of hindsight, it is fair to say that Government spending was too lavish in the early 2000s, underpinned, as its revenue was, by rising house prices and increases in stamp duty. The economy became increasingly uncompetitive in the early 2000s owing to higher costs when membership of the new Eurozone monetary union, which Ireland had joined in 1999, should have induced far greater thriftiness.

House prices were high and increasing. And the public knew there were housing shortages at different price levels. But banks, building societies and other financial services were at their beck and call, with lavish resources, generous and liberal terms. The seeds of future trouble were being sown. The media also played a significant role in artificially increasing house prices. 'The biggest cheerleaders for the property boom, the Celtic Tiger, were the broadsheet property supplements, which was essential to their finances,' points out Martin Mansergh, a Junior Minister in the Department of Finance in Cowen's Government. He explains:

I'll just make the point: with the benefit of hindsight some people might say—and correctly—that we were not rigorous enough in dampening down the construction boom, even to some extent. But I don't accept the idea that the government were the only players in that—look at all those property supplements? We are being criticised by papers who are now—in many incidents [sic]—in considerable financial difficulties because they are no longer getting the income from the heightening of property that took place in property supplements. The guide prices were very often way off the mark and, so I am told, the results of the prices were quite often manipulated. The print media played a very big part in the unsustainable property boom.

Wise voices, even then, counselled caution, and were right, in objective terms, so to do. But two-thirds of the population ignored the advice and lived for present laughter and self-indulgence. The wise voices were both domestic and international, stretching from the sober old European Union, censuring us for our taxation and other economic policies, to the commentators, who so sensibly explained that what we were doing was almost certainly unsustainable. So? Unsustainable? Let tomorrow look after itself. Ministers were not quite saying this, but they were forcefully rejecting the EU judgment on what we did, none more vociferously than Charlie McCreevy himself, and Mary Harney. And politically they clearly decided they were right to do this.

Bertie Ahern won the 2002 pre-election campaign handsomely. He presented a solid, bland vision of collective and personal competence.

He had lasted in a minority coalition Government for five years, and was justifiably proud of that fact. He delivered a legislative and management package of average conviction, but one that was hugely reinforced in its impact by the great good fortune of national wealth. There was validity in his claim about 'a golden era', validity not untinged with nostalgia.

He presented the country with a lively and original interpretation of what leadership is about. Surprisingly accessible, always ready with brief and generalised comments, Bertie Ahern was in reality a remote and protected leader, his public appearances stage-managed with the intention of making him non-vulnerable.

The Irish economy required reform and had the money to allow for this. It needed a huge programme of social reform and it had to be paid for. Health, the transport system and roads, rural and small-town employment, how we dealt with the imbalance between the east of the country and the west, the aged, crime and endemic poverty, drugs— these were all issues that took the shine off the economic progress of 1997–2002. Nevertheless, the country's infrastructure and a great deal of good building before the bubble burst is Ahern and Cowen's lasting testimony.

Some key issues were not economic. Peace in Northern Ireland, rightly claimed up until then as an achievement by the administration led by Bertie Ahern, was in an uncertain state, with doubts expressed in the North about the lasting power of the administration and of the Peace Process. In our midst, as a party contending many seats in the south, was Sinn Féin, with its unacceptable prevarication over links with the IRA and the continued involvement in terrorism of IRA members. The constitutional bedrock on which Irish society had flourished was threatened by the southern focus of the party. Its appeal, often to younger voters, and the failure of the State to make Sinn Féin exclusively part of our democratic system, was a worrying new political phenomenon. The public wanted the Sinn Féin ties with violence permanently cut.

The first few days of the 2002 general election campaign defined the strengths of the parties, naturally raising the profile of the Opposition but leaving a certain inevitability in the expectation that the Fianna Fáil party would be the main partner in any new Government. It was even argued that the prospect of an overall majority was not beyond sight. Indeed, Fianna Fáil began the contest embarrassingly strong in the public opinion polls. The other parties, for various reasons, were carrying handicaps.

It was an election dominated by issues. It provoked serious and highly important judgments among voters about the shape and style of their then future Government. It had the longest possible preamble to the contest, with an infinite range of speculations about how it would go. It cleared away most of the debris that usually litters the beginning of a general election campaign. Some hard debating was ahead.

The election produced an interesting proposal, later to be espoused by Enda Kenny. This was the suggestion from the Progressive Democrats to fund the public capital programme for the next five years by the sale of what were described as non-essential State assets. The target figure was €6 billion and the proposal was essentially a policy of privatisation. By definition, this was open-ended, and in reality the target figure they gave could well have been conservative. The party's manifesto referred to three quite obvious utilities—the ESB, Aer Lingus and Bord Gáis—with the commercial ports thrown in as a slightly less obvious candidate. The principle was an attractive one. It allowed for a more positive approach to the need to conform to European law on competition. It recognised the State's general failure previously to run the utilities in a way that logically balanced service and profit. It recognised at the same time the need to free up State companies for better management.

The consensus on the economy was central to the 2002 election. Eccentric argument focused on the Bertie Bowl project, which introduced contention between Fianna Fáil and the Progressive Democrats. Michael McDowell was right in claiming that to spend as much money on a sporting extravaganza as would build ten major hospitals, or fund the running of a sizable part of the health service, was nonsensical. It rendered all debate on key economic issues absurd when the largest party in the country was committed to something that was unrealistic in the economic climate. It speaks volumes about Ahern's character that when asked during one interview if he had any regrets about his tenure as Taoiseach, he spoke about how he wished he had gone ahead with the Bertie Bowl.

The new Fine Gael leader, Michael Noonan, failed to engage the sympathy or support of the public. He seemed a bit at odds with the media, presenting himself a shade pompously in the guise of an alternative Taoiseach when most voters wanted simply to hear what he was made of and why the public should rescue his party. There were many reasons why such a rescue was worthwhile, but people needed reminding of them. He of all people should have been entering each and every debate without preconditions. The Labour Party, in debate anyway, was beginning to hold valuable fresh territory. The Progressive Democrats were setting the pace, and Mary Harney and Michael McDowell were making an impressive case for the separate identity that is so difficult for a junior coalition partner to achieve at the end of an administration.

Charlie McCreevy had adopted a crisis strategy and this was broadly correct. He was a traditionalist and believed that politicians are elected to lead countries, make decisions, accept responsibility. He also believed that Ireland always had an extravagantly large and expensive public service to provide answers to problems and to help the political leaders through crises. That is why the civil servants get security of tenure, generous salary and pension arrangements, and protection from too much public scrutiny. The role of presenting and arguing the case is a political role, either in the Dáil or with the press, and McCreevy was well able to take care of it. He made the electorate feel that it was enjoying good times and would be wise to go on with the team that had created them. The Special Savings Incentive Account scheme (SSIA) was looked on, at its inception, as a fine mark of mutual confidence between wage-earners and the Government. It had a different, elitist complexion by 2002. It was also costing more. With greater justification, what was rightly costing the Government a further billion euro was the furnishing of the pension fund, one of McCreevy's better decisions and one not to be abandoned or milked. Restraint was required in every department, and McCreevy's recognition of this, and his firm action with all his colleagues, was to be commended. What McCreevy was attempting was a sharp scaling down from a rate of increase that exceeded 20 per cent for the two years before the general election, and was in 2002 being targeted at 10 per cent for 2003 and 8 per cent or less for the following year.

McCreevy was not by nature a historian. He therefore did not argue from experience but from the kind of pragmatic realism that inspired Seán Lemass, but has not inspired a sufficient number of politicians who have come after him. In rude essentials, he was right in what he was doing. He was acting firmly at the outset of a secure term in office. He was satisfying the right wing of the partnership—the Progressive Democrats—and there was no harm in that. He was arguably not being tough enough, soon enough, but there was the old casualty of declining public confidence to avoid.

Stability was bought at a high price, much argued about during the last six months of 2002. It was the main burden of assault on Charlie McCreevy, but in fact it splattered the whole Government with the colourful evidence of public opprobrium, turning the processes of assessing the public finances and how they should be used into a lively and entertaining circus. Charlie McCreevy drew a line under that in December 2002 with a carefully constructed Budget, well-balanced and responsible to the point of being boring. Politically, McCreevy responded in an effective way to the international situation, to the domestic out turn, and to the basic security of his own and the Government's position. The inflationary impact was there, but it was modest. The borrowing was much lower than many people anticipated. The taxation penalties were adroitly placed. He concentrated taxes on existing wealth rather than on productive earnings, though of course these had to bear some increase.

Leading economists criticised the absence of a long-term strategy, notably Moore McDowell in the *Irish Independent* and Jim O'Leary writing on the same day in the *Irish Times*. But McCreevy judged the toughness of the Budget well. It was essentially stern, in keeping with the times, yet it was encouraging for business. Its main blemish was that it continued to fatten the monstrous public service while at the same time containing the admission that this creature had to be pared down in size. How the country got into the spiral of increases, some of which exceeded the Budget provision as a result of bench-marking, was a question that McCreevy should have been answering, but wasn't.

The partnership between Fianna Fáil and the Progressive Democrats was stabilised by the 2002 election. Voting strategy was skilful. Coalition voting, which meant first preference votes being given to Progressive Democrat candidates by supporters of other parties, even above their own candidates, worked and a strong endorsement of the party's role and performance was given in key constituencies, to the immense surprise of the majority of commentators. Their eye was excessively on the opinion polls, which gave a distorted and prejudicial view of the standing of the Progressive Democrats for reasons that are all too obvious: they were under-represented at the national level, their constituencies chosen where there was a good chance of success. Their success paved the way for the preferred solution of the electorate acceptable to Bertie Ahern, who recognised that the partnership with the Progressive Democrats, which both sides said had worked well, strengthened Ahern's own position within his party. It gave him an unusual authority. He was significantly responsible for it, he made it work, and he ensured that it developed away from the threatening character of earlier Fianna Fáil alliances towards a genuine, organic partnership.

Charlie McCreevy was replaced by Brian Cowen at the Department of Finance in September 2004. He spoke of the change without enthusiasm and of his new job in Brussels as an appointment that was still remote from all that he held dear. Despite rumours to the contrary, both Bertie Ahern and McCreevy claim he went of his own free will to the EU post. McCreevy was judged adversely for one major black spot in his career—the huge spending spree before the 2002 election—but that apart, he was uniquely successful, year on year, in matching his analysis of economic needs with his actions.

In 2004 the country was beginning to face the run-up to a general election. Ireland was governed by collective economics, the loosening of the purse-strings on departments, the buying back of lost popularity with a view to buying seats, and the control of power for a third term. For Brian Cowen, a new and untried Minister for Finance, without the experience McCreevy had gained over long years in power and without the skills McCreevy had, the prospects were daunting indeed. The

Minister had to contend with a Taoiseach who did the wrong thing and whose motives were dubious. He had to satisfy a party with short-term objectives, mainly about holding its seats and winning more seats. He had to contend with a partnership between Fianna Fáil and the Progressive Democrats, which he openly despised.

Chapter 3

THE 2007 GENERAL ELECTION

B ertie Ahern became the first—and now probably the last—
Fianna Fáil party leader since Eamon de Valera to be appointed
Taoiseach three times in succession. At the outset of the 2007
general election he knew better than most that the party, for him, was
over. His own good standing had been undermined. His poor
performances at the Mahon Tribunal (the public inquiry established by
Dáil Éireann in 1997 to investigate allegations of corrupt payments to
politicians), and the almost endless negative stories emerging about his
dubious personal finances, made his continued leadership of Fianna
Fáil or of the new Government impossible.

He had not been defeated by any electoral backlash following the
serious allegations that had arisen from the Mahon Tribunal. Question
marks about Ahern first arose when he confessed to the Tribunal that
he had signed blank cheques—astonishingly without even enquiring
what they were for—for the then Taoiseach Charles Haughey. Ahern
attempted to pass this off as so-called 'administrative convenience', but
he was severely criticised by the media.

However, worse was to come in September 2006 when the *Irish
Times* printed leaked material from the Tribunal about allegations that
Ahern had received money from a millionaire businessman while
Minister for Finance in 1993. Ahern went on to admit that he did
receive money, but expanded on this: 'What I got personally in my life,
to be frank with you, is none of your business. If I got something from
somebody as a present or something like that, I can use it.'

This statement was in complete contradiction to Ahern's comments to the Dáil in December 1996 when he had said: 'The public are entitled to have an absolute guarantee of the financial probity and integrity of their elected representatives, their officials and above all of Ministers. They need to know that they are under financial obligations to nobody.'

After the payments were publicised, Ahern appeared on RTÉ and admitted that he had received two payments totalling £39,000 in 1993 and 1994, but he regarded the money as a loan, or as a 'dig-out' as he put it himself, during what he described as a difficult time in his personal life. He explained that he had separated from his wife and was facing financial problems during the period in question. In his TV interview with Bryan Dobson, Ahern had insisted that the loan 'was raised by close friends, people who were close to me for most of my life'.

If it was a loan, surely Ahern would have made repayments? But nothing was ever going to be simple with Ahern's Pinocchio-styled story. He conceded that no repayments had been made, and highlighted that he had attempted to repay the loan but that his friends would not accept it. Ahern claimed that he had 'broken no codes—ethical, tax, legal or otherwise'.

The embarrassment continued as Ahern also admitted to receiving payments totalling £8,000stg from a group of 25 businessmen in Manchester. He pointed out that this money was an unsolicited 'gift' and therefore was not subject to tax since it had been received when abroad in the role of a private citizen and not in his capacity as Minister for Finance. This payment had been made to Ahern after he gave an after-dinner speech at an unscheduled function. Ahern also went on the record to state that no other payments had been received by him after he had spoken at similar functions.

It later emerged, in January 2008, that Ahern at the time was actually in discussion with the Revenue Commissioners about his liability for tax on the sums received in Manchester and on his tax-clearance status. Ahern, who bizarrely did not have a bank account when he was Finance Minister, would later admit to the Tribunal, on 21 February 2008, that he did not pay tax on substantial payments that he received when Minister for Finance in the 1990s.

As the 2007 general election got closer, the situation was becoming increasingly bleak for Fianna Fáil. On 30 September 2006, it was revealed that part of this contentious payment to Ahern was actually a cheque drawn from an account of NCB stockbrokers. On 28 November 2007, former NCB managing director Padraic O'Connor contradicted part of Ahern's story at the Mahon Tribunal by stating that the payment was not a loan and that he was 'not' a personal friend of the Taoiseach. He said the payment his company had made for £5,000 was intended as a donation to Fianna Fáil. O'Connor told the Tribunal: 'It is flattering to be described as a friend. I was not a close personal friend. Since I left NCB eight years ago, I have met Mr Ahern once or twice. I have no recollection of any mention made of the money paid. I made no personal donation to Mr Ahern.'

On 5 October 2006, it emerged that Ahern's residence in Drumcondra had been purchased by the Manchester-based Irish businessman Michael Wall, who had been at the 'dig-out' evening for Ahern in 1994. Later it was revealed that Wall had written a will in which he had planned to leave the house to Ahern.

The controversy continued to grow when it was pointed out that a number of Ahern's benefactors were later appointed as directors to the boards of various State bodies. In an attempt to defend himself, Ahern lamely stated: 'I might have appointed somebody but I appointed them because they were friends, not because of anything they had given me.'

He must have hoped that the matter would be settled for good when he gave an extensive statement in the Dáil to explain the unusual monetary payments to him. But more and more damaging information continued to be leaked from the Tribunal, the majority of which was being published in the *Irish Mail on Sunday* almost on a weekly basis under the byline of freelance journalist Frank Connolly, a brother of one of the IRA members dubbed the 'Colombian Three' who had absconded from South America after being arrested for allegedly training FARC rebels in explosive techniques. There was an attempt to use this connection to smear Connolly and imply that somehow the facts or sources for his brilliant investigation into Ahern couldn't be trusted. But there is no disputing now that Connolly's reporting made a major contribution to bringing down Ahern.

Further questions were raised about an amount of £50,000 that Ahern had lodged to his bank account in 1994. Ahern claimed this was money he had saved over a substantial period of time from 1987 to 1994 when he had had no active personal bank account. But Ahern was able to weather the storm. He even managed to defend himself against some of the more serious allegations that had been made against him, most notably the claim that he had taken a £50,000 bribe from a property developer, Owen O'Callaghan, in 1989 and a payment of £30,000 in 1993, in connection with a shopping complex development of lands at Quarryvale in Dublin. Ahern won a libel action against these allegations, but there is no doubt that his protest of innocence was slightly dampened when the outspoken former Irish international footballer Eamon Dunphy testified in the Mahon Tribunal that O'Callaghan had told him that Ahern had been taken care of to support a shopping centre development in the 1990s. This revelation by Dunphy followed the initial allegations—vehemently denied by both Ahern and O'Callaghan—by a retired developer named Tom Gilmartin, who alleged that O'Callaghan had given Ahern a payment of £50,000 and also another substantial payment in relation to tax designation of a site in Athlone in 1994.

Ahern was forced to bring forward the 2007 general election after his press secretary Mandy Johnston received a phone call from Paul Drury of the *Irish Mail on Sunday* on 28 April 2007 seeking a comment about a damaging story his paper was running the next morning about his finances. The story would reveal that Ahern had told the Tribunal that he had received a suitcase of £30,000stg cash from Michael Wall 'to be spent doing up the house' at the centre of the controversy.

With such an explosive story, a panicking Ahern knew he had no choice but to unexpectedly dash to Áras an Uachtaráin to dissolve the 29th Dáil. After discovering what the *Mail* planned to run, Ahern tipped off the *Sunday Independent* so it could cover the upcoming election as its front-page exclusive and he hoped to distract attention from the story in the *Mail.*

Other publications had been afraid to repeat many of the stories in the *Mail* because they didn't have the same information and were waiting for it to come out in the Tribunal. They didn't have to wait long because on 30 April the Mahon Tribunal was due to begin its public hearings into Ahern's possible links with Owen O'Callaghan.

All the aforementioned stories—and the fear of new ones emerging—prompted Ahern to run for cover; he refused almost all media requests during the election campaign and—apart from the leaders' debate on television—he chose to deal primarily with the *Sunday Independent*, which, as the country's largest-selling newspaper, was also astonishingly the only publication not to attack the Taoiseach's unorthodox financial arrangements. It later emerged that Ahern and Cowen had dinner with the paper's proprietor, Tony O'Reilly, before the general election.

This cosy relationship began when the paper's editor, Aengus Fanning, bumped into Ahern at the Irish cricket team's homecoming from the World Cup and, striking up a conversation, sympathetically said: 'You're having a hard time.'

'They're persecuting me!' was Ahern's bemoaning reply. He agreed to do an interview with Fanning. Fanning has no qualms about the *Sunday Independent*'s decision to support Ahern, whose exclusive interviews were pushing up sales. As Fanning admits himself:

> He gave you stories. Stuff that sold papers. We sold an awful lot of newspapers during that period.... From my point of view as editor, Bertie gave us stories. He revealed stuff about his own personal tribulations. He gave value for money. We often got lead [exclusive front page] stories out of him during that period. But there was plenty of criticism about Bertie in the paper. Bertie was getting a hammering from the media and I really don't think it was shared to the same extent by the public at large.

The 'plenty of criticism' was restricted mainly to a select few of their columnists, such as Gene Kerrigan, widely perceived as the paper's 'token leftie'. Labour leader Eamon Gilmore was furious with the *Sunday Independent* for being 'a cheerleader for Bertie' and his Fianna Fáil-led Government. 'If a newspaper group and a title goes onto the pitch as a player, it is no longer offering fair or objective comment,' Gilmore pointed out.

It was also speculated that the *Sunday Independent*, which had been campaigning to get rid of stamp duty for all first-time buyers, agreed to endorse Ahern if he pushed through the tax changes on residential property. After the election, the stamp duty change was pushed through—even though Cowen, as then Finance Minister, had clearly stated before the election that he had no plans to revamp it.

Eyebrows were further raised about the paper's close relationship with Ahern when one of its star columnists, Eoghan Harris, went onto 'The Late Late Show' to support publicly Ahern and later was appointed to the Seanad as a Taoiseach's nominee. A coincidence? Harris says:

> There's all this shit about putting me in the Seanad as a reward for 'The Late Late Show'. Bertie Ahern would probably have put me in the Seanad as a mark of appreciation for my relentless support since 1988. I have never written a bad word about Ahern since 1988. In the 2007 election, Ahern was up against it with the media and I felt I had to do my little spin-doctoring bit to shift the pendulum and make the Irish people look at Bertie Ahern as he was really—a fucking man without a bob!

It was difficult for journalists trying to be fair, diligent and judgmental to believe they were in the same profession.

According to an RTÉ exit poll, 82 per cent of those who voted in the general election were simply unconcerned about Mr Ahern's Byzantine financial arrangements. 'What does one say to that? He can certainly look back and say that, far from damaging him, it actually helped him, which is amazing,' recalls the then Labour Party leader, Pat Rabbitte.

It appeared that the election was Enda Kenny's to lose, with virtually every opinion poll showing a surge in support for a Fine Gael and Labour coalition following the two parties' 'Mullingar Accord', a pact to effectively run as a team to offer the electorate a genuine alternative to an Ahern-led Government.

There is little doubt that if the Opposition went on the offensive and attacked Ahern, they could have damaged Fianna Fáil, but, somewhat strangely, they decided not to raise the controversy over Ahern's financial affairs during the general election. Enda Kenny stated:

> I can give Bertie Ahern one guarantee: there will be no descent into sleaze politics with me as leader of Fine Gael. We will fight the election on the issues that are before the people—health, crime, value for money, and taxation. That is going to be a hard political battle but, for me, it will be a fair battle.

It was clearly a mistake—Ahern was against the ropes. Why didn't they go after him? In retrospect, the decision not to challenge Ahern about his financial affairs during the course of the election came to be regarded as a tactical mistake by many within the Opposition ranks. Pat Rabbitte points out that the Opposition 'never considered' aggressively targeting the Taoiseach over his precarious money issues because there was a consensus back then that 'people don't personalise politics in Ireland to that extent'. After one attack on Ahern, Labour actually dropped in the polls and the Opposition feared that further attacks would only alienate voters even more.

Eamon Gilmore, who replaced Rabbitte after the election as Labour leader, believes they should have continued to target Ahern:

> I disagree with Pat when he said that 'We shouldn't have done it because the previous time we did it we went down in the polls'. There are some things that you have to make a call on—irrespective of whether polls are going up or down for you. There are certain standards that have to be maintained in public life. I do not think that an office-holder should be getting large sums of money, whether from friends or business people, or whatever, for personal use. Now, that is my standard.

Without going on the offensive, Rabbitte said he still could not offer any rational explanation as to why Ahern's 'unorthodox finances' didn't produce any substantial backlash against Fianna Fáil in the general election, as had been predicted by the political pundits. 'I cannot say why it worked against the Opposition parties. I cannot explain why he gained from it and we lost support—the Labour Party wasn't in Manchester at all.'

But if the electorate wasn't perplexed by Ahern's personal finances to such an extent, the media certainly were. Nevertheless, the first ten days of the campaign were taken up by media pursuits for answers on Ahern's finances. 'It tended to dominate the campaign and precluded our capacity to discuss issues that were important. I probably have some regrets now that we didn't make the economy a bigger issue,' says Pat Rabbitte.

The constant revelations of further allegations were making it next to impossible for Fianna Fáil to get its media campaign up and running. The party was constantly on the back foot—and some of its press people were refusing to return media calls or answer queries even as close as four weeks before the general election. 'It got to the stage where you couldn't fucking believe a word coming out of Bertie's mouth,' states one of his former Cabinet Ministers.

At the time, most political pundits were predicting that it was almost inevitable that Enda Kenny would be the next Taoiseach. Fine Gael represented a serious and admirable challenge. Unfortunately, Enda Kenny, who had replaced Michael Noonan, was seen as not up to the job, not experienced enough, lightweight, not a match for Bertie Ahern. The party should have done better. Unlike Fianna Fáil, which seemed at the outset of the campaign to be less well-prepared than the situation required, the main Opposition party had carried out a root and branch reorganisation in every constituency which had brought it back to a well-deserved level of power, which paid off in seats. Despite this work on the ground, many thought less of the achievement in 2007 than the party deserved, and both 'The Man Who Would be Taoiseach' and the party he led were repeatedly written off. Kenny proved himself on the campaign trail but not in the leaders' debate, where his performance was terrible. However, his election campaign sustained the party around the country in the self-respect and confidence that had been induced over many months. There was undoubtedly a gap between this countrywide achievement and Enda Kenny's own performance. There was too much emphasis on the 'Contract for a New Ireland'. Too much of its content was seen as a device. Novelty politics, some would argue. It only partly worked, but it gave to Fine Gael some things that the party had lacked for many years: a focus and a direction.

Enda Kenny had proved himself a leader of the Opposition with growing muscle. He had, as he showed convincingly in the 2011 general election, those vital requirements for political warfare: an easy manner and a gracious handling of the public. He was trusted throughout. So were his team. This was in marked contrast to the dishonesty displayed in the closing stages by Fianna Fáil, the factual inaccuracies over tax and the economy. Enda Kenny faced into the 30th Dáil with many new strengths.

In 2007, two factors went against Fine Gael—the first was the emergence of Fianna Fáil's deputy leader, Brian Cowen, who famously declared he had the 'bottle for the battle', to lead his party's media campaigning. The second was Kenny's weak performance in the debates with Ahern. However, Ahern's 'winning' performance was hyped up—he may have shaded Kenny, but that doesn't necessarily mean his performance was that good either. The presenter of the debate, Miriam O'Callaghan, recalls that both men were clearly 'nervous'. It's obvious why Ahern was nervous: he feared hard-hitting questions from O'Callaghan about his personal crisis; but it was revealed only as late as 2011 that Kenny was considerably shaken prior to the debates because he had been door-stepped at the entrance to RTÉ's television studio by two Fianna Fáil 'supporters' purporting to be reporters asking him uncomfortable questions about a supposed story about to break concerning his party. There is no doubt that this dirty trick worked in shaking up Kenny.

With Ahern out of the picture for most of the general election campaign, Cowen was frustrated by his party's inability to mount an effective offensive. With Ahern's obvious reluctance to front a media campaign, Cowen, nicknamed 'the Rottweiler', decided to come out fighting. He was seen as the party's primary spokesperson and was even later credited with almost single-handedly winning the election for Fianna Fáil. There is no doubt that Cowen's robust intervention at this critical point had a decisive impact in steadying the nerves of the party faithful and in galvanising efforts to put their campaign back on the front foot. This action by Cowen distinguished him from his peers and can be seen now as the moment when Ahern decided to mark him out as his 'heir apparent'.

Cowen was equally frustrated by the fact that the Opposition parties' political manifestos, particularly those of Labour and Fine Gael, were not analysed or scrutinised by the media. He put across the argument that both Labour and Fine Gael's political manifestos were 'con jobs' and argued that two of Labour's seven promises—in relation to health and pensions—were 'flawed'. During every single media interview he gave, Cowen stated that both Opposition parties had different spending commitments out of the same €2.9 billion Government fund. Both parties were making different election promises—but within confines of the same budget. 'They are not the same commitments, but they are spending the same money twice. People need to analyse what is going on here. This is a con job—plain and simple. It is all dishonesty,' stated Cowen.

Bit by bit, Cowen pulled apart the Mullingar Accord. His argument that when the election was over, Labour and Fine Gael were going to say, 'Now we must negotiate the €2.9 billion' clearly resonated with the electorate. He pointed out that all the promises of the Opposition would have to 'be funnelled into this €2.9 billion magic can that they have, which they are going to negotiate after the next election'.

The polls were predicting that Fianna Fáil would lose between 13 and 15 seats, but Cowen confidently dismissed this, since he believed that the momentum was behind them, with their canvassing confirming it. He was also finding on the doorsteps himself in his own constituency that the Ahern controversy wasn't a major issue. Nobody was really interested in the economy, he was finding—it was local issues that were of most concern. So, in the end, contrary to the mid-campaign expectations, Fianna Fáil managed to return a total of 78 seats.

In 2007, Fianna Fáil gave us all the most dramatic lessons in the nature and use of power. The party stormed back, led more by the impressive performance of Brian Cowen in attempting to gut the policies of the Opposition than by any other single figure, Bertie Ahern included. Yet the personal comeback by Ahern, against a mixture of legitimate criticisms, the misfortunes of revelations about his personal finances and his own incapacity to explain himself, was also an astonishing achievement. He kept cool under pressure, he maintained the momentum of the whole campaign and he used every opportunity—and there were many such coming from his good friends Tony Blair, Bill Clinton, George Mitchell and Ian Paisley—to recover his position. Only once did Ahern show his true emotions on the campaign trail. When out canvassing, he was asked by Scott Millar, then a journalist for the *Mail*, about the Tribunal and he appeared to momentarily crack when he muttered bad language and made derogatory comments about the journalist's British nationality under his breath.

The party ran a formidable political machine. Countrywide it went into overdrive and sustained this throughout the most unfortunate mixture of bad moments and own goals, as well as considerable achievements. The gap between Bertie Ahern, public and international figure, endorsed by world leaders aiding him in his dark hour at home, and the muddled domestic circumstances he faced with the media here, was a large one. He steamed on through it all, as did the party and its daily team of spokespersons.

After the election was over, the sure-footed confidence about the Irish economy with which Brian Cowen, Bertie Ahern and others carried the country through the campaign did not take long in turning into uncertainty, prevarication and a rather feeble appeal to the commentators not to talk us into gloom and doom. The optimistic future that guided their words turned into a number of doubts and imponderables. Brian Cowen, once on the attack, was now on the defensive. So was Bertie Ahern. They didn't quite know what language to use. An example is how Ahern caused controversy when speaking at the biennial conference of the Irish Congress of Trade Unions in Bundoran, Co. Donegal in July 2007 with his insulting and wounding remarks about suicide when dismissing those forewarning about the impending crisis. He said: 'Sitting on the sidelines, cribbing and moaning is a lost opportunity. I don't know how people who engage in that don't commit suicide because frankly the only thing that motivates me is being able to actively change something.' It was, as Enda Kenny points out, insulting and wounding to those who had lost family and friends through suicide. He said: 'I hope his comment about the economy and what people should do was a slip of the tongue. I have stood in 200 kitchens where that phenomenon has brought untold grief on families and leaves a mark that lasts forever.'

And the initiative for sound judgment and a balanced reading of the future—insofar as this was possible—was back in the hands it should have been in, that of the professional commentators who were telling us that the property boom was slowing down, as were growth and expansion. The shadow over the country was that of a dying Tiger not of a living, vibrant animal, full of strength and self-assurance.

Morgan Kelly's controversial report, issued alongside the ESRI (Economic and Social Research Institute) Quarterly Commentary but carefully separated as independent of the main economic forecast, resonated very accurately with opinion among house buyers and those trying to sell their property as a sensible attempt at cooling a grossly over-heated aspect of the economy. Property prices were at a high point that was truly ridiculous; it had few parallels anywhere else in the Eurozone; and it occupied a substantial cycle of employment, marketing, borrowing, investment and, not to put a tooth in it, gross greed.

Side by side with the property boom was enormous State investment in public expenditure. The welcome improvement in the road network was the most visible demonstration of this, marred by further work that seemed to have every good highway in the country partially covered by reconstruction activity. Lavish expenditure was an offshoot of the building boom, employing many of the same companies, and funded out of the enlarged tax revenues in the years previous.

Because it was so welcome in a world where the commuter's nightmare appeared to be slowly going through a cycle of solutions, the Government took courage and went on spending. But the nightmare was still there and the tax revenue was no longer supporting the level of expectation. Brian Cowen had been remarkably lucky in riding the Tiger while it was strong. He now faltered in trying to manage it in its infirmity. Cats are as unpredictable as economies and, when wounded, can be hard to handle.

Chapter 4 ∾

| COALITION UNDER COWEN

It was the late Seamus Brennan's idea to form a coalition with the Greens. There was an argument that the Greens weren't needed, but Ahern looked at the numbers and agreed that the Greens would help put together what they thought would be a solid Government that would last the full term. Cowen was appointed chief negotiator for the Fianna Fáil team tasked with the coalition talks with the Green Party. Fianna Fáil's decision to negotiate with the Greens came as a surprise to many, particularly considering that their leader, Trevor Sargent, had vowed not to go into Government with Bertie Ahern, whom he believed should have resigned because of the revelations emerging from the Mahon Tribunal. Therefore it came as a surprise even to the Greens when the call came through from Fianna Fáil about discussing a deal. John Gormley recalls: 'We had a number of days where we thought, "Is this for real?" Once we found out it was for real, we then had to ask ourselves, "Will we go for this?"'

The Greens astonished many of their core supporters by agreeing to the talks. They may have been politically inexperienced, but even the Greens were not naïve enough to believe that they would achieve any of their main election promises—primarily the banning of US military flights landing in Shannon Airport; to block the ring roads around the historical Hill of Tara shrine; and to oppose the Corrib gas project. Instead, the Greens turned 'yellow' and shamefully agreed to break all these promises as part of their power grab.

However, before agreeing to go into negotiations with Fianna Fáil, the Greens desperately sought to put together a coalition with Fine Gael and Labour. But there was a major problem: Enda Kenny had made a solemn pre-election vow not to go into Government with Sinn Féin.

Why? He claimed that Sinn Féin—despite acknowledging that as a party they 'have moved a long way'—still had an 'Army Council in situ' and 'there are things that are not cleared up at all—the consequences of the Northern Ireland bank raid, the murder of Joseph Rafferty here in Dublin, and all of these things'. He was adamant that he would 'not be sharing power with Sinn Féin'. But with the figures not adding up for a coalition between the Greens and Labour, Kenny evidently had a change of heart. At first, he privately mulled over the concept of Sinn Féin not joining the coalition but only supporting it from 'outside'.

Brian Hayes, the Dublin South-West Fine Gael TD, who later played a pivotal role in orchestrating Richard Bruton's botched heave against Kenny in 2010, admits that such a proposal was 'a fine line' between keeping your 'word' and simply being yet another hypocritical political leader desperate for a power grab.

'I'm surprised that he doesn't admit the fact that he was trying to speak to people. I think the question was would they support it from being outside Government. The question would they back it—i.e., a change of Government—without being part of the Government, that was the question,' recalls Hayes, who became a Junior Minister in Kenny's eventual Government in 2011. He continues:

> His [Kenny's] argument at the time presumably was he wanted to form a Government. The first priority for every TD is: Do they want to be part of that Government or not, in terms of supporting his candidature for Taoiseach. So, I think his suggestion was, 'Would you support a Government, albeit not be part of that Government?' Needless to say, they were going to say no to that. The idea that it was going to happen was quite fanciful.

But even though Kenny insists that his 'word' is his 'bond', it does appear that he was so desperate to put together a coalition after the 2007 general election that he considered going back on his word and doing a deal with Sinn Féin.

Trevor Sargent insists that Kenny rang him and asked if he would approach Sinn Féin to enquire if they'd consider supporting him as Taoiseach. Kenny has always denied this, while Gerry Adams also confirms that Sinn Féin had been approached by the Greens about supporting a Fine Gael-led Government. However, Kenny still won't admit that he contemplated the uncontemplatable by getting into bed with Sinn Féin.

After the general election, Kenny demoted the party's national director of elections, Frank Flannery, for suggesting in an interview with the *Irish Mail on Sunday* that Fine Gael would consider doing 'business' with Gerry Adams. It has been suggested that Flannery was told to purposely drop the Sinn Féin idea in print to test the reaction, but it received a negative response. After this, in an interview in *Hot Press*, outspoken Green TD Paul Gogarty claimed that Kenny had approached Sargent, and this was picked up by the *Daily Mail*, which got the former Green leader on the record to confirm his conversation about Sinn Féin with Kenny. But Kenny's people denied it because, as Gogarty points out, Kenny 'didn't want to be embarrassed' by the Sinn Féin connection after the Flannery incident. Gogarty recalls:

> It got to the stage where Enda Kenny rang Trevor and said, 'Listen, you wouldn't mind talking to Sinn Féin about forming a Government?' He, in good faith, spoke to Caoimhghín Ó Caoláin about an alternative to Fianna Fáil after being contacted by Enda Kenny. Now Enda is casting aspersions on Trevor's good name by suggesting that Trevor isn't telling the truth. What he said was, 'Who do you believe? Me or Trevor Sargent?'
>
> I think Trevor's integrity is not in question. He showed tremendous integrity when the mistake was brought to his attention and he immediately resigned. He didn't brazen it out.
>
> I'm really pissed off with Enda Kenny over blackening Trevor's name and not having the moral courage to admit that he was looking to talk to Sinn Féin. I think questions still need to be asked of Enda Kenny about that because he hasn't come out and called Trevor a liar, he just insinuated; he said, 'Who do you believe? Me or Trevor Sargent?'
>
> He's behaving like a sleeven because if you're setting yourself up as Taoiseach, then you should be beyond reproach. If you make a mistake you should say, 'Yeah, I did that. I had my own reasons. It was politically sensitive at the time. But that was the only way we could form an alternative Government.' Ultimately, he should have

said, 'Yes, I did contact Trevor Sargent; we needed a new Government and Sinn Féin were the only option, we had to discuss that.' But for his own reasons, he denied it.

It was an issue that Enda Kenny, who portrays himself as a straight talker, was never challenged on directly in any media interviews—bar one previously unpublished. In the following excerpt of the recorded in-depth interview with Jason O'Toole, as soon as the Trevor Sargent phone call question was put directly to him, Kenny started to stumble and then he danced around the question:

'Em, I don't recall the detail of that. But obviously if you were to put a Government together after 2007, you would have needed everybody to get up to 84. And obviously I wasn't in a position to talk to Sinn Féin.'

'So, would you have let the Greens talk to Sinn Féin?'

'Well, my conversation with him [Trevor Sargent] was with him about his party. And our conversations were in Irish because I always spoke to Trevor in Irish. And obviously we discussed that I had spoken to Mary Harney. And it didn't work out. It's over. It's history.'

'But would you have accepted them at the time then to make up the numbers?'

'I think there were a lot of exercises going on about mathematics, how you might reach 83 or 84. But my conversations with Trevor were about the Green Party.'

When it was pointed out that Paul Gogarty mentioned he was standing beside Trevor when he made the call, Kenny replied, 'I didn't know Paul Gogarty understands the Irish language. Maybe he does. I don't know. I might fault the man. When you're ringing somebody, you don't know who's standing beside them.'

'So, you didn't mention Sinn Féin to him?'

'I don't know that it was recorded. Obviously people will say, "If you're going to make up numbers between Fine Gael and Labour and Greens, Independents, PDs, or whatever, how do you make up 83/84?"'

'So, basically Paul is probably lying?'

'I wouldn't accuse any man of lying, but all I can confirm to you is that I spoke to Trevor Sargent *as Gaeilge*, if Paul Gogarty understands what I'm saying....'

'Well, Gogarty says that Sargent told him this immediately after your conversation.'

'Listen, that's history. We are where we are. I've ruled out Sinn Féin the next time and I've given a very clear reason for that. And we're focused on winning the next election. I've no interest in going back to the past; we're focused on the future. That's what the people want.'

It was a subject that Kenny clearly did not want to discuss but it was interesting to note that he almost admits to it all when he says he 'ruled out Sinn Féin the next time'—but what about the last time? To this day, Kenny denies ever contemplating such a shift in his political ideology.

But the Greens certainly did dramatically shift their own thinking. After the 'tough negotiations', as John Gormley describes them, were finalised, the Greens had a difficult time selling the deal for Government to their grassroots members. At an emotional vote in the Mansion House, the party members endorsed the deal by the narrowest of margins—making them the first all-Ireland party to be in power since the foundation of the State.

Patricia McKenna—who made political history for the Greens in 1994 by topping the poll and becoming their first ever MEP—recalls that Greens' meeting as almost akin to a convention of a cult sect:

First of all, we didn't see the Programme for Government until we got into the Mansion House. We weren't allowed to take the Programme for Government out with us. We had a massive document to try and read through in a very, very short space of time—and then vote on it. It was all very strange. We were told they got four ministers—I've never seen the fourth one. The people who were not happy with it felt it was a strange set-up where you had people placed all around to 'work' on people to get them on their side. It was a very, very well organised event by very clever people.

After the vote was effectively 'pushed through', as McKenna describes the situation, Trevor Sargent dramatically resigned as party leader because of his pre-election promise not to lead his party into a coalition with Bertie Ahern. However, despite stepping down and being replaced by John Gormley, Sargent effectively did lead his party into the coalition by urging party members to vote in favour of the Greens going into Government. McKenna states:

> Trevor said he would not lead the Green Party into Government with Fianna Fáil—yet that day in the Mansion House he urged everyone to support going into Government with Fianna Fáil and asked them to vote in favour of it. He was instrumental in getting the members to vote in favour. And when the result came out he said it was the proudest day of his life! I don't understand it. I just find it schizophrenic!

If Sargent clearly felt uncomfortable leading his party into coalition with Ahern, it must surely have been puzzling, even smacking of double standards, that he had absolutely no qualms about agreeing to work under the Fianna Fáil Taoiseach as the Junior Minister of State for Food and Horticulture.

The Greens in Government with Fianna Fáil was a 'temporary little arrangement', to paraphrase Albert Reynolds, which was never going to sit comfortably—one look at the picture of the Minister for Communications, Energy and Natural Resources, Eamon Ryan, standing shoulder-to-shoulder with the Rossport protestors before he entered Government speaks volumes about the Greens' volte-face. Perhaps Paul Gogarty later summed up how the Rossport protestors felt when he confessed that his party had 'prostituted' itself and had been 'screwed' by Fianna Fáil.

When the new Cabinet was announced, Cowen kept the Finance portfolio, but Ahern chose this moment to promote Cowen to the role of Tánaiste. As an obvious acknowledgment of Cowen's significant contribution to both ensuring Fianna Fáil's success in the general election and his invaluable input to negotiating the programme for Government with the coalition partner, during an interview with the *Sunday Independent* Ahern declared that his new Tánaiste was his 'heir apparent', which annoyed some of the other obviously ambitious

Cabinet Ministers, such as Micheál Martin, Dermot Ahern and Noel Dempsey, who all had designs on the highest political office. But the argument put forward at the time was that none of them had the same level of Government experience as Cowen, who had held more ministerial positions than any of the other members of Cabinet. It's hard to imagine now any of them doing worse than Cowen when he eventually became Taoiseach.

In the immediate aftermath of the general election, Ahern even spoke publicly about how he would not be making any major moves without first consulting Brian Cowen. 'Obviously the party will ultimately decide, but [from] my point of view, he is the obvious successor to me in five years' time or whenever,' Ahern stated during an RTÉ radio interview with Seán O'Rourke.

But political pundits did find it unusual that Ahern decided, merely days after the election, to publicly push forward Cowen's candidature for the leadership of Fianna Fáil and, thus, the likelihood of becoming Taoiseach within the lifetime of the new Government. Did he do this as part of an agreement made with Cowen to keep his support?

Other political pundits wondered if Ahern's public declaration for Cowen was akin to his public support for Albert Reynolds's presidential nomination. It was the consensus amongst Cabinet members that Ahern clearly had his own motives for bringing Cowen close by identifying him in this way. He knew that in all probability he would soon come under even more extreme pressure when he had to go before the Mahon Tribunal within the coming months—and who better than Cowen, who was dubbed 'the loyal politician from the loyal county', to have by your side? All agreed that it was an astute move on Ahern's behalf, as Cowen did indeed go on to defend his boss on several occasions before the situation became untenable.

As soon as the new Government was formed, the Opposition adopted a very different approach to their pre-election handling of the Ahern saga and now relentlessly pursued him at every given opportunity, as they pressed for his resignation. A motion of no confidence in Ahern's Government was moved by Kenny after Ahern's appearance at the Mahon Tribunal on 23 September 2007. In a stormy Dáil debate, Ahern was accused of telling 'lies' and was called upon to resign. The no confidence motion was defeated by 81 votes to 76.

On 13 September 2007, Ahern had begun four days of testimony at the Tribunal. He acknowledged that he had not been fully cooperative with the Tribunal when the counsel stated that information supplied 'did not encompass all of the material questions that had been asked of you', replying: 'I accept that, yes.' The following day Ahern changed his story on the infamous dig-outs. The Tribunal chairman, Judge Alan Mahon, stated that there were 'significant gaps' in the money trail that 'would have made it impossible for the Tribunal to follow the trail'. In a subsequent opinion poll, it was revealed that less than one-third of the electorate believed Ahern's accounts of his finances; it got even worse the following January when 78 per cent stated they didn't believe Ahern had given a 'full picture' of his finances.

The Tribunal continued to uncover an ever-increasing number of questionable financial matters relating to Ahern. On 2 February 2008, it emerged that Ahern's former partner, Celia Larkin, had purchased a house in 1993 with money donated to Ahern's constituency organisation in Drumcondra.

On 28 March 2008 it was revealed in the Tribunal that lodgements of £15,500stg had been made on Ahern's behalf by his former secretary Gráinne Carruth to building society accounts for him and his children. She had previously stated, on 19 March, that she had made no sterling lodgements; while Ahern had told the Tribunal in February that the lodgements to his daughters' accounts came from his salary as Minister for Finance, because he didn't actually have a bank account at the time. But Carruth changed her testimony after she was reminded by Des O'Neill SC that she could face a two-year prison sentence or a staggering €30,000 fine if she was found to be lying under oath. At this point, Carruth broke down under the sustained pressure and asked if she could leave. It disgusted the public. How could the Taoiseach put a mother in this position? Ahern would later blame the Tribunal for the sorry sight.

Ahern had originally stated that he would not be making any more public statements on the issue until his next appearance in front of the Tribunal, but the position in which his former secretary had been placed was giving rise to public disquiet and presented Ahern with an embarrassing dilemma. For some of Ahern's Cabinet colleagues, the public's perception of a crying mother being placed in such a difficult position while testifying in an investigation into Ahern's affairs was making them uncomfortable. To make matters worse, Ahern did not make any public statement to defend Carruth at that time. Rightly or wrongly, the public had the perception that Ahern was now hiding behind his secretary.

On 28 March 2008 the unease at Ahern's testimony having been contradicted by his former secretary at the Tribunal was highlighted when the acting party leader of the PDs, Mary Harney, who had traditionally been perceived as a steadfast supporter of Ahern, publicly called on the Taoiseach to make a statement. The Green Party leader John Gormley followed suit. Pressure also emerged within the Fianna Fáil parliamentary party for Ahern to make a public statement on this latest twist in the Tribunal saga when the Dáil reconvened the following Tuesday.

Ahern realised that he was quickly losing the support of his Government colleagues. Word was put out that he was now thinking about stepping down after the local elections in May. But this didn't stop the disquiet—Fianna Fáil councillors were starting to believe that they would lose their seats in an electoral backlash over Ahern. Ahern heard that a group of backbench TDs had made a discreet approach to Cowen to see if he might consider making a move to oust him. 'Brian said a few fellas had been ringing him moaning about the situation, but he didn't seem overly bothered about it,' Ahern recalled in his memoir.

But the party was 'bothered'. When Cowen was in Malaysia for the St Patrick's Day's festivities, there had been behind-the-scenes manoeuvring at senior levels of Fianna Fáil, and Ahern was clearly feeling pressure to announce his departure date. Mary Coughlan refused to back Ahern when she appeared on RTÉ. Ahern was in his local pub, Fagan's, enjoying his usual tipple of a pint of Bass, when Micheál Martin phoned him and told him to resign. It was speculated that Martin had made the call at the suggestion of Cowen, who says he doesn't know 'anything about it'.

Cowen received several phone calls from senior Fianna Fáil deputies when he was abroad, but he insists he was 'noncommittal' and that he was 'too far away to be making any judgments'. While Cowen was away, Anglo Irish Bank suffered the so-called St Patrick's Day Massacre when the bank's share price was attacked in London while the Irish Exchange was closed, with hedge funds selling the stock down. Panicking, Seán FitzPatrick was advised by Fintan Drury, a fellow director of the bank and friend of Cowen's since university, to phone the Finance Minister and explain the crisis. 'I told him that [Quinn] had it in CFD, I think. I am not sure. What I said was what was really happening was that pressure was coming on from the shorters, these guys, the hedge funds, trying to get Quinn,' says FitzPatrick. He recalls that Cowen 'just said yeah. He was taking it all in.'

At the time of the crisis, Cowen's spokesperson tried to reassure the market by claiming that the crisis was 'an international development as opposed to a local development'. Cowen has confirmed that he contacted his Department and the Governor of the Central Bank, John Hurley, when he was away in Asia.

As this messy nightmare played out in Anglo, surely Cowen would have been fully aware that if his close connections with Anglo directors were to emerge, it would ruin his career?

Following a short holiday in Vietnam after his St Patrick's Day duties, Cowen returned to Ireland on 26 March. Later that evening, he says he phoned Ahern to discuss 'some important issues concerning the financial markets'; no doubt Ahern's latest financial crisis would have been also briefly discussed. The two men agreed to meet the following day in Ahern's home—not in his constituency office of St Luke's, as had been speculated in the press at the time—in Drumcondra. According to sources close to Cowen, he was 'fuming' during the drive to Ahern's home—a house that was central to the Taoiseach's financial crisis, the irony of which wouldn't have been lost on Cowen. The source says Cowen went to Ahern's house with one purpose only—to give him his marching orders. But Cowen and Ahern have always denied this. Why? According to former Fianna Fáil deputy leader Mary O'Rourke: 'I suppose he didn't want to put Bertie further in the mire. Bertie had anointed him as leader, which I think now, in hindsight, was a huge mistake.'

Cowen is adamant that 'at no stage' did he 'indicate a withdrawal of support', but it's interesting to note, however, that he also said that he had discussed all the 'scenarios' with Ahern. Cowen acknowledged that Ahern had been badly served by the constant leaks from the Tribunal, so surely both men knew that the latest contradictory evidence from

Gráinne Carruth had made the situation untenable? It was no longer just an issue for Ahern alone—it was now an issue for Fianna Fáil. The party's reputation was being damaged and surely this was not tolerable to the self-confessed 'loyal to the party' Cowen? During their meeting, surely Cowen pointed out that there were growing fears that this situation could seriously weaken the Government's efforts to secure a Yes Vote in the upcoming Lisbon Treaty referendum, as well as in the local elections? And surely both men agreed that there could be an electoral backlash?

According to Cowen's and Ahern's versions of events, their conversation started with a discussion on the 'problems facing the financial markets', which was obviously a vague reference to the crisis facing Anglo. Cowen says they then 'discussed things generally' about the worrying allegations brought up in the Mahon Tribunal. Cowen says that despite the 'wild speculation', there was 'no blood on the walls' in their meeting. He insists that he never pushed Ahern or told him 'home truths'. Cowen says:

> It wasn't that sort of a relationship. To suggest that I was going around laying down the law is not true, that was not the situation. The Taoiseach was assessing the situation himself and my role was to be supportive of him, provide him with the time and space to do that—whatever he wanted to do, he could come back to us on.

According to Ahern's memoir, Cowen's 'uncle had died recently and he was obviously upset about that, because they had been close'— basically implying that Cowen had enough worries himself to be concerned with Ahern's problems. This is factually incorrect for, according to Cowen, after the meeting with Ahern he travelled to Mullingar Hospital to visit his dying uncle, Father Andrew, who had been a teacher in the Roscrea boarding school Cowen had attended. Two months previously, Cowen's other uncle, Michael, an engineer with the local authority and a former vice-chairman of An Bord Pleanála, had also died.

Ahern says he had made up his mind by now that he was going to go, but he did not inform Cowen immediately. As Cowen was leaving his house, Ahern said that he would be in touch shortly to discuss the situation further. During the weekend, Ahern phoned Cowen and asked him to visit his St Luke's constituency office in Drumcondra on the Monday. According to Ahern's autobiography, Cowen was taken aback when Ahern told him he planned to go without fighting—and go within a month. It was a perfect time for Ahern's swansong departure, since with the tenth anniversary of the Good Friday Agreement approaching, he had scheduled formal engagements at Westminster and in the US Congress. These allowed him to step down not in disgrace but with glowing plaudits, both from home and internationally.

'In my mind there was no question of him not doing that. He would have to do that. When he said, "Look, I think I'll step down", I said, "You'll have to do that, anyway." It was obvious to me that would happen,' recalls Cowen.

Bertie Ahern was forced to resign on Wednesday, 3 April 2008 after 11 years in power. Quite properly his departure was allowed to be seen as the result of his having fallen down on his own set of standards in public life. At the beginning of his period as Fianna Fáil leader, before the 1997 general election, he had told his party and the country: 'We will not tolerate any deviation from the benchmarks of honour. No one is welcome in this party if they betray public trust.' Yet in the end, it was his apparent transgression of precisely these conditions and standards that brought him down. In his resignation speech, he insisted he had done no wrong. But he had, and more than half the country thought so. They thought so before the 2007 general election, but saying it then was done half-heartedly; now, with power secured, his coalition partner demanded explanations about his bizarre financial dealings on the grounds that Government business was being blocked.

Ahern had promised from the outset of his leadership to put an end to sleaze and corruption in the party and in public life. Yet during the previous 18 months he had been subjected to increasingly embarrassing scrutiny by a planning tribunal looking into corruption allegations. Those aimed at him, and backed with financial statistics that did not add up, found that Bertie Ahern had more and more questions to answer. The Tribunal was due to resume the following month.

What may have been a pleasant surprise for Ahern was the relatively calm way in which the Green Party went along with what, to them, was a major change. It had to accept a new deal with Brian Cowen if it was to survive in Government and if the Government itself was to survive. Ahern had been a more ameliorative person than Cowen was. He was firmly against coalition and accepted it on sufferance. It was a necessary evil. On the other hand, as far as the Green Party was concerned, Brian Cowen, unlike Bertie Ahern with a Haughey-like safe full of cash, was 'clean'. He was not immune from investigation, which he regarded as part of the new 'journalistic culture', to use his own phrase, which had seeped into the Irish media since the introduction of Tribunals to investigate planning corruption, but the worst that could be laid at his door was a modest example of 'guilt by association'. The nearest the papers managed in connecting Cowen with a controversial developer was on 5 April 2007, when the *Irish Times* ran a news story highlighting that 'several major property development companies' had contributed to a golf classic fundraising election event for Cowen at Hollystown Golf Club, near Dublin Airport. One of the contributors to the €1,000-a-team golf event in September 2006 was Oliver Barry. He had been found by the Flood Tribunal to have 'obstructed and hindered' its investigations into Raphael Burke's handling of the awarding of the Century radio licence.

The Greens had felt they had flexed their muscles with Ahern's departure. In the background, they had told Fianna Fáil that they could pull out of power if Ahern attempted to stay on as Taoiseach. It appears his resignation was a political scalp so they could to go back to their core supporters and say: 'Look, we're playing tough here and we're cleaning up corrupt politics.' Paul Gogarty admits:

> It's like this: Why is Bertie gone? Let's just say that undoubtedly there must have been a Green influence! I don't know to what extent, but I know we did have an influence in him making that decision.

Ahern's timing was impeccable—he resigned only hours before he faced a grilling from the Opposition in the first sitting of the Dáil since the Carruth testimony.

But it was the wrong time for Cowen, who became the next leader of Fianna Fáil and thus Taoiseach without a contest. Even Ahern admits that Cowen was hoping he would have more time, that he would have liked Ahern to stay on longer. And no wonder—there was never going to be a more difficult time to step into Ahern's shoes with a first task of attempting to push through the highly contentious Lisbon Treaty referendum within his first month in office. Failing, Cowen felt, was unthinkable.

Chapter 5

THE LISBON TREATY
REFERENDUM DEFEAT

I t perhaps sounds implausible now, but Brian Cowen's tenure as Taoiseach began on a buoyant note, with the *Irish Times*/TNS MRBI poll showing an increase of 8 per cent in Fianna Fáil's popularity. Damian Loscher, managing director of TNS MRBI, stated that Cowen's appointment had 'created a feel-good factor which has distracted voters from news of job losses and store closures which otherwise would have acted as a drag on support for Fianna Fáil. The almost carnival atmosphere created everywhere the new leader went last week served to confirm how capable he is of energising his party and the public.'

But this 'feel-good factor' soon evaporated. Batt O'Keeffe says:

> From day one, I think Brian Cowen realised that difficult times were going to come but I don't think he or anyone else realised the extent of the difficulties that were going to emerge. I suppose nobody envisaged the damage the banks were going to do overall, and the extent of their exposure and the extent of the bad management that had been part and parcel of it.

When Cowen came to power, there was little sign of the impending storm that had recently engulfed the financial markets. Cynics suggested that the incumbent Taoiseach, Bertie Ahern, saw it coming better than most and decided to make an exit that by common consensus was somewhat hasty, while the going was still relatively good. Cowen, in effect, was left to clean up the mess.

The Lisbon Treaty referendum in June 2008 was Cowen's first major political task. Cowen acknowledges that the anti-Treaty campaigners had 'pressed a lot of buttons that raised fears and concerns among people', but he didn't help matters with his admission during an RTÉ radio interview that he had not read the current Treaty text in its entirety. 'I haven't read it from cover to cover. I know exactly what's in it,' Cowen said. As Minister for Foreign Affairs during the Treaty's gestation, Cowen claimed he had read countless previous drafts and had been briefed fully on the Treaty's final version, but that did not deter the media from stating that he had not even bothered to read the document he was asking the country to approve. The media spin on Cowen's comment invigorated the anti-Lisbon campaign. The founder of the anti-Treaty organisation Libertas, Declan Ganley, said: 'I have read the Treaty in full. Brian Cowen has not even read the entire Treaty. You wouldn't sign a contract on a house unless you had read it in full.' Ganley's comments resonated with a now sceptical electorate, who—unable to comprehend the impenetrably worded Treaty manifesto—would henceforth instead rely on the media debate for information and guidance on which way to vote. Libertas, moreover, was skilful in getting across its message.

Even though Cowen insisted that the Treaty could not be renegotiated, it didn't prevent the widely held perception that it could be altered if it was rejected. It was a statement that would come back to haunt Cowen, who was forced to seek amendments and clarifications when the Treaty was rejected.

Cowen also managed to insult the Opposition during the campaign. When speaking at a public rally in Portlaoise he said: 'I'm glad to see our own party, the support of our own base, is certainly highest among all the parties and I'm sure the other parties will crank up their campaigns now as well.' Afterwards, he expanded on this statement by declaring:

Well, from the Fianna Fáil point of view, what I think is a very important point is that you know we are the most pro-European party. We are getting most of our supporters out to support this thing in the hope that . . . colleagues in other parties now can crank up their campaign, which I'm sure they will, to make sure that we see the same level of support from other parties.

Enda Kenny said that Cowen's remarks had caused a 'great deal of antagonism and difficulty for people supporting the "yes" campaign who are not supporters of Fianna Fáil'. He called for an apology, but Cowen never did apologise.

Fine Gael described the comments as the 'final straw'. This was a reference to an extraordinary confrontation in a Dáil debate on 21 May 2008 when Cowen, while attempting to answer a question about the health service, was interrupted half a dozen times by the Opposition during a Leader's Questions session. In retaliation, a clearly irate Cowen commented that he could arrange to have people 'roaring and shouting on this side' every time Kenny 'completes a sentence'. By this stage, the session was rapidly descending into farce, with the Opposition attempting to taunt Cowen by interjecting every time he tried to address the issue at hand, and Cowen growing visibly annoyed as the Opposition shouted out: 'Answer the question!' or 'He can't answer the question!' every time he attempted to make a reply.

'Listen to me, I want to answer the question but I will make one point. If you keep that tactic up, I will make sure he,' a furious Cowen snapped, waving his finger at Kenny, 'will not be heard in this House .... It can be organised.'

Afterwards, Cowen sat down and turned to Mary Coughlan, Tánaiste and Minister for Enterprise, Trade and Employment, to have a private conversation. Unfortunately, the microphone in the Dáil picked up the exchange word for word. 'Ring those people and get a handle on it, will you? Bring in all those fuckers,' he fumed. It was presumed that Cowen was speaking to Coughlan about the National Consumer Agency and the controversy over British retailers overcharging Irish consumers. The *Irish Independent* declared that it was 'unbecoming' for a Taoiseach to use bad language. Later, Cowen was forced to apologise for his swearing.

The Fine Gael leader described Cowen's performance in the Dáil as 'quite astonishing', explaining that he had 'never seen any Taoiseach in my years in the House lose control the way that Brian Cowen did . . . and that's after thirteen days in office'. Kenny later stated: 'Brian Cowen is having a problem being in control of himself and wants to set out to prove that he is a freak in control of the leadership of the party.' At the time, rumours started to emerge about Cowen having a 'dictatorial' style of leadership, which was turning backbenchers against him.

Cowen then had appeared to affront Kenny again by canvassing with Labour leader Eamon Gilmore. At the time, it was suggested that some Fine Gael voters felt slighted by Cowen's hostility towards their party leader in the run-up to the Lisbon referendum and had opted to reject the Treaty as a result. True or not, it's clear that the dispute distracted attention from the real subject of the referendum. On 5 June 2008, the *Irish Times*/TNS MRBI poll suggested that 40 per cent of Fine Gael voters were planning to reject the Treaty

From the start there was significant opposition to the Treaty and a degree of public relief that the people were being consulted. Even so, this view was not in accordance with Fianna Fáil thinking or with that of the two major Opposition parties. This factor—of the three main parties in the Dáil all being committed to fighting in favour of a Yes Vote—gave what appeared to be an unfair advantage to that side of the argument and created a set of perceptions about the No Vote side: that they were putting forward views of an extreme and dishonest kind. The huge imbalance represented by this created unjustified complacency on the Yes Vote side, theoretically supported by at least two-thirds of the voting public who had exercised their mandate in the previous year's general election and strong determination among the disparate No Vote supporters that the referendum was an entirely different issue.

Most people struggled to understand what they were told about the complex changes contained in the huge Lisbon Treaty text. Very few people read it, and leading campaigners, if they were honest, confessed to not having read it either, or if they claimed understanding often then proceeded to confuse the issues on which the Irish people were being asked to vote. The more the people looked into the unread Treaty and the increasingly mixed views on it that made up the early stages of the debate, the less sense it made and the less attractive it became.

There seemed to be deliberate deception in the way it was being put before the people. It was offered as something absolutely vital, not just to Ireland but to all the people of Europe; yet its presentation was surrounded by platitudes and assurances that undermined its very credibility. The arguments in favour were fundamentally confused: it would make all the difference, but it would not change rights. It was a new Constitution; it was not a new Constitution. It would change the balance of power between individual states and Europe but it would not threaten the Irish people's integrity. But then, are the Irish a people any more? What about citizenship? If Ireland adopted the Lisbon Treaty, the people would have two citizenships to enjoy, not one. Was that a good thing? How would it work? Would it increase democratic rights or decrease them? The answer to both was Maybe. No one knew. And the text of the Treaty was so dense, and so dependent on other treaties, agreements and multifarious documentation, that there was no way of finding out. This central argument, about democracy, was there from the beginning. It was argued, clearly and cogently, by many leading opponents of the Lisbon Treaty; it was fudged by the three main parties, which put forward other arguments about jobs and trade but generally ignored the intractable issue of the growing European democratic deficit.

There was a wealth of material on the table well before the debate came to dominate thought on Europe as it developed in Ireland in the spring of 2008. One of the sensible European leaders friendly towards Ireland was quoted in this respect at the time. This was Jean-Claude Juncker, Luxembourg's Prime Minister and chairman of the ECOFIN, the European Finance Ministers, who had said on 26 May 2005: 'If it's a Yes, we will say "On we go", and if it's a No, we will say "We continue".'

'On we go' is not quite the same as 'we continue'. It suggests a great heave forward instead of just continuing as we are. This and many other comments reflecting ambiguity and uncertainty, as well as deliberate concealment, prevarication and outright deceit, fuelled the debate and strengthened the will of the No Vote side.

Other voices were more blunt. Major political figures from different countries in Europe had clearly stated what a deception all this was. Valéry Giscard d'Estaing, the former French president and chairman of the Convention that drew up the earlier European Union's Constitution, said at the end of October 2007:

> ...the difference is one of approach, rather than content. The proposals in the original constitutional Treaty are practically unchanged. They have simply been dispersed through the old treaties in the form of amendments. Why this subtle change? Above all, to head off any threat of referenda by avoiding any form of

constitutional vocabulary. But lift the lid and look in the toolbox: all the same innovative and effective tools are there, just as they were carefully crafted by the European Convention.

What we were doing was being demanded of us by the larger states and we were agreeing to this without seeing in it any real enhancement of our democratic control over what was happening and what lay ahead for us. In fact, opinion polls commissioned by the EU after the 2002 Nice Treaty referendum showed that the Irish public was increasingly concerned that the EU was becoming too powerful, too centralised and too much under the influence of the larger states. The disillusionment and scepticism had been growing ever since the first Nice Treaty referendum in 2001.

Ireland's difficulties were made far greater by the fact that the country was the only one of the 27 EU Member States to hold a referendum on the Lisbon Treaty. Although Ireland was confronting many referendum problems to which no other states were contributing through a parallel debate, the legal effect was 99 per cent the same as the 'Treaty Establishing a Constitution for Europe', which the French and Dutch peoples had rejected by referendum in the summer of 2005. Ireland faced an unusual form of desertion by the rest of Europe.

What was clear and frightening, though only to what appeared to be a limited minority, was that the new Constitution for Europe, represented by the Lisbon Treaty, would rule, taking precedence over the Irish Constitution. And it would do so mainly through control mechanisms that are not answerable to elected representatives running a Parliament for 500 million people, removing for ever the idea of a national veto of some kind that used to be there to protect Irish sovereignty. A natural Irish constitutional safeguard was being surrendered without the traditional Irish protection of two sides to the argument being presented by the majority of public representatives.

Ireland had lived for 70 years with a workable and, essentially, a good Constitution. When it was offered to the people, it was in language they could understand. It was debated for a year, nationally, and scrutinised in detail by the Dáil before its enactment. Constitutions are living things. They change with time and are enriched by legal challenge and by legal definition. The lifetime of the Constitution has been punctuated by amendments, which are the legal and moral life-blood pumped into the protective and defining words that have served the nation well for the greater part of Ireland's independent history.

The Lisbon Treaty had not a single one of these qualities, safeguards or protections. It was, and remains, rigid in the supposed protections about taxation, neutrality and defence. It could not be like this if it was to be the future law, embracing our governance as citizens of the European Union, since laws—as seen in the development of the Irish Constitution—change their meaning and people's lives.

Changes within Europe in defence, neutrality and taxation are as inevitable as the rising and setting of the sun. But the Irish were being told—quite wrongly and dishonestly—that Europe's moon had risen and was stuck in the sky for ever, like the sun. All this was at the heart of the debate: the living reality of Ireland's powerful and protective Constitution set against a huge, poorly understood Treaty document. Among other things, the Constitution encouraged the people to trust the structures that it enshrined. These included the many definitions of how democracy works. It was a central plank of the document. Now it was under threat.

By default, the Lisbon Treaty did the precise opposite. There was no definition of anything for anyone. The people did not know about any rights from what was given. They knew only that they were voting themselves into a new system of laws and controls that simply could not be permanently defined.

For it to work—if it ever does work in the way a Constitution should—it had to be flexible, adaptable and amendable. The nation had been taught that fundamental truth and had valued and used it as well as seeing it enhanced by previous referenda and court judgments. Nothing of this kind would be available if Ireland ratified the Lisbon Treaty.

Quite wrongly, and almost certainly inaccurately, the chairman of the Referendum Commission made a public statement to the effect that on neutrality and corporation tax Ireland had nothing to fear. It was neither his role, nor that of the Commission, under the legislation, to be supporting the interpretation of one side in grappling with the document. He was obliged by law to be even-handed. The Referendum Commission's function was to tell the people what the effect of the

Lisbon Constitutional Amendment would be and to encourage the maximum turnout of voters. It was not to give a one-sided interpretation of the Treaty.

This collective action did not give primacy to EU laws, since it was not the EU, but a community. And Ireland accepted directions about changing the status of existing laws on equality, non-discrimination, food standards and health and safety, outside the federation now proposed. This was reinforced when the European Court of Justice decided that Community laws were supreme. It was a benignly implemented jurisdiction. Under the wider blanket of EU supremacy, this could represent a quite different legal authority. The European Court of Justice would have the ultimate right to interpret a change in the law and require reform in line with that change.

What Raymond Crotty did in respect of Ireland within Europe was achieved by just such a legal reality, his result the outcome of going to the Supreme Court. For Supreme Court read European Court of Justice, and for Crotty read someone seeking justice and fairness before that Court. The 1986–7 Crotty Judgment states that the surrendering of sovereignty to Brussels in European Treaties can be done only by the Irish people in a referendum, for they are the repositories of sovereignty.

What was seriously wrong about what was being done was that the Irish people had been lied to, not for the first time, about the entirely benign structure of laws that would come into force if they voted Yes. They were not all benign and the lying was disgraceful.

Under the Maastricht Treaty on European Union, which governed Ireland at the time, there were restrictions on harmonising tax laws and these were helpful to the State's position since its preferential position did not prejudice the European Union's internal market. Under the Lisbon Treaty a new concept, where harmonisation may be enforced by the Court of Justice as a result of the distortion of competition, would affect every town in Ireland where industries have been established on the basis of the preferential corporation tax rate, or where they might be established in the future.

To save the country from this, it was argued, Ireland would need a special protocol, exempting the State from the idea that distortion of tax laws is wrong. For Ireland, such distortion would seem right, since it had been the correct solution, and successfully so, for the previous 40 years. But the argument, which appears preposterous at any time, would be simply ludicrous in the run-up to a referendum of the kind Ireland faced. In theory the protocol would have been sought, and got, if it were attempted, because the EU needed and wanted a Yes Vote, and was already prepared to buy it by deceit and lies. But the reality was that it was too late for Ireland to demand or get such a protocol in the middle of the spring 2008 campaign. The last realistic chance had been the March Summit of European Union Prime Ministers, when it could have been requested, but was not. Such a protocol would have to have been in a new treaty, substituted for Lisbon in the event of its rejection. A so-called 'declaration' would not have been enough since it would not be binding.

Any such move would have rendered Ireland the laughing stock of Europe, since it would have disproved the 'innocuous' nature of the Lisbon Treaty and would have knocked on the head the greater part of what had been said about the survival of Ireland's preferential corporation tax rate.

Voting Yes, it was argued, was a blind act; it would bring unknown penalties down on Irish heads because none of those proclaiming the wonderful advantages of the Lisbon Treaty were being truthful about the constitutional nature of power. Indeed, they were being frugal in their recognition that this was a constitution in the full sense of that term.

Nothing as dire as the destruction of the carefully created, prudently nurtured industrial investment, on which so many Irish men and women depend for their livelihoods, could possibly have resulted from voting No. Ireland would simply preserve the status quo and the rest of Europe would have to live with it.

The Lisbon Treaty was always a constitutional document. It followed through on the slow process of establishing a new federal state of Europe. It made the Irish citizens of that state, with dual loyalties. There were variations in the degree to which Ireland accepted and implemented some of those loyalties, but in effect was being drawn into a new citizenship status that undoubtedly compromises and changes the present citizenship of Ireland. The European Union was seen to be going in an entirely different way. The heart of what was seen as the EU's purpose was not democratic. Ireland did not, as a Member State, elect anyone to its law-making bodies. It elected, then and now, a Parliament, but its position was democratically marginal, not central. It did not initiate or shape the main laws. It was therefore throwing out the first principle: no taxation without representation.

It was a surprise to the Yes Vote side in the campaign how much the debate concentrated on these serious issues of constitutional and personal rights, loss of control over taxation affairs, all the legal changes covered by the Treaty and all the unanswered general questions that had been raised and over which assurances were given that did not add up or make sense.

The tax arguments were of serious concern, not just in respect of the payment of taxes but also in respect of the creation of jobs. This became part of the debate and it was made clear that, if the European Court of Justice was to deal with a 'distortion of competition' appeal directed against Ireland, it would do so on the basis of distortion, not taxation. It would order the offending State to eliminate the distortion, leaving the means by which this would be done to the National Parliament. No good constitutionalist or constitutional lawyer would wish otherwise. But it would have the same effect as a challenge against the inequality of our taxation system, which is undeniable.

It was one of the pieces of Yes Vote nonsense to point to the supposed 'locking' clauses in the Treaty—which had every appearance of having been put there to ensure support for the Lisbon Treaty, in particular by Ireland—to treat them as sacred protection. Life and the law, particularly constitutional and human rights law, and laws dealing with competition, do not operate like that.

It was widely argued, by the Yes Vote side, that the new amendment to the Constitution, which is central to the referendum wording, had been in Ireland's Constitution since 1973 when it joined the European Economic Community, which then became the European Union. The distinction was important; however, it was construed quite wrongly by the Minister for European Affairs, Dick Roche, who was careful to phrase what he had to say on the subject solely in terms of 'what is now the European Union'. He skated over the all-important fact that Ireland amended the Constitution in 1972, in support of the leadership of Jack Lynch and Paddy Hillery, in order to get into the European Common

Market, another term used; this was a quite different legal entity, with a quite different and much looser relationship with Ireland, the UK and Denmark.

What the State was now doing was fundamentally new and, in the judgment of many opponents of the Lisbon Treaty being adopted by Ireland, this raised major issues about the continued survival and prosperity of the country and ignored the huge difference in circumstances as well as the constitutional point about how the entities that existed had changed between 1972 and 2008.

The Yes voters invented a case where Ireland was not able to do, on its own, what Lisbon would make possible for it to do if the Treaty was passed. This was essentially a piece of vague speculation. There was little or no proof of its value. The No Vote response was that Ireland would, as always, manage, and play a part in Europe that would be more dynamic the more independent Ireland was. The country did not need to prove its credentials all over again. It was often necessary to repeat Juncker's wise words in 2005: 'If it's a Yes, we will say "On we go", and if it's a No, we will say "We continue". And that is how it will be.'

There was an even more dishonest argument, also put forward by Roche, that passing the Lisbon Treaty into Irish law would 'enable' Ireland to continue deriving benefit from EU membership. What exactly would stop the country doing the same if it voted No? This was not spelt out. Even more emotive was the declaration: 'Not for the first time, fate more than choice has placed the key to Europe's future in the hands of the Irish people.'

Two much-admired politicians who took part in the debate were John Bruton, who was first elected to the Dáil in 1969 and became a Junior Minister under Liam Cosgrave, and Garret FitzGerald, who was an outstanding Minister for Foreign Affairs in the same administration. FitzGerald and Bruton both subsequently served as Taoiseach.

Their political integrity and courage made them credible and impressive contributors, though in respect of the first referendum campaign in 2008 they both took positions that were excessively biased. John Bruton was then the European Ambassador to the United States. It is unusual for an international diplomat to speak in a domestic election campaign of the kind that was being conducted for the Lisbon Treaty, but Bruton did say, at the outset, that his views were being given in a 'personal capacity'. In the unlikely event of him having held a personal view that was not in favour of a Yes Vote, it is difficult to see how he could have expressed this, personally or otherwise, but then that was the way the debate was shaping up.

Bruton wrote about democracy, mentioning it about five times. This was refreshing. He talked of the Lisbon Treaty making the European Union 'more democratic by opening up the Council of Ministers to the public and giving the Dáil and Seanad, together with other national parliaments, a chance to block EU laws before they even got to the European Parliament and Council of Ministers'. Much of the debate, in 2008, was centred on levels of democracy, and it was sensible to question the phrase 'more democratic'. If the European Union moved in the opposite direction, towards a 'less democratic' regime, democracy would vanish. What Bruton wrote about were trivial matters. Opening the Council of Ministers to the public was long overdue, and would have little or no impact on the drafting of legislation since the detail was always worked out before their meetings and consideration by the people—as opposed to the PR gesture of them being represented there—would not follow.

As to the Dáil or Seanad having any kind of worthwhile debate on European issues, it was insulting of John Bruton to Irish voters even to mention democracy in this context. Any worthwhile input into the drafting of EU legislation from the Houses of the Oireachtas would be negligible. They were already having a minimal impact on domestic legislation. What time would be given to new EU laws?

When Bruton claimed the European Union as 'the world's only multinational democracy', he was stretching a point that was central to the whole debate. There was a whiff of democracy about the provisions of the Lisbon Treaty but only a whiff. In essence the European Union was no longer democratic; No voters felt that strongly and said it while Yes voters talked of other things. Bruton himself spoke from a position of great knowledge, since he was in Washington as Ambassador on behalf of the 500 million European Union citizens-to-be. And he spoke to the people of the greatest federal democracy on earth. It was sensible to read what he said. And what did he say? Among other things he told the electorate: 'The other member states might look at other options to go forward on their own.' It was an amazing distortion of the Lisbon

Treaty. There could be no such move, and everyone knew it. If the electorate said No, we would be part of the answer to what we would do next and we would remain part of the answer.

Garret FitzGerald's views on the Lisbon Treaty were blunt and also heavily biased. He had a habit, at the time, of issuing grave but unspecific warnings about the motives and truthfulness of No voters. He talked about Ireland becoming a 'pariah'. The word, of Indian origin, related to the caste system, means social outcast. Such a possibility was quite contrary to EU laws and to custom and practice throughout the Union. He also defined the stance of No voters as 'misleading' in what was said and 'shown to be wrong in every instance'. This was opinion, not fact, and was a hugely exaggerated position to adopt. FitzGerald described No voters as acting 'perversely' and 'frivolously'. He described their 'total ignorance of, and lack of interest in, this European structure'. He said they were 'prejudiced'. He mocked them as indulging 'hang-ups' and described them as using 'mendacious propaganda', 'spurious claims' and referred to 'skilful misreadings'. In the article in which these opinions were contained, FitzGerald never once mentioned the word 'democracy', yet it was constantly raised as a serious problem in what the constitutional referendum was dealing with. He claimed that those seeking a No Vote were trying 'to wreck the entire European reform project'. If he redeemed himself in this stance at all, it was his very clear disdain for the Government Ministers campaigning for a Yes Vote and not knowing the answers to basic questions about the Lisbon Treaty. In summary, this acknowledged Irish statesman considered that the important thing was to 'get it through', not to examine and acknowledge the Treaty's serious shortcomings.

As the Yes campaign deteriorated into squabbles and disagreement, Brian Cowen turned on Fine Gael and Labour to do more and to do it better. Fine Gael and Labour had already failed the electorate by their own unquestioning espousal of the Treaty when they had a duty to voters, which was to ensure that the Government and the public service honoured their duties and obligations in achieving a fair and balanced assessment of what the changes to Ireland's Constitution would actually mean. The Yes campaign was becoming inept, the performances of individual Ministers part of the problem.

Another powerful and experienced Yes campaigner was Pat Cox, former MEP and president of the European Parliament, who argued that the European Parliament 'acts as a legislator' through 'co-decision', holding the executive to account. The truth was that the European Parliament does not make laws; it amends laws that come from the Commission and the Council of Ministers. It does not originate laws nor does it have to pass them. The Commission has the monopoly of proposing EU laws, but the Council of Ministers makes them by means of weighted voting. The European Parliament has power of amendment of such laws as long as the Commission agrees to the amendment. It also has the power to veto any law coming from the Council of Ministers by an absolute majority of all its members. Such a veto rarely happens, because the Parliament wants ever more supranational laws anyway.

Cox remained one of the better informed of the Yes Vote protagonists. It was not a difficult position to occupy. The Yes campaign was based on a eulogy of the European Union, with emphasis on what Ireland had got out of it. The State meant to be humbly grateful for this when gratitude was beside the point.

As bad news about his campaign intensified, Brian Cowen made another misjudgment, trying to frighten the electorate over jobs. This was not what the referendum was about. Its purpose was to change for ever the status Ireland had enjoyed up to then in Europe. The Lisbon Treaty was designed to make ordinary people all over Europe more subservient and to be less democratic. Only in the hands of ordinary Irish people, however, lay the task of stopping the process.

The second strategy of the Yes campaign, after it had made a poor stab at getting its side operating sensibly, was to demonise, wrongly, the No campaign by suggesting it was 'Right-wing', narrowly based and somehow dishonest. How can that apply to 35 per cent of the population? This insult was made worse by the casual 'buying' of farmers' votes by Cowen. His alliance with the other parties escalated into a kind of collective panic. If there was dishonesty and distortion, it was in the pretence that Ireland's legal status would not change. The price being paid weakened the Constitution, lost the basic representation of a permanent Commissioner, risked jobs, threatened to reduce Irish attractiveness to investors and made the nation subservient in a huge State of 500 million people.

Another Yes Vote debater of great experience was former Attorney General Peter Sutherland. He roundly attacked self-interest, blaming it on the No voters. Yet every Yes Vote poster was based on self-interest. He described Ireland as sleepwalking 'towards catastrophe'.

Sutherland claimed that every Government supported the Lisbon Treaty. This was not true of the people of the United Kingdom, Austria, Denmark or France. The difference was they could not express their negativity. Peter Sutherland argued that completion of the EU's internal market enabled Irish foreign investment, 'harnessed to sound governance and hard work, transform our economy'. This was not the case. Governance was not that good, resources were squandered, and wealth and confidence were falling apart even as Ireland made its Lisbon Treaty decision. Sutherland also said that the Treaty was no more than an attempt to make good obvious deficiencies. Not only was this a poor justification, if it were true what a pathetic summary of what the Lisbon Treaty represented! But it was not true. The Treaty was a constitutional document that fundamentally changed people's lives and the status of their citizenship. The serious debaters ignored the fundamental constitutional changes in the Treaty. And though Sutherland praised the Referendum Commission for 'confirming the truth', that legal body did not explain the constitutional issues and largely ignored its own legal duties. The Commission fumbled over the loss of the Irish Commissioner, the halving of Ireland's Council vote and the delegation of powers from Ministers to the Commission.

The country watched while various political leaders bumbled their way into the Lisbon Treaty referendum and then commenced a campaign, as outlined above, full of confusion and misrepresentation. They were caught short on the Fianna Fáil side by the inept disposal of the political corpse of Bertie Ahern. Allowing him a month's grace after his decision to go was a fatal error. On the other side—that of the two main Opposition parties—an equally mistaken position was taken, of siding with the Lisbon Treaty and abandoning most of the issues that it was their duty to analyse. This created a vacuum into which stepped Declan Ganley, the leader of Libertas.

Ganley focused his Libertas movement in a clear and exclusive way on what was wrong with the European Union. He mounted a campaign that was unwavering in its presentation and at heart was supportive of the EU. He assumed, with ease, the leadership of the disparate No Vote parties and groups. He did so in a detached way, making no alliances, dismissing many of the ideas that were central to other No voters. He therefore emerged as the real focus of doubt and disillusionment. This concerned the growing abandonment of all semblance of democracy within the Union. Ganley declared there was a better way and set out to prove it.

Against quite extraordinary odds, the No vote won. With the enormous power of three major political parties, theoretically commanding four-fifths of the electorate's support, the combined Government and Opposition lost to Libertas, the voluntary group Cóir, Sinn Féin and the other No Vote campaigners. Ganley was undoubtedly the new EU-critical element in the referendum campaign, the most important and the most media savvy.

From the outset, the Government, which effectively had control of the campaign, made a mess of it. Fianna Fáil was lukewarm and over-confident. Fine Gael was uncertain and divided. The Labour Party also had mixed views. The Green Party—committed to being 'in government' for what it called 'the long haul'—presented no convincing campaign at all. The party was officially on the No Side in the first Lisbon Treaty campaign, but changed its policy to support the Yes side for the second. Sinn Féin's opposition was in keeping with its traditional 'nationalism' but it was limited because of the party's association with the Northern Ireland troubles. Its appeal was more of a discomfort to Libertas than a help and this was true of other groupings also.

The eventual victory for the No Vote was the principal achievement in Declan Ganley's political success in 2008, making him the most successful politician of the year. He not only triumphed over the main Yes Vote thrust coming from the three main political parties, he triumphed also over the media, parts of which, notably RTÉ and the *Irish Times*, conducted quite deeply prejudiced campaigns against him.

What Ganley tapped into was a deep-seated public suspicion about the European Union and what it had come to stand for, the heart of this being a form of collective Government for 500 million people that had no credible basis in democracy as it was understood by the alert and experienced Irish political mind. This force, which became the deciding factor in the outcome, had little to do with campaigning organisations. The doubt was widespread if in many ways inchoate. Generally, there were doubts about the levels of democracy espoused by the EU. It seemed that the Commission, the Council of Ministers and the bureaucracy governing from Brussels, Strasbourg and Luxembourg had a distinctly cool view about the nature and interpretation of democratic answerability and transparency. They insisted on this for Member States. Firm democratic principles and institutions were a primary requirement in the accession process for new members. But many of the elements in what was demanded from past and future EU members did not apply to the central government of the EU itself.

This argument put forward by Declan Ganley struck a chord with views that were held much more widely among voters than even Ganley expected and in the end proved conclusive in the result. To an astonishing degree this element in the campaign was simply not addressed by arguments from the Yes Vote side, arguments that tried to sell the benefits of membership, while the organisation for which that membership was endorsed struggled to prove its democratic credentials.

Jobs, grants, preferential treatment, favourable tax provisions, the veto, Ireland 'being at the heart of Europe', Ireland owing a Yes Vote in response to the huge help given to the country since its accession in 1973: all these were put forward. The democratic issue was ignored or dismissed or lied about. The campaign touched on the idea that 'more democracy' had been 'granted' under the Lisbon Treaty, as if democracy were like European grant-aid—something that had to be rationed.

Declan Ganley consistently argued that this was not enough. The democratic deficit was much deeper than that and required, in the first instance, the rejection of a treaty that would stifle all future efforts to change Europe into a true democracy. How this would be done was open to question, but that it needed to be done was increasingly realised as the campaign progressed.

In the closing stages of the campaign, those favouring a Yes Vote were accused of going round Ireland inducing apathy. This was close to the truth. Brian Cowen, in his already embarrassing performance as the new leader of the Fianna Fáil-led coalition Government, appeared on the hustings at old-style outdoor political meetings, his free hand slapped to his worried forehead—the other hand holding the microphone—telling his audiences: 'It's about the enlargement of the Union …. It's about showing solidarity with the new nations …. It's very important not to be misled.'

His audience of bewildered listeners, benign, impassive, levelled their ignorance like an electoral shotgun at him. 'No one is telling us anything,' they said. 'Everyone is telling us something different.' Brian Cowen wanted idealism. The audience wanted answers and explanations. 'I appeal to the young to show idealism,' Cowen said. 'They must show solidarity with their peers in the newly joined states, to recognise the wider sense of the landscape, sending a signal that would be understood. A No Vote will not be understood.' There were few enough young people in his audiences. There were children with grandparents; the young were at work. The middle-aged eyed their leader inscrutably.

The Irish, one of the most shrewd political populations in the democratic world, politely waited their turn. Their scepticism had a note of doom about it. But their wisdom in elections was acute and sensitive. Not many could name the 'newly joined states' to which Cowen referred. Even fewer cared. But they knew, in their hearts, a No Vote would be understood. What does anyone have to explain about No?

Cowen campaigned with Garret FitzGerald, leader of the party Cowen has opposed all his life and doyen of European pundits. Both men admitted that things were not going well. The early June apathy was greater than it had been in May. FitzGerald agreed with Cowen: 'it's very hard to get people out. We get a sense of more negativity now.'

And so it proved. The turnout, at 53.13 per cent, was a respectable 1,621,037. Those voting 'Yes' and supporting the implementation of the Lisbon Treaty numbered 752,451, or 46.6 per cent. The No Vote attracted 862,415 voters or 53.4 per cent. It was a sensational defeat in Cowen's first major test as Taoiseach and new leader of Fianna Fáil. It reflected badly on a poorly planned and at times inept Yes campaign. It revealed a powerful and unexpected rejection of the conventional guardians of power in the State and the emergence of what would become a new and angry electoral force.

It could be said that negativity defeated apathy, but it was a close-run thing. This interpretation fails completely to recognise that the No Vote side was as sophisticated and determined, even more so, than those who had based a whole campaign on deriding them for negativism and for misleading people. In fact the whole No campaign had been outspoken and logical, its main contention—about the lessening of democracy in Europe—one that was widely, and with hindsight correctly, believed to be basic to the whole referendum campaign. On this central argument—however much it was supported by minority groupings arguing quite different points—the victory of the No Vote side was politically momentous and forced Brian Cowen to face a huge problem, that of losing his first big contest as leader by a wide mark.

Many tried to lay blame on the peripheral aspects of the No campaign. Garret FitzGerald described No campaigners as 'voices from the margins'. One voice was Sinn Féin's, for whose candidates in the general election few enough people had voted. Yet it is attributed with a new Lisbon Treaty debate achievement of a telling slice of the 850,000 No Votes. In no sense was there any credible argument that these were voices from the margins. Declan Ganley, with Libertas, using a cool, measured technique mainly focused on business and taxation questions, convinced the country to support him.

The victory established a bond between the Irish people and a wider but disenfranchised body of men and women across the European Union. It represented a less successful aspect of Declan Ganley's Libertas movement and his campaign. Outside Ireland he over-reached himself and was damaged. But both Ireland and many voices in Europe felt they had a right to share in deciding their democratic future, a right that had been denied many of them.

A web of deceit had been woven around the Lisbon Treaty. This had been put before the Irish people by an inadequate body of politicians. Those who originally signed it had not read it. Those who had tried to sell it to the Irish people had represented it to them incompetently and quite falsely and had pilloried as dishonest the case put for rejection.

The result of the Lisbon Treaty referendum restored confidence in the people, convincing them that they had a voice that mattered in Irish democracy. It represented an expression of the true viwepoint of those who actually had the determination and judgment to go out and vote, showing that half the country took its democratic responsibilities seriously. Some feared for the future of that democracy and they turned out to be the majority, thus causing the defeat of the Lisbon Treaty. The other half expressed faith in Europe and in the judgments made by other people, supposedly their leaders, though those leaders got it wrong in a number of different ways.

This placed as a central issue democracy at home and democracy as it had been shaped in the broad, 27-country partnership of which Ireland formed a part. The No Vote enhanced the country's European standing—at least in democratic terms—by taking nothing for granted and by making clear and intelligent judgments about what is lacking in the future shape of Europe. Sadly, all this would in due course be lost.

The process for this began immediately, even during the counting of votes. When it soon emerged that the No Side would win, Cowen was reported as having made a call to José Manuel Barroso to tell him that Ireland's advice to other EU countries was not to call off their own ratification of the Lisbon Treaty—a polite metaphor for Juncker's solution.

Later that day, Micheál Martin confirmed on RTÉ that EU ratification would go on. This was supported by the Department of Foreign Affairs. At no stage while the count was going on and after it had been concluded was there any consideration of the Government being consulted about the result or of the view of Parliament being first considered.

Chapter 6 ∿

COWEN IGNORES THE
REFERENDUM RESULT

T he second Lisbon referendum, held on 2 October 2009, was born out of fear, dishonesty, deceit and a deliberate breach of the Irish Constitution. The people had made a democratic decision about the country's future and it required a response from the European Union. Instead, the EU decided that Ireland had been wrong in its choice and should choose the opposite route for the future by holding, and passing, a new referendum. This approach was entirely accepted by the Government and its implementation orchestrated, planned and presented to the people all over again. The country's law and practice, over decades, were set aside. Well-tried decision-making processes, outstandingly the referendum system itself, was now aligned with a deliberate and hypocritical enslavement to Europe. The conspiracy that had been present in the first referendum campaign, between Government and Opposition parties, was put in place for the second referendum campaign.

No single act of the Fianna Fáil-Green Party coalition in its period in power did more damage to its standing than the decision to re-run the Lisbon Treaty referendum in obedience to the EU. This presaged, more than anything else, its defeat and dismissal from power two and a half years later in the most dramatic and powerful electoral defeat in Ireland's history. As to the Opposition parties, they gained nothing from repeating their previous approach, endorsing a dishonest set of reasons to vote in favour.

No one, certainly no significant spokesperson for the Yes campaign, either tackled the democratic deficit or explained the constitutional reasons for the amendment. Foreign Affairs Minister Micheál Martin, who, on behalf of the Government, carried more than his fair share of the initial debate, even before the final result came through, expressed the view that the issues were defence, neutrality, the right to life, militarisation and taxation. This was a misleading and dishonest narrowing of the issues and one that could not possibly account for nearly 900,000 No voters. They were singular and minority issues accounting for an unmeasured but limited part of the rejection.

Martin's interpretation for Europe of what had 'gone wrong' in Ireland left aside the huge matter of deliberate confusion and obfuscation about what the Lisbon Treaty really meant, the fact that it altered for ever Irish citizenship, reduced democratic strengths and safeguards, took away key rights, such as the one for a permanent Commissioner, and never explained these things.

In January 2009, in an address to the Institute of International and European Affairs, Micheál Martin said Ireland's goal was to 'chart our way forward' with a process of 'reflection'. This was a poor response when he and everyone else involved in the campaign had been doing just that and getting it all wrong. Their own attempts at 'reflection' seem to have been deliberately misdirected and false, and though, at the end of the campaign, some of them realised, too late, that it was not going well for this very reason, they had no escape clause. Whatever about there being no 'Plan B' for Europe, the three main parties certainly had no Plan B for themselves.

It is a singular reality that Sinn Féin, a party that was ostracised comprehensively during the six weeks of campaigning in the first referendum campaign, got it right and did so as part of its response to what was demanded from it, which was to turn to exclusive democracy. The party seemed to be complying. Change confronted it and it dealt with it. To continue demonising the party was another of the rather smug and mistaken attitudes taken by the other main political parties.

Fervent Yes voters and Europhiles had interpreted the No Vote as based on extreme left- and right-wingers and eccentric religious groups. This was of course wishful thinking, a frantic search for a scapegoat to be bypassed in a future re-run of a re-tinkered—and possibly renamed—Lisbon Treaty. It was also a mistaken response to defeat by Cowen and some of his Ministers to concentrate on the idea that different minority groupings had been responsible for defeating him. That this was not the case was the obstacle immediately facing Brian Cowen. It was clear from the vote and was an obvious problem to be faced by the leaders of all the main parties in Ireland. They did not do it well. Apart from anything else, they had to come to terms with close on a million No voters, including many of their own supporters.

For Cowen, the test was immediate. His Foreign Affairs Minister preceded him to Europe the week after the vote. Both men had to answer to the Council of Ministers. Not in relation to new Treaties such as Lisbon. Here the European Council of Prime Ministers and Presidents representing the EU Member States—the so-called 'summit meetings'—were the relevant body. These were Cowen's opposite numbers across the EU, representing the other Member States. They had all approved the Treaty and wanted it passed in Ireland.

Micheál Martin's approach—to blame minority voices and ideas—was a mistaken one. How could this be true when it had delivered a majority? The expectation was that Cowen would concur with the widespread calls to ignore the vote and advise all the other members of the European Union to go ahead with ratification. Cowen, new to his job, had made major mistakes in the first referendum campaign. Now he was set on a course repeating what had gone before. He was modestly supported with promises of uncalled-for amendments and reassurances. Ireland would get its permanent Commissioner—who is there until 2014 anyway, a date that can be extended without the Lisbon Treaty. Other sleights of hand were aimed at reassuring an angry electorate, allowing for a re-run.

All this indicated a deep misunderstanding of the No Vote, as well as disrespect for it. If Ireland's leaders were going to do this, then no other country would respect the No Vote. Such a course would also misunderstand the subtlety and discrimination of the Irish electorate. The poll was a forthright rejection of the three main political parties and of the 'wise and good' in Ireland. It said No to trade unions, management organisations, farmers' representatives, lawyers, businessmen and former leaders of the country.

Every attempt to present the Treaty as an urgent, appealing option fell on its face. The No campaign had all the hard questions. And the soft answers coming from figures of experience and lofty confidence fell largely on deaf ears.

The No voters were not marginal. A majority of voters said No firmly and without giving reasons. The catalogue of post-hoc explanations of what they meant and how they could be answered would not wash. And Cowen, who said firmly that the voice of the Irish people had been expressed and would be respected, risked his political future by betraying that clear statement.

This early set of responses to the defeat of June 2008 was all set in place before the Irish banking crisis threw everything into confusion. The second half of 2008 descended into financial crisis and the Lisbon Treaty was rendered more defective and irrelevant as Europe itself floundered. But before this happened, the Cowen-led Government had made the extraordinary decision, making virtually irreversible that there would be an attempt to change the legal approach of the Irish people by re-running the referendum.

What might have passed over, with the decline in activity of Libertas and other proponents of the No Vote, went in an entirely different direction. The Government could have achieved its objectives much more subtly by ensuring that the motivation for trying again came from Europe and was put to a reluctant Irish Government trying its best to stand behind a democratic decision of the State. Instead, Dublin led the charge. This probably astonished Europe.

It also brought Declan Ganley back in an even stronger position, confirming him in his earlier declared intention of Libertas seeking European Parliament seats and continuing to fight for a better and more democratic EU that way.

The Government made further mistakes, notably in pretending that it had obtained big and valuable concessions from Europe at the December Summit in Brussels, when in fact it had obtained trivial political promises, which would leave the Lisbon Treaty unchanged, but dressed up as major achievements. The question of democracy in the EU was still ignored, not just by Ireland's politicians, but by most of the media as well.

The period immediately following the 2008 Lisbon Treaty referendum defeat was significantly affected by unease over the nature of Ireland's democracy. This was aggravated significantly by the very poor quality of debate, much of it sustained by men and women who supposedly valued Europe and wanted Ireland's continued success as a member of the European Union to go on. They did all the wrong things to achieve this, before the first vote, and afterwards continued on that path of error in the belief that the Irish democratic system could sustain another bout of chicanery and dishonesty. This approach put many senior politicians and parties at risk from the electorate in the future. Brian Cowen should have told the heads of the other EU governments that, in the light of the Irish Vote, further ratifications were pointless. The onus was on the European Union to respond to Ireland, not on Ireland to respond to its own decision.

Cowen did nothing of the sort. Of course he could not stop ratification, but he could have said it was without any point; this, in European Treaty terms, was the case. What he told British Prime Minister Gordon Brown, the day before the Summit, which led to Brown almost, but not quite, completing British ratification, was not revealed. But his basic position was a determination to keep the Lisbon Treaty alive and his support for doing this was a minority in the country, and a very questionable Department of Foreign Affairs conviction that stupid Irish voters could be sweetened into changing their minds.

This was a bending of the knee to the essential outcome of the post-referendum European Summit where the tables were turned on Ireland and the absurd process of labelling a 'No Vote' electorate as a pariah, to be left to change its voice and stance, was resumed. The 'Pro-Yes-Vote' media rowed in behind this deeply dubious and flawed situation with a gusto and scorn that was remarkable. Ignored was the minimal No Vote idea that the Lisbon Treaty might be opened up and amended. That had happened with its predecessor after the French and Dutch said No.

There was no amending or 'freshening up' of Lisbon. If Ireland ever thought there was this chance, and acted on that assumption, it would have proved straightaway the truth contained in one of the major criticisms of Europe—one that persuaded voters to vote No: its flawed and limited democracy. Furthermore, if an attempt were made to invoke provisions in the Nice Treaty—much talked of in the aftermath of the first vote—this would have negated the Lisbon Treaty. Change to Nice, for Ireland's benefit, would have been a de facto recognition of the validity of the referendum decision.

The Irish people judged the Lisbon Treaty to be a bad Treaty and said No to it. If there was a fault in its presentation, that lay with the Yes campaign as well as with the Referendum Commission, which failed to complete its statutory obligations. There were *mea culpas* about some of these shortcomings, though they carried little weight and gained even less sympathy.

All politicians were slow to wake up to the post-Lisbon reality and this was primarily because of their presumptive stupidity before the campaign. The change of heart was aided by other shocks to the political system, putting wages and a wage deal and the economic slump into the forefront of all their minds. Politicians needed to think for themselves, their voters, their mandate and their parties; and they needed to think very hard indeed.

The same applied to Europe. Rather as the EU did over Kosovo— which was to stand idly by while human rights were abused and genocide committed—they stood idly by again, looking at Ireland for a solution to a problem that was mainly Europe's.

It was truly astonishing how much at sea European leaders were in facing a crisis that was theirs more than ours. They couldn't or wouldn't accept what was wrong in Europe, mistakes that turned away a favoured country, Ireland, which did not lose its loyalty or interest in membership, but simply disdained what was done to the body politic as it was being reshaped by the Lisbon Treaty.

Some realisation emerged in Ireland. Eamon Gilmore recognised the constitutional dilemma as such and said that the country should not go through with a second referendum. His thinking on this was not entirely clear and it may have been partly in response to the internal Labour Party view on Lisbon. But it was a step in the right direction or seemed so. As WikiLeaks published revelations in early June 2011, Gilmore simultaneously was telling the US Ambassador in Dublin that this was for public consumption only. It was owing to 'political necessity', presumably the 'internal Labour Party views, while he, Gilmore, really supported a rerunning of the referendum'. Enda Kenny's problems were of a different order. Part of his thinking was that it would be seen as poor judgment to enter some kind of Government-inspired pact sustaining the ill-fated cross-party unity that took such punishment in the referendum vote. Nevertheless, this view was a limited one, largely confined to the elite among No voters who saw that the Opposition parties had been operating not in the interest of those who elected them, but in the interest of a defective European idea, one that was poorly conceived and presented to the Irish people without any serious judgment of their political nature. Fine Gael and Labour were part of the problem. The two Opposition parties were largely in confusion, failing to make the correct adjustments to changed times and changed thinking among ordinary voters. The situation remained serious for both parties.

Enda Kenny and Fine Gael faced a greater problem than Labour. Kenny was then the Father of the Dáil, longer in the political tooth than he appeared. He had become leader after a long and undistinguished period in politics, and had made a fair fist of the job, certainly better than his immediate predecessor and with a greater sense of party cohesion. But in 2008 it looked as if it was over, further emphasised by the fact that the topical issues—the economy, jobs, unemployment—were not issues on which he enjoyed much authority. The need for this key decision was an urgent one, best taken with the Government in disarray and the Opposition parties waking up to the new realities facing them.

The greater moral strength of the Labour Party, under its then relatively new leader, was based on policy and its articulation. And the strength was evident all the time, when Kenny and Gilmore were on their feet in the Dáil. It was a different matter with Fine Gael deputy leader Richard Bruton, who had demonstrated, in the light of the drastic economic crisis Ireland was facing, that he was outstandingly more competent than his leader. He was consistently right on crucial economic and social issues and this was itself the key to where we next needed to go.

Most of what Micheál Martin said following the 2008 referendum damaged his otherwise balanced performance after the leadership change in Fianna Fáil. His suggestion that the all-party Oireachtas Committee on European Affairs should find out why we had voted No was foolish. We already knew. We did not need committees to tell us or to tell Europe. We did not need all-party pacts. We did not want to be governed from Iveagh House. We did not want to be told how to re-run what those in power thought was a botched job without understanding why.

Micheál Martin, like Brian Cowen, had his eye firmly fixed, after the result of the first referendum, on reversing the Lisbon Treaty decision. Even while the votes were being counted, Brian Cowen was telling the Commission president enough to have him declare that ratification elsewhere should continue, and Martin reinforced this. It was blatant, this indication, privately, of a wrong message while public assurances of respect for voters' wishes were being declared.

Europe was in confusion about Ireland's first referendum decision on the Lisbon Treaty. The EU did not know how to proceed. For this reason it put an entirely undemocratic obligation on the Irish people to think again. The idea that the Irish people might not think again took time to sink in. It took more time with Nicolas Sarkozy than with others, an indication of the odd and eccentric way in which the European system of governance works, transferring enormous power and authority to a man who was ill-informed about the circumstances that prevailed in other countries in the European Union, and therefore sought to apply the judgments and protocols of his own nation, from which he was sprung, for a brief six months, into the additional limelight of Europe's presidency. A curious footnote to the meeting was revealed in June 2011 by Fine Gael's Billy Timmins, who met with Sarkozy in the French Embassy. No Side people were also present. Timmins revealed from notes he took at the time that Sarkozy assured his Irish audience that Ireland's 12.5 per cent corporation tax rate would never be interfered with. France, he said, supported lower corporate taxes and that his country intended to move in the same direction as Ireland on tax.

Nevertheless, Sarkozy arrived in Ireland in July 2008 largely unaware that he had irritated everybody, yet determined to tell us what to do. He insulted the No Side with his prescription for a re-run. He enraged the Yes Side by making their task—at that time a forlorn one—far more difficult.

The Yes Side clearly wanted to change No into Yes. Since, democratically speaking, they represented four-fifths of those who thought they governed us, before the referendum, they also were in confusion as to where the No Vote had come from and how to change it. For the titular head of the European Union to come roaring into Ireland promising, first, a public debate with the perceived No Vote representatives, then changing the programme to Embassy drinks, was arrogant, worsened by the suggestion from the French Embassy that Alan Dukes should chair the encounter, alongside Maurice Hayes, chairman of the National Forum on Europe. What about MEP Patricia McKenna?

This was how the referendum debate proceeded. The rigidity of Europe's position was clearly perceived and helped to produce a parallel firmness in Ireland. It was at least likely, at this early stage, that the Lisbon Treaty would again be rejected. After Ireland voted No, Europe started going soft, as it did in Poland, with undemocratic appeasement and deal-making.

The very idea that Ireland's 'No' position—adopted by nearly 900,000 Irish men and women—could be effectively parsed and analysed seemed a further absurdity. There were far bigger issues here that created more opposition to the Lisbon Treaty than the high-profile minority groups. Understandably, they claimed credit. Yet to many No voters they were an embarrassment; this did not, however, stop a powerful and natural reaction against the Lisbon Treaty.

It was still commonly accepted in Ireland that the European Union had been a hugely beneficial development in the modern world. It had brought great advantages for everyone. Ireland has probably benefited more than any other country among the 27 Member States and this was widely realised. There could be no question of leaving it or of turning against its fundamental presence in Irish life. But it was losing the capacity to communicate and had become comprehensively arrogant about its own rights. After the first referendum, 'reflecting' should not have been confined to Ireland. The European Union also needed to reflect and to do so in legal and constitutional ways.

As is so often the case in politics, Europe did the opposite. The new text was a complete turn-off. The Yes voters could not speak in favour because they did not know how. The No voters had ready-made jibes to issue against almost everything in the Lisbon Treaty. Both sides had been deprived of what the original Laeken Declaration had attempted seven years before—clear principles and general rules; instead, they had chaos. What they wanted was a simple constitutional statement of where we were and where we were going.

And so we came to an invitation from the Government, endorsed by the EU, asking for a 'pause for reflection'. This was the new 'escape clause' put forward by Brian Cowen. It meant nothing of the sort. Its true meaning was 'Reject what has happened, re-do it in another way, to suit us, not the people'. Evident in Brian Cowen's approach and in Tánaiste Mary Coughlan's, as well as being the line followed by Micheál Martin on Lisbon, it soon became a mantra for those endeavouring to govern us. Into the vacuum of 'reflection' were sucked many words. Stephen Collins, for example, in his 'Inside Politics' article in the *Irish Times* on 2 August 2008, told us that the Government 'has made the winning of a second referendum almost impossible by compounding its botched referendum campaign with a poor tactical response to the Lisbon defeat'. He then presented this 'reflection' in the form of a question: 'So how can the Government find a way out of holding a second referendum while not ignoring the will of the people as expressed in June?' And answered it himself: 'The only way is for the Dáil to ratify the Lisbon Treaty while simultaneously opting out of areas such as the Charter of Fundamental Rights, which probably does require referendum approval, and the new defence arrangements whose misrepresentation prompted so many women to vote no.'

The enormity of this 'reflection', which threw the June referendum out of the window and embarked, all over again, on putting through in another way the defeated Yes Vote intention, seemed astonishing.

The suggestion of ratification by the Dáil had no legal basis. Such an approach would have been profoundly unconstitutional and an undemocratic course for our political leaders. The Lisbon Treaty established a constitutionally new European Union, with its own legal personality for the first time, legally different from the European Union established by the Treaty of Maastricht. What was proposed was the replacement of the Maastricht-based EU by a federal EU based on the Lisbon Treaty, making us real rather than symbolical citizens for the first time. The key message in the debate during the summer and autumn of 2009 and affecting Yes and No voters equally was that the constitutional and political character of the Union, its Member States and of Irish citizens would be transformed fundamentally by the ratification of the Lisbon Treaty. Of course no vote in the Houses of the Oireachtas was constitutionally capable of doing this.

In August 2009 a rather rueful Pat Cox re-entered the Lisbon Treaty debate, encouraged, it appeared, by a speech by Dick Roche at the Humbert Summer School. Roche put forward the view that a second referendum would be required. Cox agreed, saying it would be 'the least bad option'. He did so having criticised sections of the Irish media. Cox was an undoubted 'big hitter' as a former president of the European Parliament, someone who should have known the score on the workings of European democracy. The occasion of Pat Cox's main entry into the Lisbon debate was the launch of the Yes campaign by the Progressive Democrats, the party of which he believed he should have become leader. His original intervention had been in mid-May 2008. At that time sectoral interests—those of farmers, trade unions and middle-of-the-road groups—were dominant.

Cox dealt with the reduced number of commissioners. He used a pivotal phrase, talking about 'the available Europe' being bad for Ireland and he skilfully countered criticism by those who felt this to be true. It was prescient. This turned out to be a major problem, possibly *the* major problem, and subsequent events—in the economy, employment, international affairs, including the dismal performance of the EU on the Russian invasion of Georgia, within NATO and at the UN—showed that 'the available Europe' needed a good deal of attention unconnected with the Lisbon Treaty reforms.

Pat Cox made a major statement in early June of the same year (2008) that was a highly impressive analysis of the arguments. It was probably better than any other presentation of the issues being examined in the Lisbon Treaty, such as taxation, neutrality, the right to life, subsidiarity, even the 'Citizens' Initiative' idea, where not less than a million Europeans could 'invite' the European Commission to act on their proposal!

Wise or not, Cox spoiled his excellent case by focusing attacks on the supposed 'enemies' of the Lisbon Treaty—Sinn Féin, Libertas and 'ignorant' commentators on law-making processes—and made the EU seem even more forceful and heavy in what it intended than had been accepted by ordinary people up to that point. He talked of Irish sovereignty as 'a gift won by freedom'—a meaningless phrase—and was then very distressed when the Irish people exercised that sovereignty in a way that was deeply displeasing to him. It continued to displease him. Cox was of the view that sovereignty could be hauled into line and made to give the 'right' answer on Europe and he aligned himself with Dick Roche. Roche had opened up the dangerous route of pre-empting the outcome of what was supposed to be a serious process of reflection by introducing the sovereignty issue. Two critical elements in that sovereignty debate and where it went next were the media and the combined power of Government and the Houses of the Oireachtas. Both were needlessly disparaged by Pat Cox. Having expressed admiration for the idea of sovereignty, back in May 2008 and again in the following month, his post-referendum view was that the parliamentary route to ratification was not just a mistake, it was an exercise in 'serial abdication' and had led to a dilution of Irish parliamentary democracy. This was a perverse interpretation of the democracy enshrined in Ireland's Constitution, part of which is the legitimate and much-valued use of the referendum to discover the will of the people.

In doing this, and even with the benefit of the lopsided Referendum Commission, the Government and the Houses of the Oireachtas failed in their objective and in Cox's view 'forfeited their freedom and entitlement to act'. It was not a forfeit; it was a choice. It was made by the Government, supported by the Opposition—misguidedly, in our opinion—and could therefore be laid at the door of the Houses of the Oireachtas. But it was not an abdication. It was fundamentally in keeping with Ireland's constitutional democracy and this was lost sight of during the debate about a second run at a question that had already been answered. As Charlie McCreevy puts it:

> Each country had to ratify this particular Treaty. If the only answer to the question is 'yes', there was no point in putting the question to any of the other 26 countries either. You must remember, this is a club. The rules of the club were being changed. Existing members of the club were asked to agree to the changes in the rules of the club. Ireland—by its own constitution—had to put these questions to a referendum of the people. The Irish people said 'no'. And that decision has to be respected by our European partners as well.

The second regrettable and offensive disparagement by Pat Cox was based on the fiction that there was 'a British print and broadcast media' conspiracy based on 'an Irish homespun version of classic Tory British Euroscepticism'. Worse still, it was 'aided and abetted by some Irish fellow travellers, whose visceral anti-EU instincts hold such sway in their home territory'.

There were few enough at whose feet this charge could have been laid. They included Kevin Myers, David Quinn, Vincent Browne, Brendan Keenan, Mark Dooley and Bruce Arnold, possibly among others. 'Visceral' means to be directed by the interior organs of the body, heart, lungs, intestine. Many journalists were directed mostly by their brains. Which were 'fellow travellers'?

Pat Cox made few friends by this approach. Even if it was reluctant, his espousal of the idea of a second referendum needed the willing support of the elected representatives he said had 'forfeited their freedom', together with the journalists who, in the main, recognised the qualities he brought to European political life. Bruce Arnold advised that it should not have been attempted. But the desire for it was unquenchable.

Chapter 7 ∾

LENIHAN GUARANTEES
THE BANKS

Privately, Brian Cowen was fully in the picture, not just about Anglo Irish Bank but about the other main banks and financial institutions. Publicly, he pretended otherwise. In an interview with Jason O'Toole after the Bank Guarantee had become the source of public outrage and fear, Cowen gave a global explanation, virtually absolving Ireland from having been managed through the crisis any differently from other countries.

When the financial crisis first hit the country, Cowen said, it was part of a global meltdown and that it was 'not as if something was done in Ireland that's unique'. He spoke about looking to the United States and the European economies for 'recovery as quick as possible so we can piggyback on the demand that that will create'.

Cowen also stood over his own tenure as Minister for Finance. He said that all his decisions were based on the 'best advice' he 'was given at the time'. He would argue that nobody had a 'crystal ball that predicted all that has happened and unfolding'. He claimed that the financial crisis had happened because the 'market just froze' and that 'trust and confidence broke down completely in the banking system'.

'Many people are critical, saying, "Why didn't everyone see what was coming?" No one saw a banking crisis in America that was going to have the impact that it's had,' Cowen claimed at the time.

On his knowledge of the Irish banks as Minister for Finance and Cabinet member, and then as Taoiseach, Cowen dismissed the argument that they had been running riot, or were out of control:

Irish banks—no more than other banks in any part of the developed world—couldn't get access to sufficient equity to keep the level of investment financed that was going on in Ireland. Banks are private institutions. Yes, they were regulated. Yes, there was a situation, in my opinion, where clearly the level of borrowing that they engaged in—and the amount of money that was put out into the system—in retrospect was far less stringent than should be in place in the situation we are in today.

But many of those—it has to be pointed out—financial institutions were responding to the demands of the Irish economy, for investors, for people who're involved in business, and, indeed, for consumers at a time of historically low interest rates. It was a time when the economy was forging ahead and jobs security [*sic*] and jobs creation, making us one of the best-performing economies in Europe. The consumer confidence was high and people in good times decided to get into a level of debt—both in terms of their own private finances and in terms of investment—which put some people into difficulty. But people made these decisions on their own best judgments and advice, the same as the Government. It, too, made its own best judgment and advice at the time.

Cowen accepted that the Financial Regulator could have done more to detect earlier some of the fraudulent activities being engaged in by various banks. 'In hindsight, the regulatory system didn't work as well as it should have. That's something that's clear in terms of how this whole world financial crisis has happened in the banking system. Its set-up was far less prudent and took far greater risks than should have been the case,' he stated.

This first of several interviews was an act of concealment of a truly unimaginable story of incompetence and failure. Nothing was regulated, nothing was done in accordance with good financial practice. It would be more than two years before the correct story emerged, and even then prevarication and the deliberate obscuring of what happened was still being used to protect politicians, notably Cowen himself.

What happened to Fianna Fáil in this period? The question leads to a reasonable measure of public dismay and fear, particularly as a result of what had happened in Anglo Irish Bank.

The Fianna Fáil party's political clothing was stripped off, revealing an organisation that had lost its way. It had been consistently concealing things and blaming the catastrophe on others: the property speculators were at fault, the banks were at fault, the media were misinterpreting what was happening.

It is an appropriate moment to consider what the opinion polls—the 21st-century equivalent of the biblical prophecy—were saying about Fianna Fáil's position.

At the time of Cowen's elevation to the job of Taoiseach and for some months before that, the RED C opinion poll published by the *Sunday Business Post* was showing support for Fianna Fáil at a respectable level, around 39 per cent. In March 2008 the main issue was Bertie Ahern, in April and May it became Cowen, with a slight rise for April to 40 per cent, dropping back in late April to 38 per cent. Cowen and the Lisbon referendum were seen as the main issues. This reflected a smooth and unchallenged handover of power and things promising to go on as before. The first job in hand was the Lisbon Treaty referendum, dealt with in Chapter 5.

The Fianna Fáil position was not documented for the day of the referendum vote but by the date of the next poll, in late September, before the banking crisis erupted, it was 36 per cent. Shortly after the referendum, a further poll showed the party up to 40 per cent. What made a bigger impact by far was the Bank Guarantee imposed on 28 September. This saw the party's standing fall to 26 per cent.

From then on, the level of support remained in the twenties, a clear warning of future electoral collapse. This total was pulled back up to 30 per cent in November 2009, not helped by months of media stories on former Ceann Comhairle John O'Donoghue's expenses, resulting in his resignation. The party had clearly and permanently lost ground over mismanagement that hit hard the pockets of people across Irish society, including a huge swathe of savers to whom the other defeat—on our standing in Europe—was only of academic interest. What was surprising was the fact that, although Fianna Fáil was losing ground electorally, the gains by the Opposition parties were not comparable. There was no balance to the mathematics. Fine Gael's and Labour's standing in the polls improved less than they should have done, since many of the spokespersons, notably Richard Bruton and Joan Burton, were assessing well what had really happened to the Irish economy.

Clearly the fall was more related to the economy and to the banking crisis than to the Lisbon Treaty vote, and this seemed to be the case going into February 2009, with the issues being the economy as well as the second Lisbon referendum. Polls were held at the beginning and end of February 2009 with a dramatic fall of 10 points in that period, from 33 per cent to 23 per cent.

Fianna Fáil's own declining support had become a major issue before the electorate, with property, jobs and the economy—backed by Lisbon, on which a re-run had been announced—issues in the minds of those polled. In addition, the historic outlet for an impoverished Ireland—emigration—began to grow, with well-trained and well-motivated young people departing for the new world and the old.

After the Budget—a feat of Herculean sleight-of-hand—the party's support climbed for two months to 27 per cent but then fell again to 23 per cent where it stayed for much of 2010, dropping still further, to 18 per cent, at the end of the year. Events such as the ongoing expenses scandals around Ivor Callely TD and Senator Larry Butler did not help the party's image. There it stayed, even dropping to 17 per cent in the run-up to the general election.

By all political standards this represented not only a crisis but a chronic state of crisis for which no easy answers emerged. However, so long as Fianna Fáil held together with the Greens—for whom electoral annihilation was predicted—there was time in hand. The Dáil was a little over three years into its five-year term. Cowen was soldiering on. The army metaphor is appropriate: his electoral stance and his method of campaigning were those of a blunt and at times brutal fighter.

The underlying issue of greatest significance to the electorate and the people generally was the state of the banks. The wealth of Ireland, expressed in terms of ordinary people, was widely represented by their ownership of bank shares, their deposited cash, the capacity of banks to provide investment money, their willingness to do so, their liquidity and stability, the standing of the euro as a world currency and the capacity of the politicians who ruled them to safeguard all these things. Global economics, European rules and directives, the central European Union management of Member States that got into difficulties, eventually including Ireland, were all important issues as well and became increasingly so. Nevertheless, there was a distinction between these two groupings of issues.

The first was mainly personal and private but of the deepest significance to each individual, no matter where they stood on the scale of personal wealth. The second was a collective and public concern, written about in newspapers, seen as globally important and the subject of a huge and amorphous public debate. The post-Celtic Tiger period and, more painfully, the aftermath of the Bank Guarantee saw these two fields of interest conflate. Shares fell, deposits were withdrawn, banks became frightened and stopped providing credit, the property market collapsed, developers cancelled their programmes, Ireland headed inexorably into recession and quite suddenly trust in leaders and those in power, whether in Ireland or in Europe, faltered.

Though at the time the State did not know it, European intervention in Irish affairs, in particular in respect of the faltering banks, became a hidden factor. There had been concealment and considerable dishonesty over the circumstances surrounding all the banks, Anglo Irish Bank more than the others. The fiscal difficulties brought Europe into Irish affairs. This meant not only intrusion into banking but also a great urgency to force Ireland, through the imposition of a second Lisbon Treaty referendum, into greater obedience to the EU.

The country started out being slavish towards this bullying and capitulating, without public knowledge, to a crucial set of actions towards the banks directly imposed by Europe. But quite apart from this slavish attitude, Ireland's leaders, notably 'the two Brians', Cowen and Lenihan, were increasingly at sea in what they were doing, or failing to do. This led to a situation where the Fianna Fáil-Green Party coalition engaged in collective and wholesale misrepresentation to the people in order to facilitate the EU. In a truly disgraceful way the main Opposition parties, governed by a puerile view of their electoral, moral and political duties, collaborated in this.

This period of crisis in Irish history was accompanied by poor and unconstitutional judgment, an approach that became commonplace on many public issues during the period 2008–11, particularly by the Government, leading to a steady and eventually irreversible fall in its electoral popularity which finally led to its humiliating defeat.

It was the Government's handling of the medical card debacle that outraged the public most. Cowen insists that it was a 'government decision' and not Health Minister Mary Harney's to means-test pensioners for medical cards. Cowen never felt there would be such a public backlash because 'there were an awful lot of other proposals on the table, which were more impalpable'.

According to one former Minister:

> The TDs were annoyed that the background information was simply out of date about the extent of the demand for medical cards. People in the Department of Health didn't have or couldn't find the data [on which] that could have been based. When the word got out, people on the backbenches were saying, 'You can't be serious! That doesn't make any sense.' There was a lot of rowing back. Trying to reverse the decision was almost as difficult as making it.

It was a disaster for Cowen, who lost TDs over it. Joe Behan, a deputy for Wicklow, resigned from the Fianna Fáil party over the medical card mess. Cowen felt it was 'premature' of him to resign over the matter because he had planned to speak to the parliamentary party that evening about his plans for a U-turn. 'It's a pity that we didn't have the opportunity to sit down and talk about it before he made up his mind,' Cowen recalls. However, even though Behan was now technically an independent TD, he continued to support the Government in crucial Dáil votes. Independent TD Finian McGrath also resigned from the coalition.

Secretly, in a gross exploitation of what was increasingly seen as a dangerous form of bureaucratic totalitarianism, the EU intervened in Ireland's affairs. It did so in this covert way because it was confronting, on Europe's behalf, the potential collapse of banking more generally. Ireland failed to understand this or act appropriately. It was duped by Europe, and Cowen and Lenihan were largely to blame. This did not emerge at the time of the Bank Guarantee, but it was the background, and the EU motive was protection of European banking, not of the Irish people.

On the surface the actions of Brian Lenihan provoked a huge and amorphous debate on whether he was right or wrong in what he did, whether he had a choice, whether he made the correct decisions, even whether he knew what he was doing.

While much of the knowledge of this was to emerge later, it was clear enough in the wake of the Bank Guarantee that major questions were not being confronted. The Irish people were not being told where Europe was in all this. Instead, the involvement of the European Central Bank was concealed. In the deal done between the Government and the Irish banks, it was perceived to be to the banks' advantage, again as a result of political incompetence. It was far from clear how the solution to the crisis would be regulated, and in any case regulation itself had been discredited.

One piece of foolishness was Brian Lenihan's acceptance of the brief from his civil servants, who had been informed by the banks that the debt exposure was only about 0.85 per cent of lending. In the event, it turned out to be nearer a catastrophic 50 per cent, and the crippling liability of €400 billion forced Lenihan to seek the IMF and ECB bailout.

Cowen and Lenihan, following talks between the Government and the bankers, with the Financial Regulator and the Attorney General present, managed to create the impression that they had given some kind of decisive leadership. Brian Cowen, in a speech to businessmen in Trinity College, and Brian Lenihan, in his presentation of the deal to the Dáil and the Irish public, were performers rather than serious and focused leaders. They were at a circus and not in the chambers in which real decision-making should be pursued. In fact such chambers have become an increasingly distant memory in Irish political life and certainly are not within either House of the Oireachtas. Not surprisingly, it was not long before the absence of adequate safeguards and the weighting in favour of the banks emerged as the truer picture.

The limit on what should have happened was simple enough. It was fair and sensible for the State to guarantee the deposits of Irish citizens and savers in the banks, at least up to a certain amount. This was part of the package, the limit being €100,000. However, it was a quite different thing for the State to guarantee that all those from whom the Irish banks had borrowed money abroad, mainly foreign banks—bank bondholders and creditors—would be repaid. This was especially so in the case of Anglo Irish Bank, and, in a different sense, Irish Nationwide

Building Society, essentially a mortgage bank. Neither of them therefore were, in the fullest sense, 'systemic'. The foreign banks that had lent vast sums to the Irish banks for on-lending to the Irish property market during the boom, as normal investments, were knowingly putting their money at risk. They should have been let carry the can when these risk capital ventures proved to be dud.

There is still an unresolved question mark over this aspect of the blanket Bank Guarantee. This would not have been given by Cowen and Lenihan if it did not have the approval of the ECB. Its president, Jean-Claude Trichet, told Lenihan that no Irish bank should be let fail, for fear of 'contagion' spreading to other EU banks and damaging the euro. It later transpired that he had gone much further, threatening Lenihan into following his directions. The ECB fully supported the blanket guarantee, even though some EU governments criticised it. One can therefore safely say that the ECB was largely responsible for it and should have shared responsibility for its monitoring and controlling of that night's decision. Anglo Irish was not systemic in any normal sense. It did not have branches all over Ireland, with the deposits of large numbers of Irish savers. It was insolvent, and evidence of that insolvency had been piling up for months before the guarantee. Guaranteeing Anglo Irish alone imposed a burden of some €30 billion on Irish taxpayers.

It seemed at the time that the heads of the Irish banks went to Cowen and Lenihan on the night of Monday, 28/29 September 2008 and told them that several Irish banks were going to go bust within a few days. They then proposed the deal. This was adopted as the only way out. It was a bankers' solution and it created the central issue that made it 'inevitable'—that public confidence had to be restored.

Was Ireland right with its guarantee? We think Lenihan—who did not understand what he was doing—became enamoured of himself. He thought he had worked this dramatic miracle—as a barrister he would have seen it as winning the court action—but he was not wondering enough about the comments from international economic analysts, or how he could get out of his own economic miracle if it turned out to be, as indeed it did, an economic disaster. Three things, then, were wrong. The inclusion of Anglo—despite what Trichet had told Lenihan—was an expensive and unnecessary mistake. The inclusion of the bondholders was an even more expensive mistake. Finally, making the Bank Guarantee a fixed mechanism rather than one open to regular, bi-monthly review by Cabinet and perhaps change, was perhaps the most expensive mistake of all. Even the idea of including the Cabinet in these thoughts seems to have been marginal rather than central.

For an equally brief period it was seen internationally as 'dynamic'—which it certainly was—but also breathtaking in its scale and the judgment behind it. As the *Daily Telegraph* columnist Ambrose Evans-Pritchard put it, Dublin had 'trumped' every other country. But he also said that this blanket guarantee was the most radical since the Scandinavian rescue package in the early 1990s, but with the implication that Ireland was less stable and more vulnerable. And the comment needed to be read in the context of other judgments, including that of the *Financial Times*, where the editorial had this to say:

> It is true that Ireland, like all EU member states, is responsible for the stability of its banking system. But this is not justification for a guarantee that, as the Irish finance minister himself acknowledges, amounts to economic nationalism. His defence—'we're on our own here in Ireland'—shows scant regard for Dublin's neighbours. . .

This meant the United Kingdom, but it could have been applied more widely to Europe as a whole. Which brought one to the second question, 'Where was Europe?' And where was the passionate espousal of membership of the EU that had so captivated elected representatives a few brief months before? Was the shine taken off what politicians were telling voters of the huge importance to the economy, as to everything else, of greater closeness to the EU? Dire risks for Ireland had been forecast if it chose to 'go it alone'. The nation was anticipating dire risks to the banking system, the economy and the personal savings of people throughout the country, notwithstanding membership of the EU, to which the ties were to be reinforced.

Outwardly, it appeared that in the face of the biggest financial crisis in Irish history, Ireland was going it alone. Even if other things turn out to be defective, with too many burdens on the State and too few on the banks, which was the growing fear of everyone, it seemed on the surface that the nonsense of depending on Europe had been exposed. This later proved far from the case but it governed thinking at the time.

The move Ireland had made was unilateral and illegal. It was then copied by Greece under similar pressures. For a while it looked as though it would create an unstoppable stampede across Europe: either for an EU-wide bailout of the financial system or for it to happen unilaterally, country by country.

What was becoming increasingly clear was the lack of certainty and failure of touch of the EU. This was evident in the ponderous response of the EU president, José Manuel Barroso, who was described by economic commentator Christina Speight in London as leading 'an illiterate bunch of bureaucrats dabbling in vital subjects which they don't understand. It's ludicrous to suggest yet another bunch of bureaucrats taking two weeks to make decisions needed in 5 seconds.' If that was the measure on which European confidence was being rebuilt in the face of the crisis, then the actions of Cowen and Lenihan—even as the banks won the debate—seemed preferable to relying on Brussels.

The No voters were right. Europe wanted more and more power but knew less and less about how to use it. The sudden flight into unilateral nationalism by people who told us that closer union with Europe was an inescapable requirement made more difficult any attempt to revisit Lisbon. Those who opposed greater integration were temporarily strengthened by the EU adding another failure to its lengthening list.

The European Commission's plan for tougher bank capital rules, issued well in the wake of the banking crisis, suggested that Europe's leaders are only in the driving seat on half-days or weekend visits. Their suggestion: that banks would be restricted in lending beyond a certain limit to one party, and 'colleges of supervisors' would be put in place for those banking groups that operate in several EU states. People hoped Ireland had demonstrated that it did not need or want European 'help', particularly since the EU was operating outside the legal framework within which the regulations were proposed, despite the fact that the operations were to the satisfaction of the banks.

For a time the man at the eye of the storm was Patrick Neary, the Financial Regulator. Even more than EU officials, the time he had spent in the regulatory wheelhouse had been intermittent, while his regulatory body, staffed with supposed experts, had not provided the country with the security it needed for its banking system. Dynamism was far from being the word that jumped to mind in respect of the situation facing the country. Patrick Neary gave a lamentable performance on RTÉ television's 'Prime Time' at the beginning of October 2008. His reassurances were dismal in their limited and narrow focus. He seemed not to see beyond the restoration of confidence, which had been attempted already. His proposals on regulation were no more than that, and were made to the Government. Were his powers greatly increased by the instant legislation? His answers before RTÉ cameras suggested that nothing had been done to strengthen his role; all was for the Government to judge on and act.

Fianna Fáil habitually introduces legislation or regulations that are sufficient only to the situation they are applied to. In this case the situation was changing too fast. It seemed clear that it would deal with the banking crisis in the same loose and sloppy way adopted towards corruption, ethics, tax loopholes and many other circumstances that favoured the privileged and the elite. Its laws at the time were like colanders, deliberately made with holes in them. Clearly there were statutes needing to be patched up. And as the full details of the present structure, with all its faults, became clearer, further flaws could confidently be predicted.

What Brian Lenihan was told, on the commencement of his role in the banking crisis, is important. We do not know what Lenihan was told on taking office. The conflict in what his predecessor has acknowledged about his own position during the crucial early stages of Ireland's financial collapse, including the collapse of the banking system, raises doubts about Lenihan's own knowledge.

The reaction of Brian Cowen and Brian Lenihan to their very own economic crisis had been that of elderly janitors tinkering with out-of-date fire extinguishers while the building burns down around them. Both men had had several months to adjust to the downturn. Brian Cowen's more comprehensive knowledge dated back to his appointment as Minister for Finance.

They brought forward the date of the December 2008 Budget on grounds of urgency, then revealed that their plan was a marginal and ill-conceived dithering with the welfare and prospects of elderly people and children, which they then reversed.

The single most shocking image to come out of this was the much-photographed spectacle of the private conspiracy between themselves, the employers and the unions—the so-called social partnership—as they complacently made their regular, undemocratic and outrageous deal on wages. The Government's highest priority should have been to abandon the social partnership and take direct charge of public service pay, freezing it, with a view to scaling down the size of this monstrous and expensive burden on the taxpayer.

The task was a huge one. But it could not even be started while Ireland continued to pretend that there was any merit in pursuing an expensive and inflationary agreement—itself based on the idea that the unions have some right to inflation-protection—while unemployment rose steadily, sales of goods fell, the private sector tried to adjust to this and the Dáil remained powerless to intervene.

The good times were over and the social partnership was a product of those good times. It was never democratic. The will of the people did not govern the private deals. It was one or two Ministers and a clutch of unelected civil servants—often without reference to the Cabinet—negotiating with employer and union representatives, neither of which groupings was interested in the common good. Their mandate was to help and protect well-defined sectors of the economy, and so long as there was growth, the settlements they achieved—though on the whole inflationary—were tolerated.

Since the baleful summer of 2008, during which the nation watched the whole flimsy structure of economic strength and vitality fall apart, any social partnership deal, other than one in line with retrenchment and reduction, had not only been rendered redundant; it had become an obscene mockery of the real requirements of the economy. The State needed to set aside any thought of the social partnership awarding itself anything. Then, the next year, reduce pay and scale down superfluous employment.

That simple reality was the cornerstone of future action; yet Brian Cowen and Brian Lenihan seemed oblivious to their duty. It was widely argued that social partnership works only one way. No 'partners' were going to walk into a room and negotiate reduced pay and redundancies. The only way was for those in power to do the job they were paid to do—and, it must be said, at a rate better than any other politicians in the world—resume control and act with stern and unflinching courage. It was not a question of saying: 'Can it be done?' It was a question of saying: 'It has to be done.'

Side by side with setting it in train, the Government should have confronted the terrible mess it had made by hiving off everything in sight, through the process of 'agentisation'. It had transferred the running of a whole range of activities, once sensibly managed by the Civil Service, into the hands of agencies. The biggest and most disastrous was the Health Service Executive (HSE). This had been, effectively, the Department of Health. It should have been under Dáil control, answerable to those we elect.

The HSE was only one of some 800 such agencies, costing annually close on a billion euro of public money, expensively hived off from direct public service control and put into separate offices, with new and highly paid staff and lavish expense accounts. It made a nonsense of taxpayers' money and accountability. The current Health Minister, Dr James Reilly, believes that the obscene spending in the HSE during Mary Harney's period in office was tolerated because of a laziness by her to tackle spending. He damningly described our A&E units as of 'Third World' standards under her regime. He said.

> I haven't visited every single health service in the EU, but I haven't visited one that's worse. This is the worst that I know of, absolutely. Cuts can be made, savings can be achieved from within the absolute horrendous waste within the HSE. There was a billion euro alone last year [2009] in overtime. Now overtime is not a core part of the Croke Park Agreement. And one NCHD [non-consultant hospital doctor] last year got 130,000 in overtime on top of his pay. That's not his fault, that's the stupid rostering he was put on. So, look at the billion in overtime. Look at the two to three hundred million that could be saved by generic drugs, if they were used, number one, and, number two, if the government tackled the price of drugs in this country. There's a cholesterol drug down here in the generic form that costs €27 and in the North it only costs something like £1.40. So, you don't have to go to Spain or Portugal,

you only have to go up the road. There's something radically wrong there and we need to address it. 121 million in taxis! Clearly, proper logistic control would sort a lot of that out. The list goes on.

My whole point is that the Minister [Mary Harney] is lazy. She allows the HSE to take the lazy way out, she therefore allows them to cut the frontlines because that's the easiest thing to do, instead of making the hard decisions around redundancy; the hard decisions around the cost of drugs and taking on the drug companies, and the hard decisions around overtime and having proper rostering. The hard decisions around how hospitals operate and how they're budgeted.

'Agentisation' had taken control. Because of this, the monitoring of public expenditure was outside Dáil surveillance. Ministers and their Secretaries General did not control it. And the cost in efficiency and hard cash had become enormous. The reform of this, Brian Cowen led us to believe, was a high priority when he took over. It was not a job that could be undertaken lightly, nor one that might have been achieved speedily. But it did need some preliminary acts of courage. It got none. In fact, the country witnessed a deliberate augmentation of the opposite kind of thinking, in part based on the Government's lack of confidence in its own Civil Service, in turn demoralised by the process. The hived-off nature and economic flatulence of these agencies, taking the place of what civil servants once did, had been an excuse for party patronage and inventive control. It was highly questionable with the economic downturn. No effective steps were taken to rectify the problem.

There were also more immediate decisions related to this central one. The two Brians should have requested from the Cabinet the authority to impose a tax on all unoccupied buildings in the State. Many of them were the product of surplus private wealth. Taxing them would have made their owners responsible for part of the State's huge debt, and this would have been instead of plaguing the elderly, or denying the children.

The two Brians should also have begun the long overdue restoration of domestic rates, at the same time cutting the expensive agencies that burden taxpayers. This should have been combined with the initiation of reform of local government management and expenditure. Local government, following a National Government lead, is also guilty of profligate hiving off and double charging on services.

There is a narrative to this. Since the late 1960s, with interruptions during the oil crisis of the 1970s and the setbacks during the 1980s, the country has been on an upward curve of growing self-confidence and of legitimate and valuable wealth creation. It over-indulged this, was prodigal and now must go on paying the price for years to come. That had been the case for more than two years before Brian Cowen came to power. It had been the subject of his warnings in Budgets in 2006 and since. Yet when he took over, he abandoned his own economic creed.

The State no longer accounted to itself any more. It had lost the meaning of reform and restraint. And the blundering was at the very top. And what did Brian Cowen do? He spent his time and energy, and that of a high-powered team, on creating yet another plan, requiring yet another agency, trying to build the future economy on top of the wreckage outlined above.

| THE EU STEPS IN

Europe intervened much more openly in Ireland's political processes early in the summer of 2009, seeking by every means possible to influence the electorate in advance of the second Lisbon Treaty referendum in October. This had already been set in motion earlier and at several levels, including the visit of the EU's president at that time, Nicolas Sarkozy, in July 2008. The drama of this unlocked the doors to such intervention in Ireland's affairs and led to a steady augmentation of such interventions. In fact, two European presidents visited in the aftermath of the first Lisbon Treaty vote, both coming in their capacity as president-elect of the EU. The Sarkozy visit was organised by Micheál Martin, Minister for Foreign Affairs, working with Brian Cowen. It was hardly a brilliant success. President Sarkozy was coming, then he wasn't coming, then he changed the date; he was seeing the No people, then not seeing them, then he saw them. Though they represented the majority will of the Irish people, they were treated like freaks in a circus. They were there to be assessed in order for Sarkozy to reverse what they had achieved.

This approach unfortunately set the tone, if not the manner, of political behaviour. At one point in this period, November 2008, Micheál Martin turned protocol on its head, using it like a cudgel in the hands of a rapparee. The occasion was the second presidential visit, this time a State visit to Ireland of the Czech President, Václav Klaus, who would assume the EU presidency for a six-month term in January 2009. Klaus's visit was in November 2008, while Sarkozy was still EU president and had recently visited Dublin. Klaus was a well-known international critic of the Lisbon Treaty and of attempts of ever further EU centralisation. It was a badly handled affair, not on this occasion as a result of the ill judgment of the summer event by President Sarkozy, but through the official antipathy felt towards Klaus because he was in support of the Irish No Vote of 2008 and came to encourage the country to repeat this rejection.

The Department of Foreign Affairs can at times be pompous about protocol; alternatively, it can make it up as it goes along. The Irish do not do protocol terribly well and if politicians are too much involved, it can lead to disaster. People tend to think that a casual 'Whatever-you're-having-yourself' approach is rather charming. The British, however, are masters of the art of protocol, have it for almost everything and have taught it to the rest of the world. This teaching has been least successful in Ireland, which has spent most of its history trying to undermine the protocols of its nearest neighbour by adopting a 'special relationship' in the worst sense of the term. Micheál Martin flailed around during the visit, repeatedly bashing the presence in the country of its State Guest, President Václav Klaus, on the head with this strange weapon of opprobrium. This left a trail of embarrassment and insult, in two days doing harm to himself, his Government and the country. It pivoted on the simple fact that this intelligent, truthful and diplomatically correct Czech President was opposed to the Lisbon Treaty. Cowen was unable to intervene. His own head was in danger. Nor did he himself have sufficient respect for protocol to see the enormity of the breaches committed.

Václav Klaus had added to his State visit a private one in order to meet with Declan Ganley, leader of Libertas. This was to extend his understanding of the Irish mind on the Lisbon Treaty. Ganley had been involved in bringing Klaus to Ireland and had given a dinner of welcome. He reflected in his speech of welcome that

When the current [EU] President, Nicolas Sarkozy, visited Ireland in the summer, after our referendum, he was outspokenly on the minority losing side. Yet we ensured he talked freely to those he wanted to meet, including those who had won and represented the majority. You, Mr President, as the next President of Europe, from January, have had more difficulty, but happily you join us for this event tonight which is immensely important for my guests and for myself.

The dinner, which was private, was 'invaded' by an RTÉ camera crew led by the station's then Europe Editor, Seán Whelan, interviewing guests as to why they were there. The warped protocol of the Department of Foreign Affairs was echoed too in the quite improper publication by the *Irish Times* of the full list of the Klaus dinner guests.

Klaus quite openly supported Ireland's majority on the Treaty issue. This was in direct conflict with what the Cowen Government had already decided. Behind the scenes it was already working, in late summer 2008, to undermine its own referendum, in conflict with a constitutional requirement on the Government to support the decision of the people in June 2008.

President Sarkozy had brought good news with him from Europe, mainly reassurances on issues that were not affected by the Lisbon Treaty, involving respect for Irish neutrality and other issues, including the retained status of the country's European Commissioner. There was a direct reflection of this in the sequential changes in opinion poll treatment of public concern, notably by the *Irish Times*, which in a summer poll questioned how people would vote in a second Lisbon Treaty referendum. This was based on a simple and straightforward Yes/No question about public response to a new referendum. The answer revealed that 30 per cent would vote Yes, 35 per cent would vote No. This represented 53.4 per cent voting No, 46.6 per cent voting Yes when Don't Knows were eliminated.

By November 2008 the 'question' had changed. Voters were asked, in a poll conducted on 10 and 11 November: *'If the Lisbon Treaty is modified to allow Ireland to retain an EU Commissioner and other concerns on neutrality, abortion and taxation are clarified in special declarations, would you vote Yes or No in another referendum?'* Not surprisingly, the result changed as well: 43 per cent said Yes, 39 per cent said No. The *Irish Times* detected from this outcome 'a chink of optimism'.

The newspaper went on to talk of 'modifications' to Lisbon, as though these were easy options for the EU. Not only were they not 'easy options', they were not options at all. Usually the soul of balance in evenness of interpretation of its own excellent opinion polls, the *Irish Times*, on this occasion, placed a question that invited an answer favourable to the Yes Vote, which the paper espoused editorially at all times, and then gave a favourable editorial interpretation of what had been ascertained. This included saying that the findings would 'strengthen the Government's political confidence'.

Micheál Martin at the time rejected the idea of doing nothing, equating a second referendum with restoring Ireland's supposed 'favoured status' in Europe and placing the country 'at the heart of European decision-making'. When the poll was published the next day, he put the retention of an Irish Commissioner at the centre of his argument. The retention of Ireland's Commissioner had nothing to do with the Lisbon Treaty and was not concerned with representation of Ireland 'at the table'.

Martin's lead was followed generally by politicians, blamed that week by Maurice Hayes, chairman of the National Forum on Europe, for not helping voters to link Lisbon to their daily lives. In fact, politicians tried to do this, mainly by telling lies about jobs and opportunities. And the same politicians were even worse on this score the next time round. The fact was deliberately overlooked that EU Commissioners do not 'represent' their countries at all; they are the creatures of the EU. That is where their oath of office places them, loyal to the EU, not to the countries they come from. In any case, the retention of an Irish Commissioner was taken care of already. Under the Nice Treaty, which Ireland approved, there was a requirement to reduce the number of Commissioners, but by how many is not specified. EU thinking in 2008 was that it would be by one Commissioner, and his place would be taken by the country not having a Commissioner but having instead the post of the EU's High Representative for Foreign and Security Policy. Ireland did not need a 'Declaration' on that.

On tax there was a difficulty. It was to be a chronic difficulty related to Ireland's low corporation tax rate on which it depended heavily in order to attract foreign investment. The argument would be intense well into the period that followed the humiliation over the 2010 bailout. Everyone knew that there would be tax reforms and that they would apply to Ireland, but no assurances were given on the retention of the country's special tax regime on this vital matter.

There was no meaningful declaration on neutrality. Ireland has been ambivalent on the issue, trying to treat neutrality as an established circumstance for a State, something into which it could lock itself, when in fact neutrality is a strategy, part of a country's set of desirable objectives but not immutably so. Finally, on abortion, it was not Europe that dictated what Ireland might do; Ireland was able simply to stop it, but did not know how and therefore adopted 'an Irish solution' and did nothing.

On 24 November 2008 Micheál Martin, who had become the main spokesperson in Government on European questions, spoke of the commissionership as something that could be dealt with 'in discussions with European colleagues'. This was simply nonsense. It could not be done that way. He did not address the key issue, that the European Commission wanted Ireland to indicate a way forward. There were two options: a second referendum, or doing nothing, which is what was voted for, in June 2008, when the Lisbon Treaty was rejected.

Charlie McCreevy, the former Minister for Finance and the European Commissioner, said: 'You must remember that each country had to ratify this particular Treaty. If the only answer to the question was "Yes" there was no point in putting the question to any of the other 26 countries either.' On that occasion he also rubbished the idea of Ireland being somehow 'isolated' if it did not conform. 'There is no provision to throw out anybody, unless unanimously all the existing members of the club agreed to throw you out. And I doubt now, or in the future, any Irish Government is going to unanimously agree to throw themselves out.' McCreevy also pointed out that the referendum vote indicated that a 'considerable segment' of the 53 per cent who voted were those who failed to vote in 2007's general election. 'So, therefore, people did take the issue very seriously. That has to be respected.'

What shocked the country most, according to McCreevy, was the fact that Declan Ganley decided 'to front a campaign to get the Irish people to vote no. He was singularly successful in that, against the might of all the political parties in Ireland, against the might of practically all the established media. He won the argument because the Irish people listened to him more than anybody else.'

Europe, in the form of the European Council—constituting heads of Government and Foreign Ministers—met over two days, 11 and 12 December 2008, putting on a display of compassion and concern for Ireland. The impression given was that the country had got itself into a mess over the Lisbon Treaty and needed rescuing. The Council is a profoundly undemocratic group of men and women. Their sessions are secret. No minutes or notes are kept, no details of voting—if they do vote—revealed, and they issue ex cathedra decisions, for all the world like a papal conclave.

The Commission's president, José Manuel Barroso, *thought*—he was not sure himself, but he *thought*—that Ireland could be reassured. In the course of Mr Barroso's interview with Seán Whelan, shown again and again on the night of 11 December, the use of the word 'think' was emphasised. In subsequent reporting it was dropped. Micheál Martin, perhaps because of his office as Foreign Minister, rather than Brian Cowen, wrestled publicly, on 'Prime Time', on the same night, with his democratic soul and then promptly replaced it with the new realism. The whole Brussels event was a jolly piece of theatre, made familiar to all by frequent repetition. Public displays of solidarity, with much embracing and laughing, kissing even, seem to coincide with political hurdles faced by the European Union. It then clears them and they are resolved. The more difficult the problems are, the more funny they seem to the leaders. But that is Club Life, you know. At heart they all eventually think the same. That's the difference. The people don't.

The EU claims it is democratic, with a strange system that rotates around the 'single-party' or 'no-party' form of power which operates out of Brussels. It is essentially undemocratic but no European leader says so. What they are subscribing to, behind the EU's impenetrable wall of bureaucracy, is a form of totalitarianism, so far reasonably benign. The term has bad antecedents—possibly the worst in the 20th century—but it works on a generally favourable master-plan. This is close to British Empire administration, which was a single-minded and single-principled imperial administration, without opposition, wherever British rule stretched. In essence it is this European totalitarianism that Declan Ganley opposed during the implementation of the Lisbon Treaty: Government without opposition. He did not oppose Europe but supported it. In doing so, he marvelled at the dichotomy between democracy in the Member States and the absence of it in central EU Government.

The debate continued under circumstances that had become much less intellectual, much more fearful, as a result of the collapsing Celtic

Tiger and the fact that a steadily increasing number of people were watching, helplessly, as their life savings became undermined by the continuing crisis over Ireland's banking system.

Modest attention was paid in the spring of 2009 to the workings of the Referendum Commission. John Gormley, then Minister for the Environment, Heritage and Local Government, laid before the Houses of the Oireachtas the Referendum Commission's Report on the Twenty-eighth Amendment of the Constitution bill 2008. According to the Foreword—not an apt word for the letter of presentation by Mr Justice Iarfhlaith O'Neill, chairman of the Referendum Commission— the Report was submitted in December 2008. It was not properly debated. Nevertheless at that stage, 12 March 2009, Joe Costello, the Labour TD and a supporter of a Yes Vote on Lisbon, had to say: 'We have not seen any text of any guarantees, nor have we been made aware of any negotiations.'

The Referendum Commission was originally intended to function openly and in a balanced way as between the two sides of any argument, and, in particular, where the arguments applied to European Treaties. It was required to set out the main Yes Side and No Side arguments at the time of the first Treaty of Nice referendum in June 2001 and this may be said to have contributed to its defeat. Then the legislation was amended by the Referendum Act of 2001, pushed through on the last sitting day in December 2001, just before the Christmas break, with one day's notice and against the strongly expressed views of the Opposition parties. It removed from the requirements placed by the State on the Referendum Commission the need to explain the two sides of the argument. It was clearly designed to ensure that the verdict on the first Nice referendum would be reversed when the second one came up the following year, which indeed is what happened. The Commission still had the function of informing citizens what the referendum was about. It signally failed to grapple with the immense seriousness of the Lisbon Treaty—as opposed to other EU enactments—in the ways in which it intruded upon Ireland's Constitution, changing its status for its people.

It is important to summarise what actually happened with the workings of this important protection of referenda. The first Lisbon Treaty Referendum Commission chairman, High Court Justice

Iarfhlaith O'Neill, held two press conferences purportedly to explain issues relating to the Treaty, and he made a complete hash of one of them, showing that he did not know some basic facts about it. One could plausibly argue that holding a press conference of this kind went quite beyond the Commission's competence, because its brief under the 1998 Referendum Act was to draw up a collective statement explaining to citizens and voters how the proposed amendment would affect the Irish Constitution. Dealing with voters' questions about the details of Lisbon, especially when that was done in a biased and one-sided fashion, did not accomplish this.

In the second Lisbon referendum the Commission chairman was High Court Justice Frank Clarke. He weighed in heavily in giving one-sided interpretations of the Treaty, including writing a question and answer column in a tabloid newspaper, an intervention challenged at the time as quite improper under the Referendum Act that established the Commission. Frank Clarke was much more activist and intrusive than Iarfhlaith O'Neill in the first Lisbon referendum. The requirement of the 1998 Referendum Act was that the Commission as a collectivity of five people should issue a statement to voters informing them how the proposed Amendment would affect the Constitution. What they did was to post to all voters a statement purporting to explain the Lisbon Treaty, but in fact spending most of its six or so pages on explaining the so-called promises and guarantees the Government had been given that neutrality, corporation tax and abortion would not be affected and that Ireland would retain an EU Commissioner. These matters were outside the Treaty and had nothing directly to do with how the Irish Constitution would be affected by a ratification of Lisbon.

In due course Micheál Martin revealed a Government 'strategy' that ignored all the mainstream Lisbon Treaty issues outlined in this chapter as either significant or concerned with the democratic presence in European politics, concentrating instead on the relatively small group of voters in the first referendum who had fears over neutrality, abortion and other social or moral issues, as well as the quite unfounded fears about the commissionership. Brian Cowen, whom Martin described as 'heroic' in negotiating the Commissioner issue, and Micheál Martin sought to win over a marginal number of voters and to present themselves at the December Brussels Summit as two brave men who had solved all the problems. Combined with growing fears about money losses on the stock market and in the catastrophic fall in the value of bank shares, it worked. Martin called the second day of the Summit 'a landmark day for Ireland'. In fact, it simply confirmed all the things that were Ireland's due anyway and solved none of the issues that were stripping people of their financial and property assets.

Martin claimed that he and Brian Cowen, 'after intense negotiation', had secured Ireland's position in the European Union (never in doubt), the role of an Irish Commissioner (already agreed in principle, confirmed by the Attorney General at the time of the second Nice vote), resolved the issues of corporation tax (which by late 2010 had become very doubtful) and defence (meaning neutrality, an issue confined to 2 per cent of voters).

Micheál Martin's handling of this was a contemptuous and distorted performance. It was hardly surprising that Nicolas Sarkozy praised the 'courage' of Brian Cowen and of Martin. They did not dupe the Irish electorate but they did frighten them by their failure to regulate the country's economic policies that contributed to extensive dismay and fear. There were still problems, including a general lack of understanding of the Treaty—the failure of a flawed Referendum Commission—and widespread misrepresentation across a whole range of campaigners who were not doing it for State or Government reasons but in the muddled belief, relentlessly endorsed by the EU, that Yes was a better word than No.

Chapter 9

THE SECOND LISBON
TREATY REFERENDUM

Returning from Europe in May 2009, prior to the June Summit that was to consider responses to Ireland in anticipation of the second referendum, Micheál Martin published a moderate and balanced article calling for 'a mature debate'. This appeared in the *Irish Independent* on 8 July 2009. There was a historic parallel, more than half a century earlier, in the views of Eamon de Valera on the occasion of his return from Strasbourg in 1955 where he had been attending a meeting that was part of the construction of the future of Europe. De Valera spoke about it in the Dáil on his return and was uncharacteristically direct. He bluntly told the Dáil on 12 June 1955 that Ireland would end up losing its freedom and independence if it joined any European federation. He also warned about the dangers of a European Constitution and of getting entangled in European-led military adventures, over which, ultimately Ireland would have no control. It was a core-value speech, remarkably prophetic. Most of the issues facing Ireland in 2009 were embraced, including those that were identified and patched up at the last European Summit, and those that were ignored.

De Valera dealt with the spiritual dimension: 'We realise that, small as were our physical resources, there were spiritual ones which were of great value; and we never doubted that our nation, though a small one, in the material sense, could play a very important part in international affairs.'

Ireland did so play a part and Eamon de Valera referred directly and indeed proudly to his own leadership of the country into the League of Nations, announced before Independence, in 1919, and implemented in the period between the two world wars, though it was doomed to fail by the rise of fascism.

After his Strasbourg meeting, however, de Valera referred positively to the United Nations as the place for Ireland's international role. He went on: 'I might point out, that, on the economic side for instance, in the Council of Europe, it would have been most unwise for our people to enter into a political federation which would mean that you had a European Parliament deciding the economic circumstances, for example, of our life here.'

He then turned his attention to the statistics, which were being misrepresented to the Irish people before the second Lisbon referendum in terms of the percentage of power Ireland would enjoy under the Lisbon Treaty. For de Valera—himself a noted mathematician—the mathematics were more straightforward:

> For economic and other reasons we had refused to be satisfied with a representative of, say, one in six, as was our representation in the British Parliament. Our representation in the European Assembly was, I think, something like four out of 120 or some number of that magnitude. That is, instead of being out-voted on matters that we would have regarded as of important interest to us by five or six to one, we would have been out-voted by 30 or 40 to one.

He then made a point that was a telling part of the second Lisbon debate and related directly to one of the more absurd Yes-vote arguments, which was that Ireland still had to get away from entanglement with its nearest neighbour, the UK. De Valera said: 'We did not strive to get out of that British domination of our affairs by outside force, or we did not get out of that position to get into a worse one.'

It is part of de Valera's heritage, and a message to those who took part in the second Lisbon debate, that he focused, even then, in 1955, on the threat of a superior constitutional basis for European power over Ireland. He said:

> One of the things that made me unhappy at Strasbourg was that I saw that at the first meeting of the Assembly, instead of trying to get co-operation and to provide organs for co-operation, there was an

1. In the soup! Bertie Ahern faces an uncertain future. (© *Collins Agency*)

2. The populist who tumbled! Bertie constantly pressed the flesh and claimed, like notorious criminals, that he won his unbanked money on the horses. (© *Press Association*)

3. The much-needed leader who never was, Charlie McCreevy, a man who understood money. (© *Press Association*)

4. The Lisbon Treaty referendum was Yes to everything! (© *Photocall Ireland*)

5. Winners and Losers: Declan Ganley, Bertie Ahern and the late Garret FitzGerald. (© *Press Association*)

6. The two bankers, David Drumm and Seán FitzPatrick, architects of chaos. (© *Photocall Ireland*)

7. The Central Banker who was on Europe's side, with Matthew Elderfield who became the new Financial Regulator. (© *Photocall Ireland*)

8. Seán Quinn, the man who gambled away a bank. (© *Irish Times*)

9. Fianna Fáil lambs smile their way into political oblivion: John Curran, Tony Killeen and Pat Carey. (© *Press Association*)

10. Enda Kenny struts to victory, with Eamon Gilmore on his coat tails. (© *Press Association*)

11. Life is the Life of Brian. (© *Press Association*)

12. The 2007 general election photo Cowen professed he hated. (© *James Flynn*/APX *Photography*)

13. Batt O'Keeffe and Micheál Martin. (© *Photocall Ireland*)

14. Dan Boyle and Eamon Ryan, the new leader of the Greens. (© *Press Association*)

15. A Happy Release. (© *Press Association*)

16. Nemesis. (© *Photocall Ireland*)

17. The two Brians. (© *Press Association*)

18. Enda Kenny, the new Number One. (© *Getty Images*)

19. Brian Cowen has a word in Eamon Ryan's ear, a politician whom Cabinet colleagues felt was Fianna Fáil in all but name. (© *Press Association*)

20. Brian Lenihan and Eamon Ryan fight for political survival. (© *Press Association*)

21. Brian Lenihan in more hopeful times. (© *Press Association*)

22. David Drumm fights his corner. (© *Irish Times*)

23. Brian Cowen's first Cabinet. (© *Irish Times*)

24. John Gormley hopes that
something will turn up.
(© *Irish Times*)

25. Brian Lenihan, casualty of power and service. (© *Press Association*)

attempt to provide a full-blooded political Constitution. There were members there who were actually dividing themselves into socialist parties, and so on, as they might do in a national parliament. As far as we are concerned, whilst we wish well to all those who think that it is in their interest to do that, we certainly felt that we should not be committed as a nation to do it. Nations much more powerful with their associated states than we, were chary of that, and I, for one, felt that we would not be wise as a nation in entering into a full-blooded political federation.

On the issue of Ireland getting involved in military alliances, de Valera enunciated his neutrality views, stating the obvious, but stating it well. Less obvious, however, was the real message for an Ireland linked constitutionally and politically with other states:

A small nation has to be extremely cautious when it enters into alliances which bring it, willy nilly, into wars … we would not be consulted on how a war would be started—the great powers would do that—and when it ended, no matter who won…we would not be consulted as to the terms on which it should end.

There are many things de Valera did not cover, but in these essentials there are more issues that were not resolved, more questions that were not answered, more problems that hovered, than those that were argued in favour of the Yes Vote.

The Government published a White Paper on the Lisbon Treaty in August 2009, two months before the second referendum. It was a flawed document that did not conform to normal Government White Paper requirements. It contained a serious distortion of fact. It was unbalanced and it is heavily politicised, presenting a case that favours the defeated minority in the referendum of 2008. At the same time it met only limited and selective reasons behind the emphatic rejection of the referendum on 12 June 2008 when 53.4 per cent of the population voted against ratification and 46.6 voted for ratification on a turnout of 53.13 per cent of the electorate.

The continued Government determination to push ahead, reversing that decision, was not surprising. It began to work against the majority of Irish people on the day the votes were counted and continued to do so. While this was its right, in Irish democracy, it should have been fair, balanced and truthful. This was not seen by the public to be the case, raising serious questions for the campaign that took place in the autumn of 2009.

Initially the new chairman of the Referendum Commission, Mr Justice Frank Clarke, adopted a more balanced approach, rather different from that of his predecessor. This was doubly important in view of earlier ignorance and lack of comprehension over certain issues. There was no White Paper to contend with in 2008. In 2009 there was. Furthermore, there was a new Act of the Oireachtas, the Twenty-eighth Amendment to the Constitution (Treaty of Lisbon) Act 2009, which contained a curious addition, not present in the 2007 Act preceding the first referendum. This was a preamble paragraph to Part 2 of the Act, reading: 'Ireland affirms its commitment to the European Union within which the Member States of that Union work together to promote peace, shared values and the well-being of their peoples.' It seemed questionable if not improper for the people to be reminded, in an Act of the Oireachtas specifically dealing with a Treaty, of only the good things derived from membership over 35 years.

The most serious and deliberate misrepresentation concerned the allegedly 'new' double majority voting system: a simple majority vote by the individual EU states, backed by a qualified, or weighted, voting system. This voting system was not new. It already existed. But in its altered version, under Lisbon, it was disadvantageous to Ireland. Under the Lisbon Treaty double-weighted voting system, Ireland's vote, on a population count, was significantly reduced, from 2 per cent to 0.8 per cent, while at the same time the German vote was doubled and the votes for the UK, France and Italy would go up by 50 per cent. The importance of the system can be gauged from the fact that it lay at the heart of Ireland's influence in making or blocking laws in the EU. It seemed therefore clearly a matter for comment by Frank Clarke and his Referendum Commission.

A second significant misrepresentation lying at the heart of a great part of the No Vote thinking concerned the constitutional changes that derive from the Lisbon Treaty. The very basis of the genuine and welcomed benefits to Ireland of EEC, European community and then

EU membership was the Community that Ireland joined in an optimistic mood under Jack Lynch. This was now replaced, constitutionally and post-Lisbon, by a new European Union with a new legal personality of which, instead of having a 'complementary' relationship, Irish citizens have an 'additional' European citizenship. Because of the changed nature of that European citizenship, the attendant rights and duties are fundamentally different. Before the Lisbon Treaty, the idea of a European State was notional. It is a quite different matter post-Lisbon. The European State, however, was coming into existence under Lisbon as a sour entity without having the essential heart of any new European state in the 21st century: this was democratic control over its different forms and structures of government. The people did not consent to the laws imposed on them.

There was no proper examination of any of this in the White Paper. The relevant passage, in Chapter 3, glossed over the nominal nature of current citizenship and concealed the new kind of citizenship behind the word 'complementary', the true meaning of which—if there is one—is not explained.

The Irish people had consistently been resistant to the surrender of what they saw as the unique and valued nature of their citizenship. They did not want to surrender it for a duality of rights and duties. There were other matters of uncertainty not clarified, as they should have been, by the White Paper. These included taxation, where the White Paper was both contradictory and superficial. For many people, this issue threatened their livelihoods, even their survival.

The Lisbon Treaty clearly shifted power and decision-making from peripheral countries like Ireland to the centre of Europe, dominated by Germany and France. There was such a centre, of course, but not a place Ireland got any nearer to by voting Yes. The result was a reduction of Irish voting power in Europe and changed also the way Ireland's Commissioner was appointed.

Three senior campaigners for a Yes Vote on the Lisbon Treaty, who all played a part in the debates prior to the referendum, made strong interventions about how the debate should have been conducted. They were Noel Dorr, Alan Dukes and Pat Cox, all well-known for their espousal of the Yes Vote. The most reasonable was Noel Dorr, whose advice on RTÉ's handling of the debate was valuable. The good things he referred to, speaking in August 2009 at the Merriman Summer School on the EU, are Ireland's by right and do not need the reinforcement of Lisbon. Obviously, honesty is needed in debating that. But Dorr's real point was about quality of exchange.

The second person, Alan Dukes, was more alarmist, emphasising the lies that surrounded this debate in the past, and laying, it must be said, more blame for this on the No Vote side than on the Yes Vote side. This, too, required careful analysis.

The third person, Pat Cox, campaign director for the Ireland for Europe group, was most aggressive, helping to introduce a 'Yellow Card' and then a 'Red Card' as a means of targeting what were called 'Treaty Liars'. Side by side with Professor Brigid Laffan, who was the chairperson, he waved giant yellow and red placards on the steps of the Referendum Commission's offices. His declared target was the supposed lying by the No Vote side. He should have been concerned with the Yes Vote side as well.

Brian Cowen was not a good leader in such arguments as were provoked by the Lisbon Treaty. For one thing he was burdened by the fact that, as he confessed in 2008, he had not read it. On the night of 10 September 2009, he spoke on 'Prime Time' to Miriam O'Callaghan, telling the country why it should vote Yes.

Cowen said that this campaign was about jobs. It was not. He said it was about remaining part of Europe. It was not. Ireland was part of Europe and would have remained so, Yes or No. He said that Europe would secure Ireland's jobs and future. It consistently failed from then on to do any such thing. One vote controlled strictly the way of doing it, the other would have allowed greater discretion and greater democratic freedom. It would have allowed Ireland to decide more, and Brussels to decide less. Brian Cowen did not comment on Lisbon at this level at all. On the double mandate, the State's position was changed to its disadvantage. Its democratic voice was weakened and Irish democracy itself has been altered without any democratic debate.

Dick Roche, who should have been fighting for Ireland all along, was faced by a quite shameful sequence of defeats on fundamental issues at a very early stage in the Lisbon Treaty process. Evidence from research carried out in September 2009 by Open Europe (an independent think tank calling for reform of the EU) showed Roche to have lost on 113 amendment proposals out of a total of 149 when debating what is now the Lisbon Treaty. This failure was covered up. A permanent EU president was proposed, thus reducing Ireland's 'Heart of Europe' dream; Ireland failed to block this. Ireland failed over the new voting. Roche wanted the Nice system. He lost out, weakening the country. He lost on the main issue of the national veto. He lost on a number of democratic issues. Yet both Dick Roche and Brian Cowen repeatedly said, in Cowen's words: 'We don't need a better deal because we have got everything that we wanted in the negotiations.'

Ireland got no such thing. Three-quarters of the protections sought were rejected. Dick Roche still had on his website in autumn 2009 the pre-referendum statement from 2008: 'There is no Plan B. There is absolutely no possibility of this Treaty being subject to further renegotiation. The idea that we can reject this Treaty and have another referendum as happened with the Nice Treaty is a delusion. That cannot and will not happen.' By far the biggest lie, in the Lisbon Treaty referendum debate, was the Yes Vote lie about what Ireland would gain by a Yes Vote and lose by a No Vote. The lie was based on a carefully constructed and deliberate confusion of the European Union and the Lisbon Treaty, for both of which the people were told they were voting. It was not so.

In an article in the *Irish Independent*, the distinguished former Irish diplomat Michael Lillis wrote that a No Vote would lead to 'No legal consequences: Ireland will not be expelled from the present European Union, nor is there any legal mechanism to sanction or disadvantage us, nor will we be drummed into a second tier of membership below our present legal status.' This was totally different from the dark forebodings of the Yes campaign leaders. Lillis confirmed what others outside Ireland had been saying since before the first referendum. He might also have dealt with the blandishments, including those about jobs. Mr Justice Frank Clarke tried to do this. He suggested that the claim about the Lisbon Treaty providing jobs was 'a political opinion' and he could not comment on that. All he could say, rather timidly, was that it was not in the Lisbon Treaty. Truth, in the loaded circumstances of the time, demanded more than that.

Brian Cowen thought jobs were in the Lisbon Treaty, adding that a Yes Vote 'would be a great statement by the country about where we want to go'. He regarded the vote on 2 October 2009 as Ireland 'making it very clear to other member states of the European Union that we want to be part of reforming the union'. The decision did the opposite.

Michael Lillis's fear, which took up four-fifths of his article, was that Ireland would fall under the sway of the UK again—what he described as 'the pre-1973 cauldron of Anglo-Irish claustrophobia and dependence'. Garret FitzGerald shared that irrational fear, notwithstanding the different currencies and the clear statements Lillis made about the unchanging nature of the Irish post-Lisbon Vote status in most things. It seemed they were both saying that the nation needed to Vote Yes in order to frustrate a plot designed to put it once more under British control. Did the country have so little national confidence that it was afraid of making a suicidal social and economic return to the 1950s? Ireland did not grow in economic strength because the country, in the words of an editorial writer in the *Wall Street Journal*, 'sucked on the teat of EU regional aid for two and a half decades'. Though Ireland did do that, it had little or no effect, as those who lived through the 1970s and 1980s will know. Ireland's economic strength derived from tax reform, with the slashing of capital gains and corporate income-tax rates. Bertie Ahern undermined this valuable set of reforms. Then Brian Cowen said he didn't have the stomach for the fresh tax reform needed.

Fear, lies and an array of blatant illegalities by the Irish Government and by Europe characterised the Yes campaign in the October 2009 repeat referendum. Undoubtedly the No campaign also produced dishonesty and misrepresentation. The second referendum, much more than the first, resulted in a momentous division in Irish society. It also contributed irreversibly to the decline in the power of Fianna Fáil and in the trust that the party had previously sustained. This was because Brian Cowen had opened a breach in Irish democracy and he and his Minister for Foreign Affairs had relentlessly pursued a process of undermining the people on this issue.

The two main Opposition parties endorsed this and combined for the re-run of the referendum. This presented a formidable phalanx, collectively guilty of worse and more widespread illegalities. The Opposition parties were comfortably detached from what was done at Government inspiration, but this was no excuse for its inaction in protecting the State's Constitution and Europe's laws and for its use of EU funds. The people were told they would be made to suffer if they voted No again. It was claimed Europe would become two-tier, that Ireland would be cold-shouldered. This was entirely dishonest.

There were other toxic interventions. One of the most blatant illegalities was the placing of a European Commission propaganda supplement in all Irish newspapers on the Sunday before the referendum as a paid insert. This was an unlawful use of European taxpayers' money. The Commission has no competence in the ratification of treaties. Moreover, it presented not only profoundly unbalanced views but also misleading information. It said the Nice Treaty did not protect the concept of a Commissioner for each state and Lisbon did. This was simply not true. If Ireland had voted No, European law said it would have had one Commissioner for each State. Proposals for change lay in the future. It is inconceivable that the European Commission would not know this. Yet it lied on it. Whatever was decided, change had to be unanimous, under Nice. That was one result of voting No in June 2008. All the things in Nice are by no means the things that are in the Lisbon Treaty.

Other illegalities included the part-funding of the posters and press advertisements of most of Ireland's Yes Side political parties by their sister parties in the European Parliament. This was illegal under Irish law. So too was the Government's use of public funds to circulate to voters a postcard with details of European 'assurances' and then, later, a brochure doing much the same as the Commission did, and with as much indifference to the truth. This breached the Supreme Court's 1995 McKenna Judgment, staggeringly breached already, that it is unconstitutional for the Government to use public money to seek to procure a particular result in a referendum.

Anthony Coughlan reminded Mr Justice Clarke, in a letter, of his failure to explain the actual subject matter of the proposal to amend the Constitution and the legal text for this, as the Referendum Act required. The judge had done a lot of other 'explaining', much of it in friendly soundbites. But he did not perform his prime statutory duty, for which he had a budget of €4 million of public money and a panel of distinguished helpers whose silence was like the scattering of ash on Ireland's future.

Many people who genuinely supported the Yes Vote regretted a great deal of what was done in their names and would like it to have been done otherwise. Wherever the campaign process could be loaded in favour of a Yes Vote, it was so loaded. This tainted the outcome irreversibly. Worse still, there was official determination to ignore all this. Worst of all, however, a vacuum surrounding those who voted No was created. Because of this, those who voted No the second time round represented a new 'Fourth Force' in Irish politics.

The Lisbon Treaty was passed into law on 1 December 2009. There was a lash of vengeance in its tail, against those in the country who said No to it twice. The European Council of Prime Ministers and Presidents, which had become a 'European Institution' for the first time—similar to the EU Commission, Council of Ministers, Court of Justice—now decided, under the Lisbon Treaty, that Foreign Ministers had no formal role in EU foreign policy. The Prime Ministers and Presidents themselves seemed quite happy with this change, which left them deciding the key issues of future EU development among themselves. Within a month, as a result of this, they imposed the first sanction on national sovereignty when the Swedish Foreign Minister, Carl Bildt, declared that, under Lisbon, Foreign Ministers of EU countries would not attend EU Summits. Within days such a Summit took place and indeed the change meant that Europe's neophyte High Representative for Foreign Affairs and Security Policy, Cathy Ashton, would be there in their place. In Europe Ireland would now have only 'domestic policy'. Foreign policy was extraneous. It could be argued that this was fortunate, since every attempt at it was flawed. Nevertheless, it was decided that foreign policy would be conducted by European embassies around the world, staffed by European employees and clearly representing an enormously more powerful, 500-million, human political entity whose interests and objectives could be clarified and presented with a simplicity unknown to Iveagh House. Legally speaking, making the European Council into a formal EU institution rendered its actions—and its failure to act in accordance with the Treaties—subject to appeal to the European Court of Justice; however, it is likely to be some time before anything like that happens.

The initiative was clearly not Sweden's. Though the Swedes were nominally in charge, as all presidencies have been throughout the EU's history, it was clear from the way Carl Bildt put it that the new 'law' on foreign relations had been dictated by the EU. Announcing the change, he said in December 2009: 'As it happens I am persuaded it's a very good idea. But I can't say all the other Foreign Ministers share that opinion, to put it politely.' To all of them it came as a surprise. To Micheál Martin, the surprise was far from welcome. Did it put us at 'the heart of Europe'? It did not.

In the UK the point was seized on that the creation of a common EU foreign policy and independent embassies round the world, answerable to the EU Commission, meant the UK and other Member States could be overruled on crucial diplomatic matters, 'such as on how to respond to human rights abuses in a conflict-ridden country'. For Ireland, there would be an effect on development aid, and missionary work would need to conform with Commission foreign policy, expressed from now on in a side-by-side situation with far better-funded and staffed EU embassies in capital cities in Ireland's hallowed Third World territories.

In the immediate aftermath of the referendum, the Yes campaign was not upbraided for bias or dishonesty and this was overlooked after the vote on the Lisbon Treaty. But the residue of people who were angry, cheated, abused and felt widely dismissed, prevailed as a political force and would wreak a terrible vengeance on the main architects of their humiliation, the Fianna Fáil party.

In terms of non-governmental expenditure on the campaign, the point is worth making about the vast imbalance of expenditure as between the Yes and No sides in the second Lisbon referendum. Intel and Ryanair's Michael O'Leary weighed in on the Yes Side with vast amounts while at the same time Declan Ganley was persecuted over his modest finances. If Ganley had spent only his own money—even if it were up to millions—it would have been perfectly legal, but once he or anyone else accepted donations of over €150 or so, they had to register these with the Standards in Public Office Commission (SIPO). In the event SIPO said all Ganley's accounts were satisfactory. The *Irish Times* ran a campaign on this. Intel and Ryanair spent their own money and were legally entitled to do so without limit.

| THE COWEN RESHUFFLE

There were no good grounds for a significant reshuffle in February 2010 and all idea of it should have been abandoned. It arose in the context of one arguably necessary change, the replacement of Willie O'Dea in Defence, a portfolio of no great social or economic significance, and one without reform on its agenda. O'Dea had claimed in an interview in March 2009 that a Limerick house owned by the brother of Maurice Quinlivan, a Sinn Féin candidate in the local elections later that year, had been operating as a brothel. It is a criminal offence to publish a false statement about an election candidate and O'Dea signed a sworn affidavit denying the statement. A recording of the interview emerged and O'Dea paid an undisclosed sum in damages to Quinlivan, settling the matter with a statement read out in the High Court.

In February 2010 Fine Gael announced a motion of no confidence in O'Dea. The Government responded with its own motion and won, though the Green Party chairman Senator Dan Boyle made clear, on Twitter, that he had no confidence in O'Dea, whereupon O'Dea resigned. Publicly, both Brian Cowen and John Gormley sang from the same hymn sheet—O'Dea had resigned of his own volition—but Gormley had given Cowen an ultimatum: to sack O'Dea or the Greens would leave Government. In the past Cowen would never have been pushed by a junior coalition partner. The event showed he was losing his grip on power. Enda Kenny maintains:

We were on the brink of the Government led by Taoiseach Brian Cowen getting away with an extraordinary and disgraceful political stroke. He was transgressing the trust of the public in him and the members of the Government. He was duping the Greens and making them party to the outrageous protection of O'Dea. And in the case of O'Dea himself, we were witnessing a high officer of state being protected and kept in office at a time when a Garda investigation had been initiated into whether he was guilty of the criminal offence of perjury, together with slander and lying. And this process of protection was being done simply because the numbers game seemed to ensure his survival.

Attention was diverted by the reshuffle. The necessity for the appointment was arguable. There was precedence for the job being held by the Taoiseach, obviating any need for the appointment at all.

Yet if he was going to do it, Cowen should have been comprehensive. By 23 March he was faced with the loss of a second Minister, Martin Cullen, who resigned, citing a back problem, rendering Cowen's Government even more reliant on the Greens just as it reached its 1,000-day milestone. Instead of announcing a radical shake-up in his Cabinet at the time, Cowen opted to take the unusual step of promoting two older TDs, Tony Killeen and Chief Whip Pat Carey, who were almost at retirement age. In fact, Killeen, who was facing a private battle with cancer, went on to become one of the Ministers who resigned dramatically as part of a foolish orchestrated move by Cowen in January 2011 to inject young blood onto his front bench for the impending general election.

Carey had not faltered as Chief Whip in managing the party, despite resignations of both Fianna Fáil and independent TDs from Cowen's Government. There were a 'few' dissidents but the vast majority of TDs were never a problem. Carey had a routine of 'talking to people who had already talked to people'. He also had his 'listening posts'. Mattie McGrath was unpredictable and problematic, John McGuinness was publicly truculent after he had lost his ministerial position and later formed the Lemass Group, named after Seán Lemass, in March 2010 because there was a 'deficit of information'. The group started out with somewhere between 35 and 40 backbenchers attending the meetings on Wednesday evenings in Leinster House and it was thought at first that it might turn into a force to overthrow Cowen. Chris Andrews, who was a prominent member, dismisses the theory that they were an anti-

Cowen brigade. 'On the Lemass group, I feel that this is a group without any agenda other than making ourselves, as public representatives, available to groups in society that have concerns, an opportunity to speak to members of the Fianna Fáil party.' Cowen's view was concerned with his own self-interest. He thought the group lacked any real substance and he was probably right. Being 'probably right' could be said about much of Cowen's thinking.

In early 2010 it was anticipated that Cowen would elevate several Junior Ministers and backbenchers. Conor Lenihan was confident of promotion and apparently was telling close acquaintances that he was convinced he was going to be selected. Cowen was advised that if he was only 'going to go for a limited reshuffle', he should act quickly. One former Minister expressed the view: 'I actually remember saying it to him at the time, but instead he let it play out for a week and, of course, by doing so he let everybody get the ambition up that it was going to be a big shake-up.'

Those who had their hopes dashed were dismayed when Cowen announced in the Dáil that he was appointing Carey as Minister for Community, Equality and Gaeltacht Affairs, and Killeen as the new Defence Minister. 'He put two guys in that were as old as the fucking hills! As old as Christmas. That was another disaster,' recalls one former Minister.

Backbenchers quickly dubbed the two new appointees Statler and Waldorf, after the two 'Muppet Show' puppets who share the stage left balcony and heckle at every aspect of the show. In the reshuffle, Mary Hanafin was demoted to Tourism, Culture and Sport; Mary Coughlan was transferred to Education and Skills; Batt O'Keeffe was moved to Enterprise, Trade and Innovation; Éamon Ó Cuív was sent to Social Protection because 'we felt he was going to be very good at it', explained one of Cowen's advisers.

Cowen also appointed Dara Calleary as a Minister of State at the Taoiseach's Office and at the Department of Finance, in addition to his responsibility for Labour Affairs. Ciarán Cuffe, Mary White and Seán Connick were elevated to Ministers of State; and John Curran, one of Cowen's drinking companions in the so-called Bar Lobby, replaced Pat Carey as the Chief Whip.

Making the appointments, Cowen also revealed that he was

restructuring some of the Departments of State in an effort to 'ensure that political leadership and administrative capacity are aligned with the core objectives of economic recovery, job creation and support for those who have lost their jobs'. While acknowledging that he was 'restructuring departments and agencies' and that this 'inevitably entails disruption and costs', Cowen said he hoped the planned benefits would outweigh the expense.

'A major focus of the changes I am making is the jobs agenda: creating the conditions for sustainable job creation, ensuring our people have the skills and competences to fill jobs, especially those with a high value-added content, and supporting those who have lost their jobs as they prepare for future employment,' he argued in the Dáil.

Cowen spoke about how 'for the bulk' of his time as Taoiseach, his Government's focus had been on 'stabilising the deterioration in the public finances and banking sector as well as protecting those who have fallen on hard times and continuing to protect and create as many jobs as possible'. Optimistically, he then tried to claim the worst was behind the country.

> By taking some hard decisions and making tough choices we are now in position to rebuild from a more solid base and focus on the future with confidence. Although I believe the worst is over, I also believe that, as a country, we have major challenges and decisions to make, but we are on the right track and I know that if we remain committed and resolved, we can overcome the obstacles we are facing.

Unfortunately, Cowen's changes didn't have the desired effect, his broader intentions were not believed and, in the words of Eamon Gilmore, 'this so-called new look Cabinet has an air about it of a clapped-out car that needs to be scrapped'.

If the relationship between the coalition partners had soured after O'Dea's resignation, it was made worse by the resignation of Trevor Sargent as a Junior Minister shortly afterwards. Both parties felt the other had played a significant part in forcing their respective Ministers to leave office. The replacement of Sargent was not the Taoiseach's responsibility. Constitutionally, Junior Ministers are a Government responsibility, involving the participation of the Green Party, something John Gormley seemed unaware of in a comment made about Brian Cowen's right to appoint.

It might also have been desirable to remove Mary Coughlan, both from her post as Tánaiste and from her responsibilities as Minister for Gaffes. These included her outrageous misrepresentation of the power and capacity of Government to respond at Dublin Airport to Michael O'Leary of Ryanair, who was seeking accommodation for a high employment centre for his company, thus aiding the country's primary need of job creation. She was seen to be blocking this. Whatever Brian Cowen's arguments, then being widely debated, they were not about good governance.

This was the key issue, and at the head of any list of reasons for the foolishness of a fundamental reshuffle must be this: that to move senior Ministers in the interests of a supposed reform programme was the height of folly and in defiance of the need for stability and continuity in the public interest.

To remove the political instruments of change, and shuffle them about, was simply to set any programme back by months, as new incumbents plead that they need time to assess what their predecessors had theoretically—if reluctantly—absorbed over the previous year or so. It was more like buying time until electoral opportunities improved. Undoubtedly, actual reform was replaced by further consideration of it, thus delaying it. This was not going on anyway, but the nation lived in frail hope and tenuous trust of it being seen out of the corner of a few politicians' eyes.

Reform was always a fundamental issue for the Greens. They once had expressed a taste for it as a real part of their agenda and in their election manifestos. They had also tried, in their frequent pharisaical conferences, to demonstrate they were not like any other politicians. They favoured widespread reform of the system and of the objectives of Irish society. Having turned into putty in Brian Cowen's hands, they welcomed the reshuffle. They did so for another political reason. They supported Cowen's desire to draw a line as quickly as he could under the Willie O'Dea affair because it also helped to pass on from any hint of a political assassination of Trevor Sargent.

Sargent had resigned as Junior Minister of State for Food and

Horticulture after it emerged that he had inappropriately written on his department's headed notepaper to the Garda on behalf of a constituent, who had been the victim of an alleged assault. 'I made an error of judgment,' Sargent said before tendering his resignation. The senior coalition party was flabbergasted that he had resigned without even being questioned in the Dáil about an issue that was not a criminal offence. But the irony of it all was not lost on Sargent himself who in 2002 had said that it was unacceptable that the then Junior Minister Bobby Molloy had contacted a judge in a rape case. 'Any representation relating to a court case ought to be acknowledged with a warning about the need not to interfere in any way with due judicial process,' he told the Dáil on 17 April 2002.

The Green Party clearly believed it was not coincidental that the leaked letter conveniently surfaced only days after O'Dea's forced resignation. At first, the Greens felt the letter had been leaked to the press by Fianna Fáil as revenge for forcing the O'Dea resignation on Cowen, who was emphatic, even categorical, in denying that the letter came from within the party. Then the Greens thought Fine Gael had leaked the information to drive an even greater wedge between the coalition parties. No one knows where it came from, rendering such denial by Cowen unreliable. The only person who could be categoric about where the leak came from was the person behind the leak.

Regardless of who leaked the information, Enda Kenny—who vowed during the 2007 general election campaign that 'there will be no descent into sleaze politics with me as leader of Fine Gael'—knew it was having the desired effect on accelerating the countdown to the next general election. 'It's evidence of a government riven by suspicion and divided now by tension and lack of trust,' he said.

The Greens toasted Sargent in the Dáil bar on the night he stepped down, full of admiration for how they were clearly—in their own self-serving eyes, at least—a party of 'integrity' because, unlike Willie O'Dea and John O'Donoghue, their man didn't 'brazen it out' but, instead, 'fell on his sword' immediately.

Once the euphoria about Trevor Sargent wore off, we should have remembered his promise not to lead his party into coalition with Fianna Fáil. Effectively he did lead them in. Overnight, he became convinced about getting into Government. The Greens' interests would have been better served by allowing Fianna Fáil to form a minority Government instead, giving the Greens the power they so readily surrendered in the well-feathered Upper Merrion Street nest.

A Brian Cowen reshuffle stifled Green Party determination to make demands on Fianna Fáil. They toed the line, filled Trevor Sargent's place, approved whatever else Cowen decided, and continued to sink in the public's estimation. Meanwhile Gormley and Eamon Ryan went on issuing absurd mantras about 'getting on with the job' and 'addressing the real issues'.

It rested at Brian Cowen's door how little was working out for the Government. He made many mistakes and failed to bring forward necessary change and the legislation for it. The record on both was dismal. His declaration, when he became Taoiseach, to rectify, by reform, the distortion and undermining of the political and public service structures on which the State depends, proved superficial. Basic structures were stripped of authority, duplicated by newly created bodies and then triplicated by an army of private advisers to Ministers. His Ministers did not follow that objective with diligence and determination, if they did anything at all. The country was absorbing departmental and civil service responses to the crying need for reform, as outlined by the man known as 'Snip' McCarthy, by committees, reports and other sources, and by wise public comment via the media.

As to Fianna Fáil itself, the party did not need reforming. It needed removing. Even at this stage it clearly had long passed its sell-by date. It should have been taken off the shelf of power and deposited on the Opposition benches. Once there, as on previous occasions, it would be forced to reform if it was to come back from the political wilderness. It was becoming daily more apparent that this enforced rejuvenation was the only reform that would work for the organisation.

It seemed excessive when Eamon Gilmore accused the Taoiseach of 'economic treason' in the Dáil, yet whether you call it treason, treachery or betrayal, it was how a majority of people regarded Fianna Fáil and its leaders, notably Brian Cowen.

Treason? Did Eamon Gilmore choose the best word to express his evident—justified—fury at what was being done to the country's economy? Treason is an old-fashioned concept, no longer a crime in Ireland. You cannot be indicted for treason, though its meaning lives on. Treason is 'the violation by a citizen of his allegiance to the authority of the State'. You may not be charged with it. You can be guilty of it. Eamon Gilmore judged correctly in his accusation.

A further definition is required as to what 'the authority of the State' may be. In the republican and democratic Constitution, in which there is no figure to whom the nation expresses allegiance, that ultimate sovereign power is the people. This sovereign power expresses itself in democratic elections, which normally suffice.

Circumstances were far from normal, with Ireland facing the worst economic crisis in its history. The conditions under which it was being handled were controversial, contentious and based on foolish acts, in particular the blanket Bank Guarantee.

In such circumstances, checking out the sovereign will of the people was an essential prerequisite to going forward in what might prove— and indeed seemed already to be proving—potentially catastrophic actions. An unequal and huge burden was being placed on innocent taxpayers in order to salvage the safety and well-being of an elite group of people and institutions which did not merit such salvage.

At the very least this had the appearance of a 'deal' or 'conspiracy' of limited and circumscribed, yet highly expensive, character undertaken without public approval of any kind from those who were being forced to pay for it. It is hard to think of a more apt definition of 'the violation by a citizen of his allegiance to the authority of the State'. Brian Cowen was there by virtue of the electorate. They put his party in power, or almost did. Another group, the Greens, then went totally against everything it had promised its supporters, thereby completing the scramble for power. They then elected Cowen to succeed Ahern; Cowen, with Brian Lenihan, did the rest.

The Irish were asked to believe a duly formed 'Cabinet' carried out the violation. Yet this was certainly not the case with the blanket Bank Guarantee of September 2008, the single most treasonable action of any administration in the State's history, an act that fully justified Eamon Gilmore's judgment. What followed was economic devastation and doom for the whole country. It was close to nauseating when Brian Lenihan, Finance Minister, had the insulting contempt to tell the people they were economically capable of weathering this storm and paying back the enormous debt his stupidity brought down upon their heads.

This might have represented one terrible mistake, understandable in the circumstances. Yet that is not easy. More than anything else what happened looked like a conspiracy between those in power and those who so badly managed the banking system that they brought down upon everyone, through greed, dishonesty and the manipulation of figures and actual cash, a catastrophe for which there were no adequate legal or official restraints. It made one wonder: who really was advising Brian Lenihan?

| BRIAN COWEN'S DRINKING

The so-called 'Galway gargle-gate' is the consensus amongst Fianna Fáil members when asked to pinpoint the moment when Brian Cowen finally lost his credibility within the party.

Rumours about Cowen's alleged large appetite for booze had been circulating for years before he became Taoiseach, but many of his colleagues 'didn't believe' and simply 'dismissed' the anecdotal drink-related stories as nothing more than mere nonsense created by sensational tabloid hacks. States one former Minister:

> I defended him very strongly when the media started that on him earlier. Jesus! The longer it went on, we kind of think it was true. The stories I've heard since have not abated. You can never stand these stories up. He certainly drank an awful lot, there's no doubt about that. Everybody thought that when he became Taoiseach he would stop, but he actually didn't.

However, when he first took up office, Cowen was blissfully unaware of the gossip about his supposed heavy boozing. 'Taoiseach,' one journalist politely began, while they waited for the kettle to boil, as he buttered some crackers and sliced big chunks of cheddar for both of them to munch on, 'do you know that there's a rumour going around that you're a heavy drinker?'

While they stood in his modestly arranged family kitchen back in the summer of 2008, when Jason O'Toole conducted a series of interviews with Brian Cowen for a biography he was writing of him, he was sure that he saw—albeit for a split second—a genuine look of horror in Cowen's eyes as he attempted to digest this. Immediately, he was left with the distinct impression that the then newly appointed Taoiseach was flabbergasted that he was being described as a lush.

As O'Toole elaborated on some of the myths about his drinking exploits, Cowen sighed and shook his head, perhaps in annoyance, or maybe in embarrassment. It was easy to see how deeply upsetting it was for him that people were spreading such rumours. It seemed at the time that those close to him, particularly his political advisers, had for some unclear reason not had this same conversation with him and, instead, had decided to ignore the issue.

Cowen quickly rubbished the accusations; he was adamant that it was all 'nonsense'. As if to demonstrate the absurdity of it all, he pointed around the pine decor kitchen and explained that he didn't even keep drink stocked in the house.

'I very seldom would ever drink at home. It wouldn't occur to me,' he once said. 'In our time, it wouldn't have been too well regarded to have a jar at home in front of our parents, but that's changed now—and that's fine. But if I have a drink, I have a drink in a pub—that might be a generational thing now.'

He admitted that he 'would always go in' to a pub 'for a couple' of pints 'on my way home from a meeting'. He did so, he said, to unwind.

It is good to talk about other things and not to have your life dominated by politics. It takes up enough of our time as it is. You sit down with friends and relax and talk about everything—except politics. I enjoy the craic and other things, local issues, local chat, sport. It's part of what you do to deal with the heavy workload that you have. Different people have different ways of relaxing. But I don't exclusively relax that way.

At the very beginning of his tenure, Cowen was advised not to be photographed in the future knocking back pints, since this would obviously add to his growing reputation as a heavy boozer. He agreed. He absolutely hated the now famous photograph of him taking a swig from a magnum of champagne during the 2007 general election. The photograph had only occurred because somebody, he recalled, had just handed the magnum to him to celebrate his impressive achievement of topping the poll, not just in his constituency, but nationally—a clear indication of the man's popularity at the time.

However, while he said he'd be more careful about drinking in public, Cowen insisted that he was still going to continue to enjoy his few pints in the pub. In retrospect, perhaps this attitude was a fatal error—one of many he has made during his turbulent tenure—because the electorate did not want the sight of their leader enjoying the 'craic', as he puts it, while the country was going down the drain. Or, as the broadcaster Gay Byrne commented in early 2010, nobody wants to see their Taoiseach sitting on a bar stool.

By his own admission, Cowen was 'born and reared in a pub'. Like his wife's family, who were also publicans, the Cowens were prominent members of the community in Clara, County Offaly, and ran a public house after his grandfather Christy—a founding member of Fianna Fáil—married Rosanna Dowling, whose family had a public house that dated back to the 18th century. In 1966, they had the pub knocked down and replaced with Cowen's Bar, which today is run by the Taoiseach's older brother, Christy. Brian Cowen says:

> I became a very good observer of the human condition growing up behind the pub. You see all forms of human life in a pub culture. Some very interesting; some very boring; and some drive you nuts; some highly entertaining. And you'd see how guys would react with a few jars in them. It's an interesting observer post to watch, as you grow up, people much older than yourself.
>
> I have always enjoyed, as a young fellow, serving in the pub to the great characters. I learnt far more there about human nature than I learnt in any university or school. I think it gave me a great insight into people. Sometimes, I reckon my political judgments have emanated from my observation of people and my understanding of what makes them tick—what their preoccupations really are, rather than what the media says that they are. I find it very relaxing and I enjoy the company.

While his predecessor Bertie Ahern could not wait to leave Leinster House after Government business was wrapped up, Cowen could be found every Wednesday drinking in the Dáil bar with the so-called Bar Lobby.

'Even when he became Taoiseach, he always had a pint with everybody on a Wednesday night. When you think about it, it was kind of fucking crazy,' says one former Minister. According to one source, it wasn't unusual for the Bar Lobby to go back occasionally to the small cottage at the front of the Farmleigh estate with Cowen to 'have some more pints after the last orders at the Dáil Bar'.

Mary O'Rourke, who believes that it was in the Dáil Bar that Cowen made many of his political decisions 'on the hoof', states:

> You could see them in the bar at night. There was Michael Finneran who used to go get the pints for him. They'd fill him up. Batt O'Keeffe, who was actually a good Minister, would talk to him and tell him he was going great. But I don't think Cowen went on benders; I just think he drank steadily—not during the day, not at work, no, no, in the evening time when he'd be finished in the Dáil.

Batt O'Keeffe acknowledges that he was perceived as the 'chef du Cabinet' of the Bar Lobby, which included approximately 13 other TDs. O'Keeffe believes the media's 'focus on the bloody drink' contributed to Cowen's eventual downfall.

> That's a travesty. It fits the caricature, you see, as a drinker. The other thing is this fucking Bar Lobby. It was a few pals having a few jars. Certainly, there would be some people who would be part of it all right who were very, very hard drinkers, but you wouldn't see Cowen in that bar all the time, only very irregularly, and even if he had four pints at night, that would be it. It was just blown up.

Unfortunately, Cowen's drinking became a national issue following his radio interview on 28 September 2010. This was when he made his infamous and 'appalling' appearance, as Mary O'Rourke describes it, on RTÉ's 'Morning Ireland'. According to subsequent media reports, it was stated that Cowen had started drinking at 10pm at the party's parliamentary meeting the previous night in the Ardilaun Hotel in Galway, but Mary O'Rourke recalls buying him a pint of stout at around 7.30pm; the papers reported that he was drinking wine at the dinner and lager later in the bar and didn't stop drinking till well after

3.30am. Cowen had spent the evening singing songs and telling jokes, which he interjected with the occasional 'this is off the record, lads, don't be printing this' to the press corps. Micheál Martin reportedly 'rolled his eyes' and Dermot Ahern was 'flabbergasted', according to news reports, as a group of 40 TDs and senators stood around listening to an intoxicated Taoiseach perform his party pieces. Cowen, who is well known for mimicry, would later get into even more trouble when it emerged that on that particular night he had been doing an inappropriate impersonation of Ryder Cup-winning golfer Philip Walton, who has a high-pitched voice owing to a childhood speech impediment. The episode so enraged Walton that he released a press statement to the Reuters News Agency explaining that he had written to the Taoiseach to demand an explanation.

The *Sunday Independent* political columnist John Drennan, who attended the event, admits that the media 'had no intention' of covering any of Cowen's 'frolics' that night if it hadn't been for his shambolic performance on RTÉ radio the following day.

Drennan recalls leaving the hotel at 2.30am and witnessing Cowen 'half-sitting, half-slumped beside two pints'. Even though the Taoiseach was surrounded by some of his Bar Lobby group, Drennan observed that 'he looked like a man who was utterly alone'. The *Irish Mail on Sunday*'s political editor, John Lee, recalls: 'At one point Mr Cowen was leaning against the jamb of the door, with part of his shirt hanging over his trousers, when he was approached and escorted back to his table.'

The Taoiseach didn't leave for his bedroom until around 3.40am. Yet he was scheduled to give an interview to Cathal Mac Coille on RTÉ's 'Morning Ireland' at 8am. This was postponed until 8.50am, obviously to give Cowen some more time to recover from his heavy session. The interview took place in the hotel's dining room while other patrons had their breakfast, to add 'atmosphere'.

'Oh, I'd love a quick mug of tea. I'm going on the radio,' he told one of the waitresses. According to Mary O'Rourke, he 'looked okay' and 'was turned out well', even if his hair appeared 'a bit unwieldy and [he] must have brushed it down'. So, on an empty stomach, Cowen sat down to begin the radio interview, which would make him an international laughing stock when his performance was mocked by Jay Leno, one of the USA's biggest chat show hosts.

None of the Ministers and TDs sitting behind Cowen initially thought the interview was going badly. 'He looked fine,' recalls one former Minister who was close by. In truth, none of them was paying close attention as 'we'd heard it all a million times before'; some of them thought Cowen sounded hoarse—probably as a result of the previous night's singing and the cigarettes that he was accustomed to smoking when he had a few beers—and their ears only started to prick up when they heard him mistakenly mention the Good Friday Agreement when he meant to say the Croke Park Agreement. Nobody really paid any more attention until Mary Hanafin came in for her breakfast and dramatically 'threw her eyes up to heaven'. Another former Minister says he then became 'a bit puzzled' when he overheard that 'they were trying to get Cowen into bed' and use a 'filler' for some of the other day's scheduled events. But if Cowen's media handlers were trying to persuade him to rest, they didn't succeed.

News of the terrible radio performance started to circulate after Fine Gael TD Simon Coveney twittered that he felt Cowen sounded 'half-way between drunk and hungover and totally disinterested'. Cowen was in the lobby chatting, oblivious to the rumours spreading like wildfire, when he was approached by a group of reporters. He looked visibly stunned when TV3's political correspondent Ursula Halligan asked him was he 'drunk or hungover?'

A rattled Cowen replied: 'Absolutely not. That's ridiculous. It's not true at all.'

Cowen, looking at the media scrum, then added: 'That's uncalled for,' before he was whisked away by his media minders, as they shouted out that there would be a press conference later that day.

Some of his Cabinet colleagues believe that coming out to 'defend him probably did more damage than good'.

Everybody wanted to know who was handling Cowen that morning. 'I don't know who was in charge of him there; we never got to the bottom of that. All they had to say to "Morning Ireland" was—smug and all as they are and popular as they are—"No, he's not feeling great and he's not doing the interview",' says O'Rourke. One former Minister points out: 'the Batt O'Keeffes of this world would have been doing a far greater service if they had gone off and had a walk with him and stayed away' from the pub all the time.

His main media handler, Government press secretary Eoghan Ó Neachtáin, wasn't at the event because it was not Government-related, but he privately told acquaintances that such a disastrous PR blunder wouldn't have occurred on his watch. Regardless of who was supposedly in charge of the Taoiseach that morning, they all knew that it had finally opened the flood gates for the media to cover in-depth Cowen's drinking.

'Why would they do that?' a frustrated Cowen pondered.

Cowen had always made no secret of the fact that he likes his pints. During his tenure as Taoiseach, he remained one of the lads and could often be found in Digan's pub, which directly faces the solicitor's firm he helped establish before his involvement in politics, in Tullamore. Here you could find him regularly having a few pints, enjoying a sneaky smoke and the occasional flutter on the horses; he'd normally get one of the regular revellers to put a modest €5 or €10 bet on for him when they were placing their own bets in the nearby bookie. Digan's also happens to face Mac's Cabs, which Cowen would use to drop him back to his house down the road.

But it's not the only pub in Tullamore he frequented and he would usually name different venues when asked for his favourite local haunt. Sometimes he'll mention the Brewery Tap, where he once recorded a song for charity.

He also prefers pubs with a good outdoor smoking facility. 'I'd only smoke now and again when I have a drink or something. I don't get up in the morning buying cigarettes. I'm a sort of casual smoker. I might spend a month not smoking and then have a few—that sort of thing. So, I am not a heavy or a constant smoker at all.'

But he'd frequent most of the pubs in the town because, as an astute politician, Cowen spreads himself around so as not to insult anybody. He even initially picked Doheny and Nesbitt's pub as a regular haunt in Dublin because, apart from its close proximity to the Dáil, its proprietor also just happens to be from his own constituency. And when he was up in Dublin during his last days as Taoiseach, Cowen preferred to drink in the Dáil bar because it is 'the only private bar in the country that you can go into as a members' bar' without having any unwanted 'exposure'. Besides, it would have been hard to imagine Cowen being able to enjoy a quiet pint in Dublin, because undoubtedly somebody would vent their anger at him. But he was also starting to feel an edgy atmosphere in some of the local pubs. In one or two venues in his home town, there was the occasional time when a drunken reveller could be heard muttering some snide comments under his breath about the economy when Cowen passed by on his way to the bar for his tipple, which was either Guinness, lager or gin and tonic. It was a sure sign that even Tullamore's most famous adopted son's popularity was not only declining nationally but also locally.

Friends from Tullamore remember how when Cowen first became a TD he would always be last to put his hand in his pocket for a round of drinks, but you'd never see him drunk or falling out of the pubs. However, Cowen would go out every night of the week if he had the opportunity. He was, as his friends insisted, simply a man who enjoys his few pints. When Cowen was once asked in an interview what he liked to drink, he replied: 'This time of the year, the summer, more lagers than Guinness.' Asked if he could hold his drink, he said, somewhat coyly, laughing: 'I'm not too bad.'

Shortly after his appearance on 'The Late Late Show' when Ryan Tubridy raised the question of his drinking, Cowen was asked if he thought the constant whisperings about his drinking had been a cynical smear campaign. 'People have views on that, but for anyone who looks and observes it, this is not an issue.'

However, immediately after the controversial interview, there was a 'big rumble' within the party about a heave finally happening against Cowen. One former Junior Minister believes that it 'was even going through a lot of people's heads' to resign from Cowen's Cabinet. 'It was the ideal opportunity to do it, but people didn't seize it. His credibility was almost shot at that stage. But most of the Cabinet were gutless. They'd been there too long; they'd become too complacent,' he adds.

But those interested in ousting Cowen had become extra cautious after observing the failed heave against Kenny in July. 'That put a kibosh on a similar thing in Fianna Fáil,' says Conor Lenihan. Another former Minister believes that there would have been an 'earlier run against' Cowen but for Kenny's victory, which 'unnerved some of the people in our outfit'. It was also believed that 'the fact that Kenny was still left there' also meant that Fianna Fáil was starting to feel 'more confident, that if it came to a face-to-face showdown between the two leaders in an election, Cowen 'would beat him hands down'.

Mary O'Rourke believes that, even though it 'became more open season' on attacking Cowen, most members were still saying: 'I know he should be gone, but it's too late now, too near the election, for anybody to make a difference.'

After the Galway debacle, Cowen was declaring to Cabinet colleagues that he was cutting back on his boozing by drinking the non-alcoholic Kalibur beer instead and proclaiming he would be focusing all his energies on the tasks in hand—primarily the financial crisis, improving his communication with the public and on the dreaded upcoming by-election in Donegal South-West, scheduled to take place on 25 November.

'Every time we'd tell him, "You need to be out there talking to the media more, brief them more," he would do it for a while and then back to the old habits again. You get to the stage where "Well, we'll see how long this lasts" was the approach we'd take,' recalls one former Cabinet Minister.

'A lack of awareness that he had to communicate was his biggest downfall, more than the Dáil bar. In a way that's his bit of arrogance. "I don't feel like communicating. I don't need to communicate, therefore I am not going to communicate". Those surrounding him didn't encourage him,' opines Mary O'Rourke.

Once again, 'there was a push' by Cabinet colleagues for Cowen to give an address to the nation. 'Why should I do that?' Cowen would ask them. 'To keep the country in the loop,' was the reply.

One former Cabinet Minister who served under Cowen believes his reluctance to communicate played a significant part in his downfall. He states:

He was very shy. Shyness with media and public was a drawback. The other mistake was that he never really spelt it out to people what the situation was and he should have done interviews when things were really getting tough. To get out into the public domain. He didn't want to be Charlie Haughey, but he mistook the demands of people, which was the openness and honesty of the situation. If that was done, I think it would have helped; it wouldn't have been absolutely significant but they might get a glimpse of the man who knew at close quarters.

Perhaps Cowen opted against the idea of addressing the nation because it had first been mooted by certain columnists in the *Sunday Independent*—a paper his political allies despised because of how it was always harping on about the 'fucking Bar Lobby', as Batt O'Keeffe would sigh in vain every time it was mentioned because he knew the unflattering image was damaging their man, and 'hounding Cowen on his holidays'—and he didn't want to give them the satisfaction of being cajoled into it, just as he had been forced into making changes to stamp duty in 2007 when the paper campaigned for it to be scrapped. At the time, it was speculated that Cowen, the then Finance Minister, was forced into the stamp duty concession as part of a deal Bertie Ahern had brokered with the paper for its enthusiastic support for him. But, in all likelihood, Cowen opted against such a dramatic televised state-of-the nation address because it would 'inevitably have been compared' to Charles Haughey's famous 'living beyond our means' speech, which would have stuck in the public's craw.

'I expect that's one of the reasons why he didn't do it,' says one of his former Cabinet Ministers, who believes that such a speech should certainly, at the very least, have been given when 'the IMF was being put together, but the game was up by this stage'.

Those close to Cowen thought part of the problem with his image was the media advisers in the Taoiseach's office. They were convinced that he had made a fundamental mistake in keeping on many of the same press handlers whom his predecessor Ahern had appointed. Some of them pushed for Cowen to sack the Government press secretary, Eoghan Ó Neachtáin, whom Ahern had appointed in July 2007. Despite having much experience dealing with the media in his roles as the former Defence Force and ESB spokesperson, Ó Neachtáin was disliked by some journalists, who perceived him as nothing more than 'an army bully' in his attitude towards dealing with them; with one ex-Minister agreeing with the assessment by saying 'he was not a nice fella'. But it must be noted that Ó Neachtáin did take up the unenviable task of manning the Taoiseach's office during an unprecedented decline in

Government popularity and was battling against a clearly hostile media. Regardless, it must also be accepted that Cowen and his team's handling of the media was unquestionably inept and was a significant contributor to his downfall in popularity.

One former Minister recalls bluntly telling Cowen that he felt that 'neither' Ó Neachtáin nor any one of his five special advisers, including Joe Lennon, who was on a salary of €188,640 a year—a wage that even surpassed that of David Cameron—was 'up to it'. He described Cowen's media set-up as a 'total joke'. Another former Cabinet Minister recalls telling Cowen that he would gladly hand over his own adviser to help him in the Taoiseach's office.

But it all appeared to fall on deaf ears. Why didn't Cowen sack some of his media team? At the time of Ó Neachtáin's appointment, it was rumoured that he had been hired by Ahern on Cowen's approval because he knew he would be the next Taoiseach. But this has been dismissed by one of Cowen's allies, who argues: 'You know now, there's no fucking way that Bertie would have looked for Cowen's approval. No fucking way.'

'It was an awful mistake. He [Cowen] prevaricated. His fucking loyalty is his weakness. He hated to be nasty to people and I say he would have hated to have said to Eoghan Ó Neachtáin, "Look, lad, I'm sorry, I'm going to have to fucking move you on".'

But perhaps it was also a case that Cowen was not only ignoring his close allies but also the expert advice being given to him by his media advisers. Batt O'Keeffe, one of Cowen's closest allies, concedes: 'I'm sure if he could start back again, he'd do it so much differently. For some reason he was just unable to make changes that he needed to make. I think he's the first person who would admit, "We made serious mistakes."'

| LENIHAN'S BOTCHED JOB

T he apparent alliance between Brian Cowen and Brian Lenihan, who between them appeared to be running the finances of the State, was really an unholy union of two politicians who thought and acted differently, were distrustful of each other, were personally handicapped—both men by personal issues and general lack of understanding of the tasks facing them—were in constant disregard of the constitutional requirement of keeping the Government fully informed on absolutely crucial decisions, and were both habitual 'instinct merchants' whose decisions were made on the hoof, in the bar or in front of the media. Though Cowen had the ultimate responsibility, Lenihan was in the driving seat as far as the fiscal sovereignty of the State was concerned and he did not know enough about it to regulate it or to save it as the crisis developed. As the *Daily Telegraph* put it in his obituary on 11 June 2011:

> Brian Lenihan, the former Minister for Finance in the Irish Republic who died yesterday aged 52, presided over the total collapse of the Irish banking system in 2008, which led to the fall of the government two years later.
>
> When the end of the property bubble revealed the enormous extent of impaired debts, Lenihan's response to the threat of a run on the banks was to legislate a blanket government guarantee to bank depositors and, crucially, also to the banks' bondholders, or international creditors.
>
> This binding promise to honour obligations to institutional lenders in the wholesale money markets proved disastrous when taxpayers realised that they had been unfairly saddled with the debts of foreign speculators, and the ensuing election last March

cost the Fianna Fáil party three quarters of their seats, while their coalition partners, the Greens, lost all of theirs.

Lenihan, who was credited with a keen academic mind, was an advocate with no business experience or acumen, and rather naively accepted the brief from his civil servants, who had been informed by the banks that the debt exposure was only about 0.85 per cent of lending.

In the event it turned out to be nearer 50 per cent, and the crippling liability of 400 billion euros forced Lenihan to seek the IMF and European Central Bank bail-out last November, to which Britain also contributed a loan of £7 billion, and which necessitated a four-year programme of austerity budgets.

...Lenihan described the [blanket bank] guarantee, which other countries soon copied, as 'the cheapest bail-out in the world', words which would haunt him.

While the *Daily Telegraph* described Lenihan as presiding over 'the total collapse of the Irish banking system in 2008', in reality the banking system continued to operate, so it did not literally collapse. Owing to the blanket guarantee given by the two Brians, it continued on life-support provided by Irish taxpayers and the European Central Bank. All the time he was searching for guidance—as David McWilliams revealed in *Follow the Money*—and if and when he took it, the act was often finite, meaning he had to come back to discover what the next step should be. On that fateful night, 28/29 September 2008, Lenihan found himself confronted by two senior legal colleagues at the Irish bar, Dermot Gleeson (for the banks) but a former distinguished Attorney General, and the then presiding Attorney General for the Government, Paul Gallagher SC. That the outcome was fraught with lack of balance and of economic wisdom may be simply stated: to guarantee people's deposits in the banks, thus saving citizens' money and thereby heading off a bank-run, was correct. What was terribly wrong, and really ruined the Irish economy, was the additional State guarantee to creditors and bondholders. Including also Anglo Irish Bank. This was irresponsible folly. Far from being a 'systemic bank', with countrywide outlets, it was an elitist bank mainly for property developers. There were strong European reasons for including Anglo Irish Bank but for Ireland it was a prime case of guaranteeing mainly foreign banks from which Anglo had borrowed vast sums to fuel private development. It might have been permissible to guarantee foreign bank loans in the future, but not those already in place. The simple truth is that the ECB told Lenihan not to let any bank fail and clearly he did not think this through. This was the heart of his and Ireland's problem then and ever since.

Brian Lenihan was suave, articulate and remarkably fluent. Trained as a lawyer, he was a convincing advocate. But he was not himself convinced about what needed to be done, so his advocacy, in political terms, was flawed. When given one case to plead, he delivered his arguments superbly. Given quite another case to plead, he did precisely the same. He was an interviewer's gift and he displayed his lawyer's skills wonderfully on radio and television. RTÉ repeatedly used him to explain what was happening and did not know enough, or research what he was saying enough, to challenge and confront the changing arguments about what, at times, was sheer nonsense.

The unholy nature of the alliance was not one-sided, however. Brian Cowen deeply distrusted the other Brian, but not on account of his lack of real understanding of the crisis. He was worried instead by the possible threat Lenihan represented to his leadership.

Sources close to Cowen say he was made aware that Brian Lenihan had been 'undermining' him at every available opportunity since the beginning of his tenure as Taoiseach. It had reached the stage where one of Cowen's closest advisers had warned him: 'Hold on! We've got to look at this.' They felt Lenihan was leaking material 'to beat the band'. As one former Cabinet Minister claims: 'The big weakness in Brian Lenihan was that first of all when he took a glass of wine he couldn't keep his trap shut! There was a danger when he had a few drinks on him even with the Opposition in what he would say to them! There was no depth; he was very bright but no common sense.'

According to one former Minister, Lenihan wasn't trusted by some of his Cabinet colleagues because they felt they were 'never told the full story' about emerging financial problems. There was a sense that Lenihan 'believed that you should tell them as much as they only should know'. And Cowen was even informed that there was a 'growing feeling' amongst Cabinet members that Lenihan simply 'wasn't up to it' because it appeared that he was 'disseminating' the information he was getting from Finance. It was an opinion concurred with by the *Financial Times*. The paper awarded Lenihan the dubious honour of being the Eurozone's worst Finance Minister for two years in a row.

Some of the other Cabinet members didn't like his aloofness, his 'superior belief in himself'. They also disliked his habit of ensuring that he always left meetings last and that other Ministers and TDs would have to go out first and give the bad news to the waiting media.

Others observed a tension between Lenihan and Micheál Martin, who was also lurking in the background, waiting for his chance to lead the party. Recalls one former Minister:

> Martin wanted to know every last thing. There was a general feeling, 'You have the same fucking memos as the rest of us and will you go and read them?' kind of stuff. It was typical stuff. Here's the Foreign Minister back from his jaunt to wherever and he's been briefed about every possible nuance of an issue and he's coming in here now and the rest of us are slumming it, you know?

However, according to sources close to Lenihan, any tension between him and Cowen was because the Taoiseach 'was very keen' on the 'ridiculous' partnership deal with the public sector. Recalls one of Lenihan's closest allies:

> How can you have partnership talks when you're cutting their wages, because they're public servants? They [members of Government] were all addicted to partnership and partnership wasn't delivering at this stage. They wanted to accept the 12 Days of Christmas proposal [to allow public servants 12 days' unpaid leave]. It was a joke. Nobody else wanted it. They thought this was a great breakthrough deal. The TDs went bananas over it. Backbenchers revolted over it and said, 'This can't happen'. It was widely known that Cowen wanted to sign off on that. It was stopped by Finance and his own backbenchers. They thought it was the maddest thing ever put forward.

Lenihan's people felt that the proposal to allow public servants to take days off in lieu of pay cuts removed an 'awful lot of the party's credibility' within the business community. Lenihan was starting to feel that Cowen was 'too soft on the hard measures' that needed to be taken quickly. One former Minister recalls:

> That was the biggest complaint Brian had about him. He [Cowen] turned out to be a bit of a softie when it came to tough decisions. He and all these ministers were out to lunch on what was happening. There was [sic] huge tensions around the Cabinet because Cowen wasn't accepting the logic of what had to be done, you understand? He thought there was some easy way out of this. It was unreal stuff.
>
> There is no Minister of Finance who doesn't have to assert himself. My experience would have been—for most of the time—Lenihan and Cowen worked quite well together. I don't think they'd have ever gone out for pints together because Lenihan would have had to buy pints and Lenihan didn't buy pints!

But, in typical fashion for a man whom his colleagues felt 'hated sacking people', Cowen didn't take any dramatic action against Lenihan. Was it a case of keeping your friends close and your enemies even closer?

To those observing the Taoiseach and Finance Minister during Cabinet meetings, it was obvious that there was 'tension' because Cowen knew 'what he was at'. But even though Cowen never appeared to consider seriously sacking his Finance Minister, he 'certainly did call Lenihan in once' to give him a dressing down. He was aware that Lenihan was talking about a possible heave to the likes of rebel Fianna Fáil TDs Noel O'Flynn and John McGuinness. It was not, however, a genuine threat to Cowen.

Cowen's Bar Lobby dismissed Lenihan's 'serious discussions about heaves' because, in their eyes, he was aligning himself with a group of disgruntled TDs 'who really had no substance and belief among the ordinary members of the party'.

Why did Lenihan not attempt to oust Cowen? According to one of his own closest allies, speaking about Brian Lenihan at a much later stage, it was because he was lacking in courage and had been 'unnerved' by observing how Enda Kenny had managed to overcome the plot to remove him. However, Lenihan's aunt, Mary O'Rourke, believes he would have challenged for the leadership if he was not only grappling with the financial tsunami but also with his own battle with cancer. 'He never went for it because he had his health [problem]; that was a big thing in his life,' she maintains.

It was first revealed in December 2009 that Lenihan was sick; however, when it was announced on 16 December that the Finance Minister had been hospitalised—on the very day the Dáil passed the public sector pay cut—a statement was released to state he was suffering from a suspected hernia problem. The statement also said that he had been due to go into the Mater Private Hospital later that week for the same operation but he had opted to go earlier because he was losing sleep and experiencing discomfort.

However, as TV3 had controversially revealed on 26 December, Lenihan was suffering from pancreatic cancer, which statistically has a low survival rate. However, Lenihan never contemplated retiring from politics; with his children grown up, he told friends he wasn't going to 'just sit at home and stare at the walls'. Mary O'Rourke says he never allowed the tumour to depress him, nor did the intensive chemotherapy and radiotherapy treatments, which took place during the summer of 2010, 'affect his personality'. 'He'd go off and have his treatment and rest for an hour or two and he'd be back again. He has great reserves,' she recalled before his death.

Others, however, believe that his illness was affecting his personality. 'As the treatment for his cancer progressed and became more intense, I think his judgment might have been impaired a bit. He wouldn't be human otherwise,' believes one former Minister who served beside Lenihan.

On the subject of Brian Lenihan's health, Dr James Reilly, the current Health Minister, says he doesn't believe 'it's appropriate' for a doctor to comment on 'someone who isn't my patient'. However, when it was put it to him that for someone with cancer to hold such an important position, it would surely not only be detrimental to the individual's health, but the chemotherapy could also affect the thought process and the way the person works, he responded: 'Well, I mean, all those things are true,' adding that 'some might agree with you' when it was suggested to him that it was surely not ideal to have someone with a life-threatening illness in charge of the country's deteriorating purse strings during possibly its worst ever recession.

Dr Reilly added: 'In fairness to him, he's made his own decisions and they are his decisions to make. He's doing his job to the best of his ability as he sees it and that's his decision. And that's a personal and professional decision for him. In relation to the job he's done, it's been a catastrophe.'

While some of his colleagues feared the worst, by September 2010 Lenihan had publicly declared that his cancer had stabilised and no longer imposed a 'clear or immediate danger' to him. However, he acknowledged that it 'hasn't gone away and is still there'. Privately, Lenihan was coming to terms with the fact that he didn't have much time left and, in an effort to spare his family as much pain as possible, he made his own funeral arrangements and picked out his own burial plot in December 2010.

This public analysis of Brian Lenihan's capacity to weather the storm of ill-health muddled together his personal trauma and the welfare of the State in a quite inappropriate and damaging way. The leaking of details about Lenihan's illness had put the public in an invidious position that could not last. At a time of great economic crisis he pledged himself to the crucial job at Finance while undergoing treatment for a most serious form of cancer, its prospective cure rate less than 10 per cent. However, he asked that 'goodwill' should not impact on 'normal political processes'. One of these processes is criticism, so here goes.

The revelations surrounding Brian Lenihan's illness created a huge emotional over-reaction. This was based on an entirely meretricious belief that respect and privacy for the man and his family should prevail over crucial news. The media are not in the business of gentlemen's agreements designed to manipulate the truth. We should not make them. If public figures have private lives, it is their business to protect them.

This issue had to be seen separately from human sympathy for the man. It had also to be separated from judgment of his public performance. Such judgment was confused by eulogies on Lenihan's 'masterly' performance as Minister and his crucial handling of the economy. Unless such eulogies stopped, they would have grossly distorted everyone's judgment as people apostrophised the man amidst the chaos of what he did and what he intended to do.

The truth about him, professionally, was harsh. He understood little about economics and he headed a department of state that was starved of high-grade economists who mainly worked outside the public service. In addition, there seemed to be no shrewd political advice about what lay behind the EU urgency over protection of the banks at all costs and their advice to that effect at the time the crisis was brought to Lenihan by the bankers for immediate action. He claimed to have been learning about absolute basics at a time when all fundamental theories and philosophies about running national economies were themselves bewildering great international economists who had spent their lives in the business.

Lenihan had certain pet theories and beliefs and was heavily influenced by the politics of each situation. His most pernicious instinct was a desire to side with the most venal groups or institutions in the State, the bankers and builders, and to compound this with a slavish response to European authoritarianism.

Secondly, he did not understand the dangers for Ireland of being within the Eurozone and being on the shortlist of EU countries that could have been forced out of that shaky, imploding partnership.

Thirdly, he seemed blind to the most obvious economic fact that faced Ireland, and that was its economic dependence on the UK and the USA—both non-euro economies—as its biggest trading partners and most vital export markets for our indigenous producers. Lenihan was not directly involved when Ireland made its biggest economic blunder ever, by joining the Eurozone, an area with which the country did just one-third of its total trade. The State joined at a grossly inflated cost to the exchange rate, thereby doing untold damage to borrowing and inflationary expenditure, from which Ireland is trying to recover. He should have absorbed the realities of this and been governed by them. He was in fact governed by the opposite: an abject, misplaced respect for the ECB and a totally illusory belief that the euro and the EU are a 'saving grace' for the country, the way it used to be believed that the Holy Ghost favoured the Irish above all other nations on earth.

Respect for the ECB spawned parallel respect for the banking system in Ireland. This was mistaken and has cost the taxpayer a huge debt without producing the recovery that Brian Lenihan blithely promised.

He was given to such outlandish prognostications in part because he did not understand the realities behind what he was saying. This also caused him to change his mind when it suited.

Fourthly, in budgetary terms, he committed the State to a strategy of cutting expenditure instead of broadening taxation. This deadened initiative and investment and produced an envy culture among workers. His approach was like that of Wilkins Micawber: something will turn up, like a revival in the building industry or a sudden splurge of bank investment in new job-creating enterprises.

This did not happen. Experienced economists knew this, though in keeping with the trends around the world, they had mixed solutions. Ireland was in a liquidity trap and exhortation from the Minister, combined with spurious promises about having 'turned the corner', did not overcome the innate fear of spending. If governments cut expenditure, so do ordinary people. The general result is deflation and recession, leading to slump, with job losses as well.

Brian Lenihan had no doubt. It is a frightening capacity in any politician. It was widely expressed by members of that Government. They were infected by an over-confidence, designed to counteract political unpopularity rather than to redress the day-to-day problems of the Irish people.

Brian Lenihan's lack of doubt was extremely damaging in the disastrous guarantee he gave to bank creditors and bondholders. It was the product of the 'bubble thinking' that brought the creditors into Ireland in order to make fast money, which they did, and were then guaranteed no loss. The UCD economist Morgan Kelly, one of the best in the business, published a brilliant paper on this. The prison of the euro, allowing Irish banks to get their hands on unlimited money cheaply, led to grossly irresponsible lending, to be repaid by the taxpayer.

Morgan Kelly said NAMA would push the country beyond the fiscal limits and would need a subsidiary support structure requiring more tax. Either way, this was the product of Lenihan's over-optimism and his limited grasp of the briefs so ill-prepared for him by what seemed to be a poor back-up team of economic advisers who went along with his facile policies.

He should have resigned: the sooner the better. Misplaced sympathy for his truly unfortunate state of health had nothing whatever to do with this case.

At virtually every level Ireland was floundering, with no political, tactical or strategic leadership worthy of the name. The State's political rulers, who had recently scrambled their way to power by buying off the fools running the Green Party into accepting complicity for what they did, were simply doing everything that such failing, corrupt and fearful political groups do.

What they were doing had little or nothing to do with government or leadership of the country. It was simply about position and how to ensure it for the present. These people wanted tenure and protection. They either did not understand power or were afraid to use it. Over the Lisbon Treaty they threw away power, squandering it on marginal favours from the 'Top Table' in Brussels. And they did not recognise what they were doing. All they saw in it was a way of keeping their position.

Theirs was a political floorshow without any real politics in it. They wished to avoid all short-term risk, make no innovations, introduce no reforms, avoid all decisions, hang on to their privileges and try to sustain the public perception of their own importance, in the hope that something would turn up.

Not surprisingly, one expression of this approach was in the banking inquiry but it could have been applied to virtually all Government actions under Brian Cowen and most of those under Bertie Ahern in respect of reform and legislation. Ireland was not governed and there was no political mechanism designed to reveal this.

Despite the belated positive news on his health, which came well into 2010, Brian Lenihan was still reluctant to challenge for the leadership. Nevertheless, he continued to 'listen', as Mary O'Rourke described his talks with the frustrated rebel TDs about ousting Cowen. John McGuinness, it is understood, later 'lost his cool' when Lenihan bizarrely came out and publicly supported Cowen not once but on several occasions. The first incident occurred when Cowen feared a heave shortly after the Galway drinking incident and was advised to get Lenihan to support him publicly. Cowen knew that Lenihan had a press conference scheduled 'for a normal briefing on the economy'. Cowen decided to hijack it by getting Lenihan to publicly support him at it.

Unannounced, Cowen strolled into Lenihan's office and nonchalantly said: 'Come on! We're going down to do a briefing on this.'

An irate Lenihan later told those close to him that he had been 'bounced into this assertion of confidence in Cowen's leadership'. Meanwhile, it was decided to put his younger brother, Conor Lenihan, on RTÉ's 'The Frontline' to further assert support for Cowen. But the ever-astute Conor was clearly ambiguous, with his vague endorsement that Cowen could 'lead if he wants to'. The clock was ticking down towards Cowen's last days in power.

As if to exploit the wider ineptitude of the politicians running the country, there was the relatively manageable cold weather chaos. Yet instead of a sensible and well-ordered response, there was the unprepared incompetence of local authorities and the almost mindless behaviour of the responsible politicians. The Minister with overall responsibility, Noel Dempsey, went abroad and stayed there, claiming that the adverse conditions were under control. Those combating the chaos on the ground could not get the grit, the shovels, the spades and brushes to clear ice and snow from pavements. Call in the Army! Ordinary walking in towns was unsafe. Streets were nightmarish scenes where people fell down and broke their arms or worse. The floods were the previous example of stupid planning, leading to ill-advised construction in flood-prone areas. The idea that John Gormley would co-ordinate fighting the cold was laughable.

Whether it was the major matter of the banking crisis, or the relatively minor matter of managing a serious cold snap, the Government had for years accepted a restrictive interpretation of the law in respect of the Houses of the Oireachtas investigating issues where public performance was in question, whether this was banking or gritting the roads.

Part of the onus of government is to tackle those issues where an impediment has blocked political progress. No case of this was more glaring, in the context of a public right for an open inquiry into the banking crisis and the credit disaster that froze business, than the Supreme Court judgment limiting Oireachtas inquiries where they might affect the reputation of individual citizens.

For nine years Ireland had been mesmerised by this absurd majority judgment. This effectively says those elected to govern cannot make findings of fact about people if there is the possibility of such findings damaging people's reputations.

Obviously, those we elect cannot engage in the criminal prosecution of people they find to have acted criminally or negligently. That is a matter for the courts, but they should be able to find that individuals did not perform their duties adequately, and that is precisely what we were—or should have been—confronting over the banks.

In such an approach there is no threat of damage that carries any criminal sanction. Such sanction can only come afterwards, when and if the judiciary, the Director of Public Prosecutions and the gardaí become involved. And recent experience of the many Tribunals has demonstrated how carefully this distinction between findings by inquiry and their process in law are separated. Not only is there—or at least should be—a right implicit in what is expected from those elected, to process actions against those who deceive or wrong the people, but in addition the Houses of the Oireachtas should have the right to refer their deliberations to the DPP so that he can determine if a criminal prosecution is appropriate.

Never was this particular fault in the system of so bright a magnitude than it was as a result of the banking crisis. The matter should have been addressed by way of referendum, changing the Constitution in the light of the Supreme Court finding. This had been blindingly obvious and Fianna Fáil in power had done nothing. Action on this would have represented a deliberate enhancement of the powers of the Oireachtas. But the Ahern years, followed by the Cowen era, had seen the undermining and weakening of the Houses of the Oireachtas. At times it had seemed deliberate and structured.

It was certainly the case that the failure to deal with the castration of elected politicians made the banking inquiry, as structured, favourable to the banks and to those in power who had much to hide. It was all a bit like one of those Russian toys, Matryoshka dolls, in which a smiling peasant is opened up in order to reveal another smiling peasant, and then another. This is a fitting emblem of what happened. One semi-private investigation opened out into another semi-private investigation, so that when it got to the Dáil, it was largely incomprehensible. In any case, the Dáil's ability to say or do anything worthwhile was rendered sterile by the Supreme Court.

How convenient for Brian Lenihan and Brian Cowen! They treated the people with disdain and the banks with kid gloves. Into the bargain the Attorney General suggested—without giving much by way of authority—that it was necessary to suspend police investigations into the actions of the bankers.

| THE SAD AUTUMN OF 2010

The mood at the end of October 2010, when the Dáil returned, was gloomy and despairing. The mood of the Fianna Fáil party was confused and distrustful. The party's *zeitgeist* was in place but no longer contained any of the magic that had held it in power since 1997, an unequalled three terms during which the country's prosperity had been raised to unprecedented heights, only to be now dashed down in pieces.

That *zeitgeist* is a clue to the paralysis of Fianna Fáil and its leadership during that gloomy autumn, a paralysis that derives from the mantra of never challenging an incumbent leader, never publicly criticising the party's so-called 'policies', never making any full commitment to coalition partnership—despite the inevitability of this sharing of power since the 1980s—and never looking too closely at its own character and seeing there the basic faults that needed to be redressed.

The party had been corrupted by power. Though Brian Cowen had committed himself to reform on becoming Taoiseach and leader in May 2008, he had soon abandoned such objectives because the heart of all necessary reform began with the party itself.

An ever-widening public view was being expressed: it was vital for the Irish State to hold an election and achieve a clear mandate for government. This would inevitably be a Kenny-led administration, whether the Fine Gael party on its own or a Fine Gael-Labour coalition. There was also much talk of a new party but this was accompanied by gloomy prognostications over the difficulties of this. What was certain was the over-riding need for the shaping of a plan that would satisfy people, giving them clear political leadership and ridding them of the stumbling confusion of those in power.

Though none of this was possible under Brian Cowen, it did not stop him putting before the people a Four-Year Plan entitled 'Securing Ireland's Future', designed in part to ameliorate a December Budget that would concentrate a significant part of the €15 billion Budget burden into the first of the four years. Brian Lenihan called it 'frontloading'. He had even brought over from Brussels Olli Rehn, the Commissioner for Economic and Monetary Affairs, who would assess Ireland's economic needs and its budgetary options.

All this was classic Fianna Fáil politics: the plan, the co-operative liaison with Europe, the incorporation of the upcoming Budget into a longer-term strategy. Lenihan wove into this continuing doubt over the Croke Park Agreement. Nevertheless, his handling of the Government presentation was a plausible performance, as were all his public statements and debate at the time. He was preparing the ground for a two-day Dáil debate. The picture he gave, however, was a very partial one. The impending visit of Olli Rehn was outlined as a briefing session for the Opposition parties and the 'social partners' on the EU's assessment of Ireland's budgetary options. On all sides, though for different reasons, the fiction of Ireland's economic sovereignty was maintained. For Fianna Fáil, the looming overseer character of EU intervention was too much to bring forward. For Joan Burton, the Labour Party's spokesperson on finance, it was obvious that the European Commission's role was 'to now take a closer interest in how Member States prepare their budgetary plans', and Michael Noonan, for Fine Gael, said the same thing in different words: 'Europe is a mirror which reflects the reality of the outside world and what the people who are expecting money are expecting'. None of them foresaw the draconian measures that were imminent.

Rehn came and went, doing his stuff with the Opposition parties, getting everyone onside. The fiction was maintained. Brian Cowen argued, in the two-day debate on the economy at the end of October 2010, that the proposed budgetary burden might 'dampen economic growth in 2011' but it would give confidence to the markets and secure Ireland's funding position. In rather similar arguments to those given by Brian Cowen all along—that the home-grown property bubble had accentuated Ireland's original economic boom and also its subsequent fall—Patrick Honohan, Governor of the Central Bank, argued that the property bubble was responsible for Ireland's public finances being 'worse than almost any other country'.

The Government was being less than honest on two main fronts. It was using a drip-feed approach on the bad news coming from the banks. This had been Lenihan's approach since the late September 2008 Bank Guarantee, made significantly worse by the growing conviction that he did not really understand what he was talking about. This fabrication of illusory reassurances was made far worse by the deliberate misrepresentation of the world economic situation and its impact on Ireland. The Government line was to suggest poor prospects for the world economy as a reason for the position being taken by the Irish Government. The trouble was that this simply was not true. When the first draft versions of the 2010 plan were drawn up, in December 2009, the international prospects were gloomy. By October 2010 they had improved significantly and looked positive for the future. Yet the Government still subscribed to the year-old downbeat version of events, blaming this on outdated figures. The EU was showing better than expected growth and the UK economy, in particular, was relatively strong, its growth rate at 1.8 per cent. The rate in the USA was even higher, so that Ireland's two main non-EU trading partners were strong and during the year there had been a surge in Irish exports.

The month of October ended with a European Summit. Brian Cowen was still on the side of the other EU members of the Eurozone in shaping the terms of a permanent rescue fund, rather than being the recipient of such a fund, as he was shortly to become. The talk was about whether or not Ireland would need a referendum!

Cowen's immediate challenge was to put on a brave face in his futile exercise, attempting to hold on to the Dáil seat in the Donegal South-West by-election in November 2010. This had been vacated by Pat 'The Cope' Gallagher, after his win in the European election in June 2009. While there is no legal obligation to do so, by-elections are normally held within six months of a seat being vacated, but Cowen—as a result of a tenuous majority—stubbornly opted to drag his heels on declaring dates for the three by-elections necessary, knowing that the Government would undoubtedly lose all of them. The other two were for George Lee's seat in Dublin South after his sudden resignation, following his brief flirtation with political life, and Martin Cullen's in

Waterford, after his retirement from politics in March 2010.

There was a major blow for Cowen in early November when Donegal North-East TD Dr Jim McDaid, who appeared to have courted controversy throughout his colourful political career, pulled out of Government and called for a general election, a call he had also made in 2009. This ultimately meant the need for a fourth by-election, and would thus spell the end of Cowen's Government if it lost all of them when his majority would be down to three. It was surprising that McDaid's resignation came to light only several days after his letter had been sent to the Taoiseach. It was clearly a stalling tactic by the Government.

As McDaid told the Taoiseach in his letter of resignation: 'We have failed to make any significant progress in relation to reducing our structural Budget deficit, which remains as our most pressing and potentially damaging economic challenge. Month after month we are informed of further challenging figures from the Department of Finance.'

McDaid lowered still further Fianna Fáil's dismal standing in the opinion polls. On foot of this resignation, they deserved to go even lower, and did. What was a matter of some surprise was how calmly the Opposition parties considered what they could not or should not do. They should instead have built a convincing case to throw out the Government then and replace it. There must have been many no-hopers in Fianna Fáil who saw it in the same way, their future probably best served by crossing over to one of the Opposition parties or joining a new political party.

Enda Kenny called for an election but this was rejected. However, two days later the High Court ordered the holding of the long-delayed by-election in South-West Donegal. The Government had brazenly fought the case brought by the then Sinn Féin Senator Pearse Doherty, incensed by the 16-month delay in announcing the by-election, which he described as 'unconstitutional'. The judge's findings were that the Government was in breach of the constitutional rights of the people in the constituency by depriving them of a representative for so long. The Government set the by-election for 25 November, only two weeks before the impending Budget. Pearse Doherty won the seat in the by-election. The Chief Whip, John Curran, vowed that the writs for the other three impending by-elections, in Donegal North-East, Waterford and Dublin South, would be moved early in the new year. It was not lost on Cowen that it appeared the Government was going to collapse. MEP Pat 'The Cope' Gallagher quickly squashed rumours that Fianna Fáil was going to ask him to run in the second Donegal by-election and contradicted the Tánaiste Mary Coughlan's view that he had not been approached, saying that she was obviously 'not in the loop' about behind-the-scenes movement at senior level within Fianna Fáil.

In contrast to Olli Rehn's rather forbidding presence in Ireland, attempting to guide Brian Lenihan's uncertain hand, the visit of another Commissioner, Michel Barnier, responsible for Internal Market and Services, and not notably well-informed about Ireland, told the country that he saw 'a light at the end of the tunnel' for Ireland and that it would maintain control over its domestic taxation policies in spite of EU plans for 'reform of the single market'. He said that the country had 'a lot of trump cards', combined with a 'courageous, hard-working population'.

The reaction to Rehn was mixed. Lenihan had persuaded him to call for a political consensus over the Budget. As far as Fianna Fáil was concerned, this was precisely what it needed to head off trouble from the Opposition. Fianna Fáil was prepared to ignore—if plunged into an election— Rehn's suggestion that Ireland, up to then a low-tax country, 'should lean towards becoming a normal tax country in the European context'. But a quite different judgment was put forward by Morgan Kelly, who was devastating then and later in his outspoken views. On this occasion he said that Ireland was no longer economically sovereign but was, instead, 'a ward of the European Central Bank'.

It was becoming inescapable that the Fianna Fáil party, from Brian Lenihan through all members of the Government, was on a wrong course and had lost both international and domestic credibility. The idea of charting a way forward, with the consent or consensus of the Opposition, was looking increasingly ridiculous. It would be the EU that would chart the way forward and this had been foreshadowed by Olli Rehn in his November visit. As for a Four-Year Plan, it was no more than an *aide-mémoire*. As far as the exercise of political power and planning was concerned, new minds and faces were needed. There was already talk, at the time, of the additional need for a new party. This was seen as possibly bringing a cutting edge not evident in the current Dáil.

The interest rate on Irish bonds—what foreign lenders charged for lending to the Irish Government—was up to 8 per cent and climbing. As one eminent Swiss economist put it:

> Ireland needs to know the Truth. Only new people in government will be capable of delivering the Truth. The bond market world-wide is not intrinsically evil, but it is unbelievably harsh when it loses confidence. Truth produces confidence. And your current administration has proven they can create all sorts of headlines, but the one headline they will never publish is Truth.

Far from coming closer to the truth, Brian Cowen was engaging in scare tactics by threatening that the banks would close if the Budget was not passed. And Olli Rehn was doing something similar in endorsing the Four-Year Plan and the Budget as the way forward and more or less demanding Opposition support for these measures. The reality was that neither of these engines of recovery were anywhere near being adequate for the storm that was gathering in the skies over Ireland. In fact the Four-Year Plan—which had yet to appear—was little short of an election manifesto, a set of soft options, the worst of them being a €1 cut in the minimum wage! Launching it, on 24 November, Brian Lenihan challenged the Opposition to do better. It had already rejected Olli Rehn and Brian Cowen over both Budget and Plan, undertaking changes after the election. But when would that be? Sooner rather than later was the answer, but no one realised how soon.

Well before the appearance of the plan, in a giveaway aside at a Department of Finance briefing during his one-day visit on 9 November, Rehn mentioned being in contact with the Irish authorities 'at least once a day'. What was intended was a paternalistic watching brief over Brian Lenihan's chronic under-capacity to sort out our finances, or the banks', was in reality an alarming claim. Dan O'Brien made this clear in an article in the *Irish Times* on 10 November, pointing out that daily concourse with one country out of 27 was not just not normal, it was not feasible. And he went on to say that the ulterior motive was to do with Europe, not Ireland. Describing the country as the weak link in the chain, he went to the heart of the matter, claiming that Ireland, if not handled adroitly, could blow wide open the European monetary order, which would then rock the whole international financial system. Rehn's attitude was indicative of the serious threat Ireland represented to the euro and to European fiscal events, rather than any care the EU had for the State. All Rehn could give to Ireland was an endorsement of the Budget and of the Four-Year Plan. And with slavish subservience, this was what Brian Lenihan, cap in hand, thanked him for.

On that same day, 10 November, the spectre of a bailout emerged. It did so in a back-to-front way, on BBC's 'Newsnight', with the claim that the Government intended to avoid a bailout but could not give a guarantee of this. Lenihan said:

We intend to return to the markets next year, and we intend to fund ourselves. That's our plan. We have put our public finances on a sustainable basis in the next two years. We have done massive corrections in our public debt and our deficit and we will continue to do so. Of course, nobody can give a 100 per cent guarantee, no state can give a 100 per cent guarantee on anything in the modern world.

Ireland struggled on to the end of that week. Bond yields passed the 9 per cent mark, their value falling for the 13th consecutive day. Moody's, the rating agency, was waiting for the four-year fiscal plan in order to decide whether to downgrade the State further. Ireland's public debt woes moved to the top of the agenda at the G20 Summit in Seoul in response to a statement from José Manuel Barroso that the EU was ready to bail Ireland out 'in case of need'. This statement itself was clearly directed at the nervousness of the world and not at Ireland's plight. The State was being steered towards asking for the bailout.

Brian Lenihan claimed confidence from the Governor of the Central Bank and the Financial Regulator's statement that they had 'identified the exposures in the system and recommended the best capital provisions for them'. It was like whistling past the graveyard in which most of the nation's hopes had already been buried. What was really happening was that Dublin was in direct contact with the offices of

Barroso, Trichet and the German Foreign Minister, Guido Westerwelle. Reuters surmised from this that Ireland was discussing the drawing down of funds from the EU Emergency Fund. If it was not precisely the case, then it soon would be.

Both Brian Cowen and the European Commission denied there had been any application for funds. Nevertheless, talks were going on at an official level, with a line drawn between that so-called 'technical' approach and the decision-makers. The mantra of Ireland having funds that would last until the middle of 2011 was put forward repeatedly. On RTÉ radio, on 12 November, Brian Lenihan said: 'First of all, the State is well-funded into June of next year, to fund the budget. I think that's important; we have substantial reserves. So why apply in those circumstances? It doesn't seem to me to make any sense. It would send a signal to the markets that we're not in a position to manage our affairs ourselves.'

Such signals had emanated from members of the Government and senior officials in an endless stream for months, if not years. The country was out of its depth and larger European powers were taking control. In a rather frantic mixing of metaphors, the *Irish Times* painted a dramatic picture:

> The bursting of an enormous property bubble has caused grievous harm to the Irish economy. As that bubble inflated, bank regulators and the guardians of the public finances were asleep at the wheel ....
> The only chance is to fight on. We are now in the last chance saloon.

Official denials became more strident as the gap widened between their assertions and the growing indications that a bailout was now the subject of widespread discussion and negotiation. Brian Cowen was furious at the BBC reporting that talks were taking place and that it was 'no longer a matter of whether but when'.

The shambles seemed deliberate. Denial became an end in itself. It even took the upper hand during the early days of the third week in November, with Cowen maintaining that there was no question of the Government being involved in discussion about an EU/IMF bailout, and Ministers declaring that talk of a bailout was 'fiction'. Confusion and anger at an inevitable and overdue response to their own incompetence was the reaction of Cowen, Lenihan and other politicians, and it was needless. Later, Batt O'Keeffe would backtrack by saying that he—an Enterprise Minister—was 'unaware' of such talks; amazingly, it appeared that both the Finance Minister and Cowen had kept him and other Cabinet members out of the loop.

By 18 November EU officials were heading for Dublin while Batt O'Keeffe, Cowen's closest ally in the Government, likened what was happening to 'a poker game. We've got to play poker over the next couple of days to see what cards these people have to play, what exactly they have in mind. We would like to see the colour of their money.'

Olli Rehn was so friendly it was worrying. Writing of Rehn's visit in early November 2010, John Drennan, in the *Sunday Independent*, quoted Louis XIV's Finance Minister that 'the art of taxation consists in so plucking the goose as to obtain the largest amount of feathers with the least hissing' and went on to ask: 'the real question': 'Why is Olli Rehn so anxious to create the sort of "consensus" that will keep the most unpopular Taoiseach in the history of the Irish State in power?'

On Friday of that same week, 19 November 2010, Ajai Chopra, of the European Department of the International Monetary Fund, led part of his team of colleagues through the streets of Dublin for talks at the Central Bank in Dame Street. They had already won the game of poker without showing their hand or revealing the colour of their money. The full team, coming from the European Central Bank and the European Commission, numbered well into the twenties. They would be looking into the Budget, the Four-Year Plan and 'whatever measures might be needed to support financial stability', obviously directed at the banks. Brian Cowen saw no reason for Ireland to be humiliated or ashamed and denied any loss of sovereignty.

In fact only hours prior to the IMF's arrival, Cowen was in the Dáil chamber still playing down events. A Fianna Fáil backbencher, Seán Power, summed up the consensus when he told the Dáil that the Government was treating the public like fools. John Gormley had believed it was better for the Government to be taking the tough decision themselves because he feared that the 'consequence' of the IMF coming in would make it 'far, far worse for people in the short to medium term'. Ominously, the Greens' chairman, Dan Boyle, was twittering his thoughts again: 'There is a question of trust and an adding to uncertainty that is making the basis for being in Government much more difficult.'

As news of the IMF's arrival broke, Patrick Honohan, Governor of the Central Bank, speculated—at times it seemed almost from outside the process, though of course Honohan was intimately involved as a member of the ECB board of governors—when he suggested that the Government would be accepting a very substantial loan of tens of billions; 'the ECB would not send large teams if they didn't believe first of all that they could agree to a package'. Brian Cowen thought this comment 'premature', saying there would be a decision 'after the talks were over'. Brian Lenihan put it more simply, saying that an aid package would be accepted and would 'have to be funnelled through the State' but denied that the IMF would be directing the Budget or the Four-Year Plan. In the event both were to be the subject of quarterly scrutiny.

It was what it appeared to be: an enormous loan that the ECB pressed on Ireland because it was alarmed at providing money for the Irish banks against dud or poor collateral at a 1 per cent interest rate. The ECB decided to push on Ireland an enormous loan instead, at a 5.8 per cent interest rate. Honohan played his part in this process. Morgan Kelly's article in the *Irish Times* in May said that rarely had a Central Bank Governor sliced off his national Finance Minister at the knees as Honohan had done with Lenihan in his 'Morning Ireland' interview on the day before the bailout. A better and more accurate term for it is 'stitch-up', given by David McWilliams. Lenihan agreed in May in his BBC interview with Dan O'Brien that the loan had been forced on him. In agreeing the loan, the IMF had initially been willing to impose burden-sharing on the senior bondholders in the Irish banks, which would have reduced the cost to Ireland, but the Americans, through Timothy Geithner, US Treasury Secretary, had vetoed this. So 'burden-sharing' was out—and still is. The burden remains Ireland's. A final note: the so-called 'bailout' was embodied in a Memorandum of Understanding with the ECB/EU Commission and IMF. This required and requires the Irish Government to send all its detailed tax and spending figures to the Troika once a week. There is also provision for formal monitoring by a visiting team every three months as a condition of the provision of the various tranches of the loan. The Troika supervises detailed Government day-to-day economic policy. The

Memorandum of Understanding is available on the Department of Finance website.

Ned O'Keeffe, something of a backbench wild card in the Fianna Fáil party, called for Brian Lenihan's removal as Minister for Finance: 'He should have taken corrective action to avoid these outside interests coming in and telling us how to run our country.' He said that Lenihan 'had not done the business as he should have done. The Minister has failed the Government, failed the Irish people and failed the Fianna Fáil party.' Many expressed fear of a general election and said that Fianna Fáil should 'serve out its mandate to June 2012. We are the best party to be governing.'

The truth was quick to emerge. Throughout the Fianna Fáil organisation there was recognition that the party could not possibly go into an election under Cowen's leadership and that if an election became inevitable, the party could easily lose half its seats. The Cabinet was so divided that Opposition help was thought to be needed to get the Budget through. Cowen rejected calls for his resignation, but his performance within the Fianna Fáil party and even within the Cabinet had been so abysmal that he had lost all integrity. He had failed to inform even those closest to him; senior Ministers such as Dermot Ahern and Mary Hanafin had continued to deny the coming bailout and no one in the party had been informed or briefed. They all followed the media briefings which were well-informed, their message relentlessly dismal. That weekend, of 20/21 November, there had crept into the opinion poll questioning an astonishing new issue to explore, whether people had become ashamed to vote for Fianna Fáil. Given the deep and growing shame of senior party figures, including members of the Cabinet, at having been exposed as ignorant of the biggest political decision made in their lifetime, this question had become an essential part of the exploration of where the country was heading economically, socially, politically. Sovereignty itself seemed to be a historical issue; it was an abstract concept not too difficult to set aside when survival, the protection of money, jobs, houses, and even continued domicile, were foremost in the public mind.

The opinion poll itself confirmed the unthinkable, with Fianna Fáil party support standing at 17 per cent, a clear indication that the population had turned against the once-powerful leading political organisation in the State and had become ashamed, not just of supporting them, but of being associated in any way. This last point was beginning to infect the circumstances surrounding the Green Party. In one sense the Greens had no way out. Their support had plummeted as well, its level threatening them with a comprehensive dismissal in the event of an election. They did not feel quite the same sense of shame; it was more embarrassment of the now distant decision to give Fianna Fáil the lifeline to power after the 2007 general election, chaining themselves to an indifferent leader doomed to fail. In the aftermath of the 21 November poll, the Green Party decided to part company with Fianna Fáil and to insist on a general election before the end of January.

They had had enough. The stand-off was on a trivial issue, the Climate Change bill, but the reaction had its own melodrama. It determined that a general election was overdue and would follow, bringing down in a majestic sweep, possibly for ever, the curtain on the Soldiers of Destiny.

During a break in an emergency Cabinet meeting to brief them on the bailout on Sunday, 21 November, John Gormley and Eamon Ryan went to meet their Green colleagues to discuss the developments. 'The annoying thing about it was they carried on the discussion as if absolutely nothing had happened during the interval,' recalls a former Fianna Fáil Minister.

The Green Ministers told their party members that they didn't think there was a deliberate intent to 'mislead' them and that—incredibly—'vague language' was responsible for their being kept in the dark for so long about the bailout.

The Greens held two face-to-face meetings and several phone conferences during that weekend. It's understood that they decided to call for a general election only when one of the TDs—believed to be Trevor Sargent—'jumped up' out of his seat and declared: 'I don't think I can support this one day longer. It doesn't sit with me for our country's sovereignty to be sold with no clarity with what is going on.'

There was a moment's silence as the other members of the parliamentary party digested the prospect of ending their coalition with Fianna Fáil and then, almost in unison, other voices said: 'Actually, you're right.'

This wasn't the first time the Greens had talked about leaving Government. John Gormley admits that it had happened on two occasions before their eventual decision in November 2010. The Greens had privately discussed finding an issue to dramatically terminate the partnership a year prior to the natural conclusion of the Government's five-year term in an effort to prove themselves as capable of standing up for their ethics and increasing their popularity among the electorate.

But even though the consensus was to immediately pull out, the Greens continually changed their mind. They got cold feet because it was believed that if they didn't have Ministers in Cabinet some of their commitments from Cowen 'wouldn't be kept' in the impending Budget. The Greens weren't concerned with the Four-Year Plan, which they believed was fundamentally a 'work of fiction' because they knew it was 'not written in stone' and felt that it was something for the next Government to deal with. But they felt the Budget was their 'work'— their chance, they believed, of pushing through a Green agenda and they were damned if they were going to go before seeing it through.

On the Monday morning, only a mere two minutes before the Greens broke their news to the media, Gormley phoned Cowen on his mobile and told him that they were leaving Government and that an election should be called in January. They decided to not tell him until the very last moment because they feared either being talked out of it or, worse, that Fianna Fáil would announce the news first to spin it in their favour.

Cowen was furious. Brian Lenihan was on air doing a broadcast when John Gormley tried to contact him. Lenihan went to an event in his Dublin constituency still talking of 'a very constructive Cabinet meeting' the previous day. Passage of the Finance bill was to be speeded up to facilitate this timing. The circumstances of this were muddled. Predicting the swift passage of a complicated measure, particularly in the bailout circumstances, was perilous. But the broad inevitability of the Government's collapse and an election were inescapable.

John Gormley and the Green Party made two constitutional blunders in their confused press conference of November 2010. First, they breached Cabinet confidentiality and overall Government agreement, over their position on the financial package. Second, they breached collective responsibility, supposedly still from within Government, with their call for an election and with their proposal as to when it should have been declared. They could not take this public stance on such key issues without jeopardising irreversibly their own position.

Their further pontifications did not make sense while members of the party were still serving as Ministers. They had to resign forthwith and give up the idea that the Green Party could continue to try to set any political agenda.

The agenda was set within the Dáil by elected representatives, either independents or disaffected Fianna Fáil members, together with those who pledged themselves to give us better Government than we then had.

The only person who, constitutionally, could call for an election was the Taoiseach. It was neither a party nor a 'Government' decision. Only if he was defeated in the Dáil would that prerogative have passed from him. If beaten, he had to go to the President and resign, advising her of a dissolution.

It looked increasingly likely that this prerogative would be taken from him anyway, but the timing was in confusion, with many people holding out on whether or not to support him, with those who intended to oppose not knowing when they would withdraw their vote.

All this could be viewed in an entirely positive way. Real democracy was at work and would not be stopped by deals any more. And that is the way of truth and transparency.

The Fianna Fáil party was flabbergasted when the Greens made their unexpected announcement. After the news conference, 'there was a nice number' of Cowen's Cabinet urging him to sack the two Green Ministers. Batt O'Keeffe reveals:

> There was a view in Cabinet that time asking him to sack them. The Greens had indicated they were going to back the Finance Bill, they were going to back the Budget, and there was a very strong view among some of the Cabinet members that we should tell them to go. Sack them as Ministers. They just didn't show collegiality, they didn't show loyalty that one would desire. They never discussed this with the Taoiseach and gave him two minutes' notice that they were

making this announcement. That's bad faith. From that day on, we couldn't trust them in anything they said or did.

I suppose I should say the most disparaging aspect of all of it was the loyalty Cowen showed to them, the patience that he demonstrated in dealing with them, the opportunities he took to make sure Fianna Fáil diehards in Cabinet would tolerate some of the nonsense that went on and look for accommodation with them. And the fact that they let him down so badly when they went out and said, 'There has to be an election before the end of January and that we're going to back the Budget and back the Finance Bill.' We really thought that was a treacherous move on their part. They've absolutely no loyalty. It showed them to be absolutely subjective and also showed that there was no collegiality at all. In my view, that's the day the Government died.

Up until the Greens pulled out, the two parties had, surprisingly, a 'very, very good relationship' at Cabinet level, according to O'Keeffe:

When the crisis came the Greens were very solid in the early stage. I think, if anything, the Greens were probably suspect in taking an awful lot of notice of the *Irish Times* and media in general. And they tended to react to the media rather than being their own people. And as the media became more hostile, I think they become more jittery and more demanding.

But even though the Greens' Ministers were mostly amiable at the Cabinet meeting, the Fianna Fáil Ministers were often frustrated by how their junior partners 'would take decisions at Cabinet but then you couldn't guarantee that they wouldn't go back to their people and then look for changes at Cabinet,' according to O'Keeffe. He believes that they 'never once stood up to their people and said, "Look, this is a Government decision. This is not a decision for backbenchers or for the organisation in general." Like Fianna Fáil had to do with their members. I think that was the big distinguishing fact [*sic*] between the two parties.'

According to one former Minister, cracks first started to appear in the relationship after Gormley raised, on 7 October 2010, what Fianna

Fáil saw as a 'ridiculous concept', a nationalised Government involving all the main parties. He said that such a move was a sensible one because a consensus was needed between all the parties. However, Fine Gael ruled out the prospect. The Fianna Fáil Minister said:

> The Greens were very honourable in Government. Cowen pissed all over them basically. Do you remember Gormley came out with an idea of a National Government, which was a great way of putting Gilmore in the corner, right? Cowen pissed all over the proposal. That was the end of the fucking coalition basically. Do you remember he came back to the Dáil the following week and reluctantly said it wasn't bad and we'd look at it? He kind of pissed on the whole proposal but you can't do that to your coalition partner. Gormley was the leader of the Greens. Cowen was down in Tullamore pissing all over the idea.

As Cowen grappled with the Greens pulling out and the IMF coming in, he was forced into a by-election in Donegal South-West. Cowen was approached in Donegal by former Tánaiste Ray MacSharry and told he should resign, according to Mary O'Rourke. 'Ray MacSharry says he spoke to him and told him that he should leave and all that. Ray told me he did in the Donegal by-election. He spoke with him and said, "It just wasn't working"', she states.

The Fianna Fáil party was openly in chaos and Brian Cowen was frantically trying to hold the Government together in order to get the Budget through. At this stage the leaders of the country were not talking to each other. The Cabinet was not operating as a body with collective responsibility, thus breaching the requirements of the Constitution. No one noticed that any more. Members were publicly contradicting each other about what was going on. It, like many other institutions in Irish life, was clearly being bypassed.

The big mistake being made on all sides was the linking of the general election to the Budget and also to the fiscal deal done with Europe and the IMF. The money issue was resolved. Europe was saving itself and the euro; Ireland was the tiny but important catalyst. The Budget was a preordained instrument, the main shape of which was clear to most people. And there was no valid argument for passing the

Budget first. Indeed, one suspected there were no valid arguments for passing the Budget as it had been first drafted.

One of the principal reasons for this was the fact that all indicators were that Fianna Fáil was intending to introduce a feeble Budget. This was crystal clear in Brian Lenihan's evasion of questions about budgetary intent. He would not answer about Croke Park and the minimum wage. He evaded all invitations to make a clear and courageous position on the Budget available to the Irish people.

He did this because it was the only possible statement of his and his party's position. They presided over a profoundly weakened administration and, after two and a half years of Brian Cowen's leadership, found themselves in confusion on almost every issue. Fianna Fáil and the Green Party knew that their last defence lay in a non-punitive budgetary strategy.

This was unacceptable to the majority of Irish people. It should also have been unacceptable to the financial gurus from Europe, doing their utmost not to notice the sick and dying political elephant in the middle of their conference rooms. They may have kept a sharp eye on Irish banking disasters and on the failure of the Irish Government to attract lenders. What they did not keep their eye on, and had great difficulty in understanding at all, was the ins and outs of Irish politics and the disgraceful absence of leadership under which the Irish people groaned while their collective public and private debts sky-rocketed.

The debt figure, which had stood at €15 billion two weeks earlier, rose to an EU loan figure that would reach €90 billion. The country's finances would be under constant surveillance and monitoring. The G7, comprising the seven largest industrial countries, gave approval to the deal. Independently, the UK offered a unilateral loan to Ireland. The UK donation was one of several. The financial instability was greatly aggravated by uncertainty over the banks. Exchequer funding provided for them was being steadily undermined by withdrawals and transfers of funds out of the country.

The reality facing the whole population, at the end of November, was of a set of fiscal circumstances about which people could do nothing and a level of anger and hatred about which they could do a great deal. The political arena would soon be theirs and the most culpable group in that arena who had lied to them, betrayed them, robbed them and misled them was Fianna Fáil.

Without full transparency, without any sense of the Government acting as a corporate entity or in compliance with the constitutional requirements, the main concern was to complete the deal quickly. It would be done before the markets opened, thus offering a form of Irish sacrifice that was clearly aimed, not at the reassurance of the Irish public, but at the reassurance of foreign markets on behalf of the euro. The dreadful deed was done. Briefly, the markets seemed to respond positively but then fell back. And another sacrifice on the altar of political ineptitude took place. Whatever was happening, whatever reactions then followed, Ireland was at the centre of them, which is what the country voted for in the second Lisbon Treaty referendum. Unfortunately, what was happening was now a long way from what Irish people thought might be Europe's way of saving the nation.

There was in fact a catalogue of sacrifices made on Ireland's behalf by the Government and this was greatly augmented, most notably when it threw away control of the public finances in order more easily to lose charge of the banks.

Irish banks were exercising a terrible punishment on the Irish economy, and on the Irish people. But that they should have been aided and partnered in this collective form of financial suicide by the whole Government rightly caused growing alarm and intense anger. Most people had a vague notion of the meaning of sovereignty, particularly in economic terms. Here it was being repeatedly offered up for sacrificial burning and had become only a charred and unrecognisable object. It became of great importance to try to define it. This was because, though concern for Irish sovereignty was shared by many men and women in Ireland, understanding what its loss meant in terms of savings and investment became increasingly difficult to grasp or to rely on its protection.

The country watched in dismay as the EU, through the ECB and abetted by the IMF, dragooned Ireland into the urgent and express need to conclude the Irish bailout agreement before the markets opened, not for Ireland's sake, but for the sake of Europe, and for what faced Europe in Portugal and Spain as well as in Belgium and Italy. And it seemed as though Ireland was duped into an exercise that appeared to be increasingly close to failure. It still looks that way.

What was done, roughly speaking, was that private balance sheet risk was moved by legal decree onto the sovereign balance sheet of Ireland. This was unconstitutional, not only in the way it was done, but in the motive behind it.

At the bleak end of November Ireland had gone round in circles. It had wasted time it had and all the money. It had been wasting them since the Bank Guarantee. And, since the banks were still there, and were more of a public liability than ever, they were still costing money and would go on doing so into the future. A substantial part of the bailout cash would be used to that end.

Can one blame the markets for not being interested in Ireland, other than to make money at its expense, and otherwise to laugh at how foolish it had been? Into the bargain the markets saw that Ireland was putting its own equity—the National Pensions Reserve Fund—into the banks and this did not add halfpence to confidence in the State.

On 7 December Brian Cowen signed into force the Statutory Commission of Investigation into the Banking Sector in Ireland, under the terms of Section 3 of the Commissions of Investigation Act of 2004, a piece of legislation created under Bertie Ahern and one that should be looked at again by the Dáil and with scepticism by everyone else. It had been seriously amended in its terms of reference to confine within narrow limits the work that was subsequently undertaken by Peter Nyberg, who conducted the third investigation into the banks. His terms of reference precluded much of the important matter contained in the testimony of both David Drumm and Seán FitzPatrick. Whichever of the two has given the truer expression of how much was known by the State and its servants in adjudicating on the banks was not within Nyberg's power to investigate fully.

From this point of view, as well as from other important aspects for judging the mismanagement of Ireland's banks, a mismanagement that has put the country in debt far more seriously than any other event in our history, Nyberg's remains a flawed investigation.

There was a further amendment added to the Government Order, which Cowen signed. This was to substitute 15 January 2009 for 28 September 2008 as the closing date for investigation, in itself a surprising and significant limitation since it cut out a substantial period—from 15 January 2009 until the bailout and beyond—when the

Government pursued covert actions on the country's banking.

The general terms of reference were restrictive in the extreme and forced on the Commission further limitations. For example, the Commission 'decided at an early stage that insofar as possible this Report should not contain evaluations or details of named individuals, their actions and inactions'. This was because 'the Commission's Terms of Reference strongly stress the need to explain why systemic failures happened. Obtaining meaningful information on this is much easier if individuals do not, at the same time, have to worry about how this information will affect their public image.' In addition, the Commission 'did not wish to prejudice, in any way, any possible future investigation into the actions of any individual'. The third reason given was 'that decision-makers and leadership in the various institutions must carry a large part of the immediate blame for the crisis'.

These Commission restrictions make little sense and virtually undermine the whole process of investigation. In a country where concern for the worries of individuals having their 'public image' affected has been continually shattered throughout the past 20 years, it is a nonsense to protect the small group of people who destroyed Irish banking by breaking regulations, rules and the law. Charles Haughey, Bertie Ahern, Liam Lawlor, Michael Lowry, Ben Dunne and many others have been taken through the Tribunal processes, exposed, humiliated and damaged—many would say in the country's best interest—and this, apart from the cost of it, was approved of by the people. In law there is no onus on such inquiries, other than the option of a fair hearing and legal representation, to step mincingly through the unscripted possibilities from having a person's 'public image' adversely affected.

As for the emphasis on the 'systemic failures', they were there but were abused on all sides. The controls that should have held in place the system structures of the banks were simply ignored. The abuse of them was callous, laconic and at times criminal. On both sides people were involved. They have already been singled out in the media for investigation and their roles are widely known and understood for an inquiry dealing with the institutions but excluding any examination of their personal actions and involvement borders on the ridiculous. Nothing that the Commission could possibly do in respect of protecting public images or trying not to prejudice future investigations justifies itself when set against the appalling and extensive damage done covertly to the State and to hundreds of thousands of taxpayers over their savings.

Then the ground froze, the snow fell and the country was engulfed in the worst winter weather since 1962.

Chapter 14 ∿

| NAMA

B y late 2010, it became clear that the commercial individuals responsible for the huge debt burden remained at the helm of much of the economic structure that had got Ireland into the mess. Moreover, their political regulators—the Government and the Houses of the Oireachtas—were determined to sustain their damaging course of action at the expense, firstly of the Irish people, secondly of the developers, who were persecuted beyond their deserts.

As a people, the Irish blamed the politicians. As an electorate, they were responsible for them being there. In three elections, the last the least seemly of all, they gave power to Fianna Fáil and its temporary appendages and let them run the country badly and, in the end, into the ground.

When it came to blame, the nation turned on the developers, vilifying them and then subjecting them to a form of economic crucifixion. The Government found a ready-made set of scapegoats in them. A substantial part of the justification for this came from the situation that developed within the Dublin Docklands Development Authority (DDDA), which replaced the Custom House Development Authority in 1997. Bertie had become Taoiseach. The area involved was in his constituency and, in Shane Ross's words, 'would become a Klondike for developers'. It attracted €3.35 billion in investment, making it the single largest urban project in the State's history. It had planning autonomy. It had direct Anglo Irish Bank involvement in funding speculators, and conflict of interest became the rule of the games there, which were elaborate and, in the end, quite ruinous. Rivalry between developers brought the conflict of interest into the open and the High Court was involved over the fast-track planning decision for the Anglo Irish Bank headquarters. Though Dublin City Council countered this move, the impending financial collapse brought the scheme to an end and the shell of the proposed building remains a memorial to the shattered reputation of the bank.

The National Asset Management Agency (NAMA) was the outcome of this extreme expression of greed and corruption, with cross-membership of the boards of Anglo, the DDDA and property company tycoons. NAMA so desperately tried to be squeaky-clean that it created a smell all of its own, part of it deriving from the climate of revenge on the whole band of developers, many of them shrewd, honest and courageous businessmen who had transformed the physical face of Ireland. The good and the bad were mortified together. Their vilification and punishment was pursued through NAMA by means of a gross distortion of fairness, transparency and natural justice.

NAMA was staffed by people who did not understand the complexities of the development that had failed largely because of a political lack of control and bankers who had lost their reasoning powers. It was protected by a blanket of secrecy, its activities fuelled by a desire to recover money in accordance with arguably flawed legislative processes, though checking on this was made difficult by the operation of NAMA. Proper scrutiny was absent. The implication was given that deals were being done that were profitable to the taxpayer. In reality, it was like a huge car-boot sale with any real actuarial standards absent, often through ignorance. NAMA worked under cover of the Official Secrets Act, or was hidden behind 'protection of commercial interests'.

The deals were worsening the country's debt. NAMA was issuing billions of euro in Government-guaranteed bonds to purchase the bad loans from the failed banks. The failed banks swapped these bonds for loans from the European Central Bank in part to repay senior bondholders. Once swapped, these NAMA loans became fully repayable with interest, and it is the taxpayers of the country who are footing the bill.

A minority shareholding of the beneficiaries from these deals—49 per cent—is the people of Ireland. The majority shareholding, however, consists of private investors in NAMA, protected within a master Special Purpose Vehicle, or SPV (which may create further SPVs). These investors were thought to include the subsidiaries and companies of the very same banks that benefit from taxpayers' funding and guarantee. In Ireland, therefore, the turkeys did end up voting for Christmas. Furthermore, it is quite possible that a group of these 'investors'—the beneficial owners of the NAMA SPV—could avail of a lenient or zero tax on the profits and dividends made from their 51 per cent ownership, and walk off with a prize at Ireland's expense. It was even possible that some of the NAMA master SPV investors were the self-same senior bondholders. If this was the case, then they were making money in many ways, with limited risk because of Ireland's banking guarantees.

Furthermore, the banks, which planned to sell NAMA bonds on the international markets, were forced of necessity to sell to the ECB. This was embarrassing for the European Commission, which had signed off on the NAMA plan, and devastating for Ireland, demonstrating underlying incompetence. The international markets called the State's bluff. The bailout was chasing after the wind, as it says in Ecclesiastes, and the Irish people are left to deal with the consequences.

In an interview in 2009 Brian Cowen readily recognised how deeply NAMA had split the country and he offered a defence, saying that the arguments were 'wildly exaggerated' and were 'reinforcing fear and worry and concern in people'. But he stuck with NAMA, saying: 'It's worked in other countries.' He claimed it had been done to help restructure the banks, to improve the flow of investment money into the economy, as well as working capital for Irish businesses 'trying to keep their show on the road and pay wages and meet debts and get their products into the marketplace, and adapt to the new situation they're trying to contend with'. He concluded:

> And the third thing to say is, banks get money from lending to two places—from deposits in the bank or from what they call 'wholesale money markets', people who trade in money, other financial institutions outside the country.
> Now, the problem is that that money isn't being made available into [sic] the Irish banks to the extent that we want it because those people [ECB] want to be clear as to what is the level of problem in

the banks, regarding the distressed assets, loans that are going bad, because until they see that then they're not able to assess what support they're prepared to give it or what money they're prepared to put into the system. The problem is if we leave things as they are, you're seeing a rationing of credit going out to the system, which is depriving people of keeping businesses that could otherwise be kept going—and that's what we're trying to do.

Virtually none of this happened. NAMA, instead of dividing the country, diminished its own share of support from the public, insofar as the public understood what was going on and they certainly did not believe Cowen's claim that NAMA would not cost the taxpayer.

We're not handing over money for these loans; what we're doing is handing over an IOU. Those IOUs are then presented to the European Central Bank and money is obtained from them at a rate of 1.5%. And that enables the banks then to lend on that money to the wider economy. What's this about? It's about turning the problem into being part of the solution. Getting those loans, valuing them down to what their present market value is; yes, it's putting in [sic] a long-term economic value on them as well because at the moment there's no market. In fact, we're making it clear that if there are any profits to be made, it [sic] will stay with the taxpayer.

Enda Kenny, in September 2009, expressed his own rejection of NAMA as an approach that was 'not fair because it protects the banks and the speculators and it doesn't protect the taxpayer'. He insisted that Fine Gael's proposal would 'allow the banks and the speculators who caused this problem in the first incidence to take a hit for it before you expose the taxpayer'. He pointed out that 85 per cent of supporters of the Green Party said they did not support NAMA. He was scathing of the Peter Bacon report on NAMA:

Normally, in a financial crisis as big as this—biggest in the history of the State— you would have expected a raft of opinions given to all the parties with these words: 'We want to sort this out. These are our views. What are yours?' Instead of that, they said during the summer, 'It's NAMA and NAMA only.' Brian Cowen said we would write whatever cheques are necessary to keep the banks going, which is an indication of what's happening here. Our view was stated six or eight months ago. Set up a recovery bank and get money for the small businesses.

Other voices were deeply sceptical. Desmond O'Malley, speaking of the banks and NAMA, said:

It may have an appalling effect on this country and this economy for years to come. It's really impossible to foretell because what we now know about it is different from what we were told two years ago when it started or the idea came up first. They were talking a couple of years ago about NAMA making a profit, believe it or not, now every penny is down the drain.

NAMA, of course, soldiered on. Its processes are brutal. It brought virtually all private enterprise development to a shuddering stop. It robbed the developers of their assets and sold off, in circumstances that can be repeatedly shown as ill-judged and simplistic, hugely important portfolios for short-term public gain.

The leadership of NAMA involved John Mulcahy, Brendan McDonagh and Frank Daly, the last a former civil servant and Revenue Commissioner. There has always been scepticism about their qualifications to assess and appraise developments in spite of 'expert' status, a term applied by Shane Ross in September 2009 when he described John Mulcahy as 'the rabbit pulled out of the hat' by Brian Lenihan in his address to a Dáil committee meeting. Mulcahy described himself as a 'bear' in the property market, advocating the strength of the property bubble, for some of its history, but hardly reassuring his audience of deputies and senators who were trying to grapple with the property downturn. Ross described him as 'national puffer' for NAMA. Ross continued:

John Mulcahy personifies the perversity of NAMA. He is being employed by the buyer [the State] to puff the sellers' properties. While Mulcahy will officially be acting for the State, the selling banks will be cheering him on from the sidelines. Quite a perverse position. The whole NAMA industry will row in behind him, including independent valuers, soon to be appointed to price those worthless NAMA assets. According to reliable reports, all the usual suspects have already tendered for work as NAMA valuers. Not surprising, as it is the only work in town.

Ross's main point was that the same people who had puffed the property market for nearly a decade would be the ideal 'independent' valuers of NAMA properties. And he added: 'They had so much spoofing practice in the boom years that puffing the NAMA properties will be second nature to them.' At that stage the claim was being made that the property market was already improving. This was 'auctioneer-speak'.

Ross quoted Morgan Kelly, whom he described as 'the noblest hero of the entire property boom-to-bust'. Two years previously Kelly had been severely criticised for predicting that property prices would fall by 50 per cent. By the time Brian Lenihan gave his spirited defence of NAMA to Oireachtas members, Kelly had more credibility on property valuations than the combined wisdom of all the flawed auctioneers, bankers and compromised economists in the entire nation. And he was predicting that property values could remain below their 2009 levels for a decade. Not music to the ears of NAMA zealots. It was Kelly, incidentally, who had predicted, in early 2008, a banking collapse.

NAMA was seen by many as being at the root of the nation's troubles and was essentially not operated in taxpayers' interests; instead, in a narrow sense, it helped create the enormous black hole Ireland faces. It is responsible for drawing Europe into that hole. Despite their high professional standing, it is questionable whether those running NAMA are sufficiently qualified in judgment to assess the wide range of development projects the organisation is taking over. Its powers are draconian, breaching or disregarding constitutional, property and human rights. There is no doubt that NAMA has distorted the property market, which in the current and foreseeable climate of operation means bringing the whole of it to a sudden halt.

It induced fear in foreign banks and both domestic and foreign market interests where the valuation process was not understood. NAMA's purpose was to recover for the taxpayer cash from the transferred 'toxic' bank debts. That philosophic Minister, Dermot Ahern, said the Government would 'mete out excessive pain on these developers....'

NAMA set the parameters for the valuation of all Irish property and thus all loans. NAMA prescribed the write-down without knowing how big the hole it was creating would be. Talk about 'known unknowns' —this was a world of 'unknown' unknowns, mainly owing to ignorance. There are instances cited of prime redevelopment sites given discounts of 80 per cent because NAMA said so, and not because the market would have said so.

In trying to rectify the climate of corruption which had boiled over in the collapse of the DDDA, NAMA offered ignorance combined with arrogance and secrecy. There was a property bubble, no doubt there was over-gearing. But the whole sorry mess, if managed properly, would have cost the State far less. The State should then have sought help from the ECB. Instead, NAMA dug on and the hole got deeper.

If Europe had cared about Ireland, it would have insisted on NAMA being reversed and its grossly offensive legal constraints repealed. But Europe did not care. Europe involved itself for Europe's sake.

With the change of Government, in March 2011, NAMA's tune changed too. It indulged in publicity stunts, such as giving a valuable painting by John Lavery (confiscated from a developer) to the National Gallery. More recently it undertook a €3 million transfer to the upgrading of derelict and deserted estates, a drop in the ocean as far as the extent of vacant and defective properties is concerned.

In respect of its costly attempt to take over Paddy McKillen's property portfolio, NAMA's ineptitude over the legal detail not only lost it the case but cost the State an estimated €7 million in legal fees. NAMA has announced its withdrawal from further legal action.

NAMA faced another legal challenge in July 2011 from David Daly and his two children, Joanne and Paul, whose property portfolio is the subject of discussions between Deutsche Bank and NAMA, from which the Dalys are excluded despite the fact that the family was responsible for bringing the German bank in to take over the finance from Allied Irish Bank.

Declan Ganley was always blunt in his dismissal:

NAMA is a pawn shop for the ECB as a means for us to extract cash out of the ECB to prop up zombie banks that should already be bust and shouldn't exist any more. NAMA should never have been established and it should be wound down and the distress loan books should be sold off in a fire sale. And we hit the reset button. We need to deliver debt relief to where it's most urgent, which is out there amongst consumers in households. Certainly, we need mortgage relief in this country. We cannot expect to see recovery in this country while we've got families across the length and breadth of this land that are sitting in negative equity with huge debt stones [*sic*] around their necks. That's who needs relief, not failed private banks. It's the families of this country who need to see relief. We need a proper action—what the market would do in this situation which is correct—by selling distress loan books off for however many cents in the euro and the buyers of those loan books and mortgage books do a renegotiation with those mortgage holders.

And in the shortest paragraph in his article entitled 'Ten Steps for the Economy', or what he would do as Taoiseach, published at the end of 2010, David McWilliams wrote:

Close down NAMA immediately. It serves no purpose other than to give the debts of the developers and the banks to the people and we don't want this. Furthermore, the whole purpose of NAMA was to ensure that the banks remained in private hands; now that they have been largely nationalised, there is no point to NAMA other than to generate fees for professionals. So close it down. The property market would clear more quickly as a result, which is an added bonus.

Chapter 15

COWEN'S POLITICAL DEMISE

It seemed that the deep snows of December and the unrelenting cold froze hearts and minds in the political arena. Ireland had been forced into the bailout. The nation had been ordered to budget for four years and the terms and conditions were imposed from Europe. An election was on the horizon, its date still uncertain but its inevitability hanging like the heavy grey clouds filled with yet more snow overhead. No one knew what policies the election would be fought on. It had been narrowed down to a much deeper issue, the complete removal of Fianna Fáil from power. This had become the overriding issue.

Fianna Fáil did not know what to do. The gap between the party and its leader was widening. Senior Ministers were speculating on the future. Essentially, as December progressed through ice and snow, they were clinging on to the idea of an election delayed until March, by which time, surely, something would turn up. Mary Hanafin predicted this on the grounds that the Finance bill would take weeks and that the country might wait until St Patrick's Day. Brian Lenihan battled his way through a draconian banking bill, having lost all the money, so that he was left trying to control bonuses. A mid-December opinion poll showed that Micheál Martin was the favourite to succeed Cowen as leader if this event were to take place.

Movement then came from an unexpected source when Bertie Ahern, in a sequence of statements, declared he would not contest his seat in the next Dáil, would not stand for the presidency and then issued a merciless attack on Brian Cowen's leadership, blaming him for the bailout and for not communicating with the Irish people. No one leapt to Cowen's defence. The only person standing up for him in public was Tony Killeen, the Defence Minister, who described Ahern's attack as 'a little unfair'.

Within a week of Ahern's attack came the publication of *The FitzPatrick Tapes* and a new range of questions for Cowen, closely followed by articles in the *Irish Independent* and the *Irish Daily Mail* giving an entirely different view of the truth about what Cowen knew in 2008 in the run-up to the banking crisis, about which he had consistently denied he had earlier knowledge than the night of the Bank Guarantee.

Fianna Fáil's blind but bedrock mantra was always to show loyalty to the leader. Yet here it had been broken by the most extraordinary figure of all, the former leader, who, by tradition, does not re-enter the political arena once he has departed. In the case of Cowen, it is still hard to comprehend how he managed to remain in power. His last political act was to resign but to stay on as Taoiseach, a choice, not a constitutional necessity, leaving him the rare and singular role of being a witness to the election, yet outside it.

There had been, during his brief tenure, several opportunities to oust Cowen. The one that was tailor-made to justify a push against him was the Galway drinking controversy. It did not happen, mainly because the obvious challengers lacked the necessary courage. It was also believed that there was no push on Cowen during the Galway debacle because 'many of the lads had pints with him and were embarrassed' by the controversy. 'It was extraordinary to be in the middle of it. It was like the party was sleep-walking to its death. They didn't seem to have the nerve or the steel within them to deal with the issue. It's like they were tired,' recalls one former Minister.

It represents an incredible death-wish on the part of Fianna Fáil that, knowing what a mess Cowen had made, knowing how unpopular he had become, knowing how irrecoverable his standing was, that he was a heavy drinker, his political character gruff, blunt and at times brutal, and that his career in office from the spring of 2008 into the autumn of 2010 had been a succession of miscalculations and grave mistakes, the Fianna Fáil TDs and senators were still prepared to go into the next general election—whenever it might be—with him at the helm.

The situation itself had become irretrievable because the obvious contenders for the leadership, among them Micheál Martin and Brian Lenihan, knew the party was in for an inevitable slaughter and did not want to be in charge. At least that was the theory. Additionally, there was a lingering assumption that Cowen could 'beat Kenny hands down' in the TV debates and sway voters, according to one former Minister, and this despite the relentless fall in the polls. This was combined with an almost mindless belief that Fianna Fáil 'were doing the right thing' and this would be recognised by the electorate.

Another prospect—that in the event of a successful heave against Cowen, the party would do better—foundered on the realisation that the Greens wouldn't stomach the idea of a yet another Taoiseach without a mandate. Rather than having the Greens pull out, party members fatalistically put up with Cowen's appalling record. The pervasive fear was of losing their own seats. Though this happened anyway, staying on left alive the hope that they would manage to turn the corner. The trouble was, according to Dr James Reilly, Fine Gael deputy leader, 'they turned the corner and went into a ditch'.

It is perhaps ironic that it is Cowen—a man who spoke about being 'always loyal to the party'—who will be blamed for blindly driving Fianna Fáil into the 'ditch', in part because of his connections with members of the board of Anglo Irish Bank. On this issue Cowen's people, according to sources, had been made aware of what was in *The FitzPatrick Tapes*. This was before the book was released. Cowen wondered if publication could be pushed back, maybe to the summer, but it was clear that this was an impossible ask. However, Cowen felt that he could easily and justifiably answer the claim made in the book by FitzPatrick that he had had only three conversations with him, the most memorable during a game of golf and lunch at the Druids Glen Hotel on 28 July 2008, which lasted for seven hours. This was when Cowen had already become Taoiseach.

The public were never going to accept that the FitzPatrick controversy was all about simple social occasions. Nevertheless, that was exactly how Cowen attempted to describe them when it was brought up during a heated Leader's Questions session in the Dáil. When Enda Kenny asked Cowen to clarify if the three meetings revealed in the book were the times he had met with FitzPatrick, the Taoiseach replied: 'I don't believe I had any other social contact with

Mr FitzPatrick since then. I don't believe so.'

Cowen described it as an 'absurd conspiracy theory' by the Opposition that he had somehow acted improperly. But then things took a turn for the worse right before Brian Cowen's eyes, there in the Dáil chamber on 13 January 2011. Sinn Féin parliamentary leader, Caoimhghín Ó Caoláin, stood up and revealed that he had been in the hotel on the same day. This forced Cowen's hand. He had to admit that Gary McGann and Alan Gray, the former a director of Anglo and the latter a director of the Central Bank, had attended the event. The other person there had been Fintan Drury, one of Cowen's closest friends, who also happened to be a director of Anglo.

In his lengthy statements to the Dáil, Cowen failed to answer crucial questions. He concealed details of significant conversations about Anglo Irish Bank held with senior bank staff, board members and other politicians. He denied exchanges that have been clearly claimed by others.

Cowen went on after that to continue with prevarications and to misrepresent the truth. He was wrong to refer to Dr Michael Somers, the former head of the National Treasury Management Agency, as having 'discredited' the Drumm claim over the NTMA. Somers, like the Taoiseach himself, could only deny this. This was what Brian Cowen had been doing over the events of the previous three years in respect of the banks, and notably Anglo Irish Bank.

According to those close to Cowen, he was still not overly concerned with the revelations. States one former Minister:

> You have to understand that Fintan Drury was in school [UCD] with Cowen and they had been friendly. It would be like you walking up to me and saying, 'We must go for a game of golf some day.' I don't think he knew Seanie was going to be there. Hindsight is great, people like Shane Ross extolling the virtues of Seanie FitzPatrick. 'We need more of these fellas.' You could make a big thing out of all this, but in politics you meet all sorts of people.

Another former Minister felt that the Drury connection 'was fairly catastrophic as well'. Even though Drury, 'in fairness was a good communication guy', he believes:

One of the biggest things that hurt Cowen was that Drury was in at the beginning doing some of the communications management and then he became too hot to handle because of the Anglo board membership he had. He had to be put out of the equation. He was in directing and advising him on PR very early in his regime. He then had to be taken out because the media started inquiring into contracts he had.... He had a whole load of contracts that people were asking questions about. And then he was on the board of Anglo. He was kind of removed from contact with the Taoiseach, do you see the point why?

Cowen thought he could brazen it all out. But then the story snowballed into an avalanche. Firstly, perhaps unintentionally, Gray put a big hole in Cowen's version of the day as a social occasion when he admitted in a press statement on 13 January that he had been invited to attend the event to 'provide independent ideas to stimulate economic growth and to reduce unemployment'.

Then the Tánaiste Mary Coughlan, who laughingly tried to criticise Drumm and FitzPatrick for 'running to journalists', claimed that the infamous meeting at Druids Glen was to discuss fundraising for Fianna Fáil. Again, this would hardly make it a social event. It appeared from looking at this unfold that Drumm had been right in November 2010 when he had said Cowen's kitchen cabinet comprised FitzPatrick, Alan Gray, Paddy Mullarkey and Fintan Drury. Drury had always attempted to distance himself from any type of adviser role to such an extent that he had previously threatened legal action against such claims.

Two days earlier, on 11 January, the *Irish Times* had published an interview by Simon Carswell with David Drumm. The interview was described by Carswell as 'out of character'; certainly Drumm had been an elusive figure, always declining questions from the media. This interview was granted in direct response to *The FitzPatrick Tapes* and Carswell put to Drumm the claim by FitzPatrick that he had not known until just before the Bank Guarantee of the crisis facing Anglo Irish Bank. This was also Cowen's claim. FitzPatrick had said that 'Drumm was running his own show', excluding FitzPatrick from central matters at the bank. Drumm's reply to this was dramatic: 'It is not credible that he did not know anything about the bank's funding problem through

2008. That is just an unbelievable statement to make. He was in my office three or four times a day lecturing me about what I needed to do.'

Drumm said that funding was a concern from 'early in the financial crisis in 2007 and remained on its agenda throughout 2008'. Drumm also challenged FitzPatrick's view that he had played no part in Drumm's succession as CEO. He 'pushed' Drumm into the job. FitzPatrick, according to Drumm in this interview, took charge again at Anglo Irish Bank in March 2008 after the failure of Bear Stearns in the USA caused losses. He was in the bank on a daily basis in an office down the corridor from Drumm's. This had a deleterious effect on bank staff, who did not know who was in charge and did not understand fully why FitzPatrick had returned to do a job from which he had resigned.

The story would not go away. Cowen refused to be drawn on the interview when Ó Caoláin asked him about it in yet another heated Dáil debate. A smug Cowen simply said he wouldn't be commenting on it because the Opposition would then come back with more dirt to throw at him. It was a feeble answer.

Earlier that morning, Dr Michael Somers went on the Pat Kenny radio show to state that he had never received an instruction from Cowen, then Finance Minister, to ask the agency to deposit sovereign funds with Anglo. However, Somers did admit that there had been some pressure at 'official level' to put more money into the banks. 'I made it very clear that if we were to put any money with the banks, I required written direction from the Minister for Finance. That was my legal advice, and I stuck to it,' he stated. He also revealed that he did receive a written request from Cowen in 2008 not to withdraw money from the Irish banking system. On the argument that Drumm had put forward about Anglo Irish Bank being discriminated against by the NTMA, since they had only €40 billion, compared with the €200 billion with AIB and Bank of Ireland, he stated:

We probably looked more favourably on AIB and Bank of Ireland on the basis that they were systemically important to the Irish country, that the country couldn't get on without them. Now we would have taken a somewhat different view of Anglo. We didn't regard it as being in the same league as the two Irish institutions. They weren't essential for normal day-to-day banking. You didn't get your salary paid in there. If you wanted a mortgage for your house, you didn't go near them.

If Somers was clearly stating that Anglo was not of 'systemic' importance to the country, why had Brian Cowen and Brian Lenihan taken the view in September 2008 when they issued the blanket Bank Guarantee that the toxic bank was, in fact, of systemic importance?

Dr Somers refused to deny that there had not been any pressure from so-called 'official level'. This seemed to confirm Drumm's story. In the Dáil debate, Cowen became annoyed with Caoimhghín Ó Caoláin and threatened to sue him if he repeated any of his accusations outside the chamber. On 18 January the Sinn Féin TD issued a press release encouraging Cowen to take legal action when he asked the same fundamental questions: 'How appropriate was it that a director of the Central Bank, appointed by the Taoiseach, would be engaged in debate on matters fiscal and economic, job creation and budgetary issues with three, either then or previous, senior directors of Anglo Irish Bank?'

His second question was:

Why did it take a question from me in the course of Leader's Questions for the Taoiseach to offer the information that it was not only a golf outing with Seán FitzPatrick and Fintan Drury, but that he was also meeting that evening with Gary McGann and Alan Gray, a director of the Central Bank and a member of the Irish Financial Services Regulatory Authority, whom the Taoiseach had appointed when Minister for Finance in January 2007? Why did the Taoiseach not offer that information previously?

He also asked Cowen to comment on Drumm's claim that he spent at least an hour briefing him on the issues in regard to Anglo Irish Bank. 'Is Mr Drumm lying or is it that the Taoiseach cannot recall all of the details?'

The press statement concluded with this allegation:

It has been reported that Mr Drumm has secured a deal with Anglo Irish Bank which will block the Garda Síochána gaining access to confidential reports which are to be revealed in the context of Mr

Drumm's court case in the US. Is there any basis to these reports? Is there any fear that Mr Drumm will evade full scrutiny in this jurisdiction and prosecution if same be appropriate because of this? Did the Minister for Finance or anyone approve such an arrangement as inferred from the reports before us?

Cowen did not start legal proceedings against the Sinn Féin deputy. It appears highly unlikely that he will ever do so.

These revelations about Cowen's connections with Anglo led to whisperings in Leinster House that Fianna Fáil was 'now fucked over' by association with the bank and would haemorrhage even more seats in the forthcoming general election. The view was that it squared the circle for the electorate. One former Minister put it bluntly: 'All Fianna Fáil, the bankers, developers—they are all in it together. The image of it absolutely ruined us. It confirmed what people suspected—part of the reason the economy went off the rail [sic] was that all these developers and bankers and politicians were in that fatal embrace with each other, you know.'

Surprisingly, none of Cowen's Cabinet colleagues had discussed the Anglo controversy with him. The ex-Minister continued: 'To be honest, I don't think it even registered. The only thing with FitzPatrick was annoyance. How the fuck is he still out there? Why is he not in prison? It was exasperating how the investigation was not speeded up.'

After the Drumm interview was published, Eamon Gilmore went to the plinth with his front bench and declared he was going to put down a motion of no confidence in Cowen. The logical thinking was that surely even the Green Party could not stomach this any longer. After all, the Greens themselves were being ridiculed with their backtracking on their call for a general election in January, which they were now claiming had been misinterpreted because they meant the date for an election should be announced in January. But nobody was buying that. Besides, independents Michael Lowry and Jackie Healy-Rae had both publicly declared back in September 2010 after the Galway drinking controversy that they would not support a new Taoiseach and would withdraw their support for the Government if Fianna Fáil tried to oust Cowen.

However, Fine Gael was aghast at the idea of the no confidence vote, fearing that, once again, it would give the coalition the chance to put on a united front and the Government's term of office would drag on for even longer.

On the morning of 14 January 2011, what was meant to be a routine parliamentary party meeting for Fianna Fáil was dramatically postponed until 3pm after rumours emerged that a motion of no confidence in Cowen's leadership was going to be put down. 'We didn't like it, the Anglo controversy. That became the subject of whispers and groups and cabals and all that,' recalls Mary O'Rourke.

Cowen was calm at the meeting. 'The old Brian Cowen I knew was an irrational Brian Cowen. He could tell you off very quickly. The Brian Cowen who became Taoiseach was very measured, his head was cool,' says Batt O'Keeffe. At the meeting, several TDs were surprised when Cowen stated he wouldn't be stepping down and that there were procedures in place if anybody wanted to challenge his leadership— effectively putting it up to the would-be challengers to seek the 18 signatures needed to do so. He then said he would consult with many TDs and senators over the coming days to decide what was in the 'best interest' of the Fianna Fáil party. This was taken as an indication that Cowen was looking for a dignified exit, rather than being pushed. One of his former Ministers says:

> There was an expectation that he would stand down himself; that was very much the mood going into the weekend. The expectation was that he was going to throw in the towel and do the decent thing. When he stood up at the parliamentary party meeting and said that he would ring colleagues to see what the feeling was, the point was generally expected that this ringing was easing himself out, that he was going to take himself off the pitch likely by talking to lads rather than it being brought to a natural vote. I don't know whether it was all just a big fucking send-up on his part? What happened then was he did the opposite.

After the parliamentary meeting ended, Cowen and Pat Carey walked back to the Taoiseach's office and chatted for 20 minutes. By the time they had finished talking, there were several TDs waiting to speak to the Taoiseach. 'At the end of the day, this is your call,' was the approach adopted by many of the TDs. The TDs who talked to him that day noticed an 'air of resignation' in his demeanour; reading between the lines they felt Cowen's attitude was, 'This is as far as I can take it. I don't think I can go any further.' They always felt that you had to be 'very tuned in' to what Cowen was communicating because 'often there were disjointed enough comments; he might say something in the morning and then in the afternoon he'd say something else, and you would try to join them together to see what he's really talking about'. But to most it was clear on that Friday that Cowen had 'certainly got to the stage where he felt there wasn't much more that he could have done'. He appeared 'aware' of his declining popularity and 'exhausted from work', they observed. So what made Cowen change his mind and decide to fight on?

'It was said that Batt O'Keeffe and a few others went in to him and put fire into his belly,' states one former Minister. Another former Minister agrees that 'something happened' that day. 'Whoever did it I'm not sure, but somebody put fire in his belly because [before this] there was an air of resignation about his approach,' he agrees.

O'Keeffe put together a War Cabinet comprising Mary Coughlan, Tony Killeen and Noel Dempsey. Cowen placed a lot of confidence in his 'good mate' Dempsey and could 'see great value in how meticulous he was' with his own Department. 'Cowen saw Dempsey as having the kind of level of detail you need in Cabinet,' states one of his former Cabinet colleagues. But even though he was 'very solid', some of Cowen's people felt that there was a 'pig-headedness' about how Dempsey would sometimes make decisions that were 'anything but political'; thus he 'pissed off people with his lower limits for drink-driving'.

While Dermot Ahern was also consulted, there had never been a good relationship between him and Cowen, but they had become close allies when Cowen was appointed as Taoiseach, even though Ahern resented how the Fianna Fáil leader had been anointed by Bertie. But Ahern was so determined to support Cowen that he would later vote for his Taoiseach in the motion of confidence from his hospital bed after recovering from back surgery.

They also knew that Eamon Ó Cuív, whom they perceived as a 'strange animal', was on their side because he had received the Social

Welfare portfolio. 'Everybody was marshalled,' as one of the ex-Ministers puts it, but they didn't approach Micheál Martin or Pat Carey because of Carey's friendship with Mary Hanafin, 'whom we didn't go near because we knew what she was playing'. Even though they didn't approach the former Chief Whip, they still found Carey to be 'very forthcoming' in his support.

'Hanafin, I think, grew to like Cowen over time. Forget the end game and the way things panned out, Hanafin was a very good Minister, solid, effective. Micheál was an excellent Minister for Foreign Affairs. He got on with it. He had a tough time as well [with tragedy in his personal life]. He played a sound game,' states one of their former Cabinet colleagues.

But Hanafin didn't publicly speak out against Cowen. According to one of her close allies, it was because 'if she has a weakness, it was her loyalty' to the leader, 'even though she wouldn't have been particularly close to Cowen'. Hanafin also gave the impression that 'she was genuinely not sure what she wanted to do'. States one of her close colleagues:

> [Hanafin was] anxious to try and be there but as deputy leader rather than challenging for the leadership itself. I think she would have been happy to be deputy leader, but there was nobody working in concert. People have this notion that everything was highly organised. Like most things that happen in most parties, there's a fair bit of shambles that goes on.

Knowing that most of the Cabinet was 'solid', O'Keeffe quickly brought in 13 members of the Bar Lobby who indicated they would be supporting the Taoiseach.

'And then before the vote we were absolutely confident we'd win it three to one. Our strength was in his enemies. John McGuinness, Ned O'Keeffe, Fucking Seán Power, M.J. Nolan. That's where the strength was, in their weakness,' recalled one former Minister.

Cowen's hopes of holding on dwindled daily. On 15 January the *Irish Independent*'s page one headline read: 'Cowen's close friends tell him it's time to go'. Cowen's great strength, up to this point, had been his outstanding electoral capacities. He had been a strong fighter on the hustings, a powerful debater in electoral confrontations and in theory a better leader to go into an electoral situation that had all the appearances of the Valley of Death. But he was now seriously flawed, in particular over the Anglo Irish Bank revelations.

Mary O'Rourke said that many TDs decided to vote for Cowen because it was 'too late to change leader' at this stage. However, even though Cowen was spending that Saturday morning on the phone talking to TDs from his home in Tullamore, many were not inspired by the conversation.

'He didn't have a pitch at all,' recalled one former Junior Minister. He said: 'I set out my views and told him that my constituents were looking for a change.' Several of the TDs also said that, even though they felt there was a need for a change of leader, they wouldn't make public their view because of their friendship with Cowen. It appeared that nobody wanted to declare publicly against their drinking buddy, even though they knew in their heart it was the right thing to do.

'I said I wasn't going to be making public my views in the contest because he was a pal of mine for quite some time,' admitted one TD.

Such is the nature of the man, Cowen remained calm and polite when TDs informed him that they felt it would be better if he resigned. 'The general view was that he wasn't the man to lead the party into the next election and I told him that. He thanked me for letting him know my position in an honest and forthright manner,' recalls Seán Haughey.

By mid-January Cowen and his Cabinet were all in confusion as the party leader undertook further consultations within Fianna Fáil. Those closest to him maintained that he intended to stay on and lead Fianna Fáil into an election. This was now broadly planned for mid-March. Cowen himself was clearly perplexed. He had no plan and no strategy. He was in the hands of a divided, confused and demoralised organisation. 'I am having a discussion with colleagues,' he told RTÉ's 'Six-One News'. 'As leader of the party, I will sit down with them in an atmosphere of mutual respect and solidarity and decide what I believe to be the collective view of the party.' There was no collective view. There was no mutual respect. There was no solidarity. And Cowen ended lamely when he indicated a spent and inadequate appeal mechanism for Fianna Fáil members. He said: 'It is within the entitlement of anyone in the party to use the procedures that are there if they wish to have any matter raised other than by myself'. At this time his own consultation process within the party had shifted in emphasis. He was no longer counting heads and assessing whether he had the support to fight on; he was assessing the mood of Fianna Fáil and discovering that, although there was no stomach for his removal by a party vote, there was no remaining faith in him to achieve any electoral recovery. At this point in the process that was leaching credibility from the whole organisation, he was the only matter left that had to be resolved. Alarmingly, instead of confronting this, Micheál Martin welcomed the consultation process.

Eventually, an exasperated Micheál Martin informed Cowen that he was going to challenge him for the leadership. He said he planned to announce it that evening at a press conference. When he offered his resignation, Cowen told him that the matter could be dealt with later. By keeping his Cabinet position as Foreign Minister, Micheál Martin delivered an unspoken but plain message that he anticipated defeat. A true leader would have gone into the wilderness first and then challenged the man he sought to replace. Martin's behaviour was at best eccentric, at worst defeatist.

'They did it in a man-like fashion. He understood where he was coming from and Micheál had to understand he was standing firm,' says one of Cowen's Cabinet members.

As soon as the conversation with Martin ended, Cowen rang some close advisers and informed them of Martin's intentions. They needed a plan quickly. It was decided that Cowen would put down a motion of confidence in himself at the party's next parliamentary meeting on Tuesday. By calling a vote of confidence, Cowen's team knew it would signal an expectation of victory. A hastily arranged press conference to announce Cowen's surprise move was organised at the Alexander Hotel later that afternoon. That evening, Martin held his news conference to explain that he intended to vote against Cowen because he believed 'the survival of the party was at stake'. Martin claimed that one of the reasons for his decision to withdraw his support for Cowen was the poor handling of the IMF saga, which he described as a 'watershed moment'.

'Ministers came out, from my information, without the full knowledge of what was actually going on,' he stated at his press conference. It appeared bizarre that Martin focused on the IMF rather than Cowen's connections with Anglo's directors. When Martin spoke at his press conference of the smoking ban in public places as his main achievement, hearts must have sunk. Where was the real man? Was he standing up at all? Astonishingly, he had no voice on reform, on remedying our collapsed sovereignty, on greater respect for the Constitution and on a different approach on our debt. Despite his ministerial responsibilities, he had nothing to offer on how to deal with Europe.

On 18 January, only hours before the parliamentary party meeting was to take place, Cowen was given a shot of confidence when Brian Lenihan went on RTÉ radio and endorsed the Taoiseach, saying he was the best person to 'lead us into this election'. He argued that the 'current financial matters made it impossible' for him to 'disrupt the good working relationship' with Cowen. One of Lenihan's close allies states:

> [Lenihan] shot himself in the foot by doing this interview where he was backing Cowen. It was really bizarre why he decided to do that interview. He should have stayed silent on the whole thing …. He did lose credibility because he endorsed Cowen and everybody knew he'd been sounding opinion on becoming the alternative at that stage. I think he just proved to be on the gutless side…. The bottom line was: he was gutless.

After the Finance Minister's public backing of Cowen, an irate John McGuinness quickly went out and told the media that Lenihan had been misleading the party's rebel TDs.

> Lenihan did express an interest in the leadership and that is what is shocking about what he revealed today, because that is not what he had to say to us during the past 12 months. I think what Brian Lenihan has been saying to you is not what he has been saying to the backbenchers. He did encourage dissent, he did encourage us to look at the numbers.

Shortly after 9pm that night, the Government Chief Whip, John Curran, announced that Cowen had won the vote of confidence. It was felt that the Taoiseach had engaged in a peculiar distortion of the principle behind the secret ballot, using a party device not only to conceal the measure of support for and opposition to himself but also to destroy the evidence by shredding the ballot papers.

Martin was then forced to resign from the Cabinet but he was still insisting that Cowen 'continues to have my full support as head of Government'. But, as it turned out, things were about to get even more curious for Cowen…. 'If Cowen hadn't made the second mistake, Micheál was fucked,' points out one of Cowen's allies.

That 'second mistake' as the ex-Minister puts it, was one of the most extraordinary moments in Irish politics.

| COWEN'S ENDGAME

After he had won the confidence vote on 18 January, Brian Cowen's ego was suddenly restored. It was this renewed confidence that, according to those close to him, led to his dramatic fall. With his days numbered in low single figures, Cowen followed desperate advice that might have helped the party in happier times but was absurd in the circumstances. This was to seek the immediate resignation of Cabinet members who were not going to stand anyway and fill the vacant places with deputies who would still be fighting for seats. It would give them some kind of advantage.

Cowen called Mary Harney to ask for her resignation. For a second time, according to a senior Minister, she warned him, 'Look, I'm not running. I have no problem [resigning] but I don't think it's the right thing to do.' Unfortunately again, he did not listen. Cowen told Noel Dempsey, Dermot Ahern, Tony Killeen, who was retiring after a battle with cancer, and Harney to hand in their resignations, which were announced the following day, 20 January. Batt O'Keeffe's resignation was later because Cowen had never planned for him to go. On the day Cowen was making his changes, O'Keeffe informed the Taoiseach that he had been planning to announce at the upcoming convention his plan to retire, but now that everybody else was retiring, he felt honour-bound to also offer his resignation. According to those close to the two men, Cowen 'wasn't pleased' about O'Keeffe's departure.

However, it was all orchestrated to appear that it was the Ministers' decision themselves to resign. Mary Harney drew up a statement saying that she had informed the Taoiseach the previous week of her decision to step down as Minister for Health because she wouldn't be running in the election, but Cowen had requested her to hold off on announcing this until then. O'Keeffe retained his Education portfolio because he hadn't made up his mind about retiring from politics. He was verging on the side of not running because a private poll was showing it was 'very tight' that Fianna Fáil would win only one of their two seats in Cork North-West but could risk losing even that if a second candidate ran. Feeling that it would be better to let the younger candidate run since he himself was reaching retirement age, O'Keeffe had mentioned in the bar one night to Cowen that he was considering not running, but was told, 'We'll talk about that later.' It seemed Cowen didn't want to talk about the possibility of battling against the tide in an election without his right-hand man.

Why did Cowen attempt to reshuffle his Cabinet? He had won the vote of confidence. He had conceded to Green Party demands for an election. He was facing a disastrous future whatever he did and would inevitably lose power. But he was still, at least nominally, in control and free to lead on. Yet he plunged himself and his party into a situation where he lost that control and became the creature of all around him, pilloried and discredited, his reputation doomed.

This was one of the most extraordinary moments in Irish politics and led first to the dissolution of the Dáil, then to Cowen's resignation as leader of Fianna Fáil, then to the inevitable defeat of the coalition— far worse than would have been the case if the choice of the moment had remained in Cowen's hands—and, finally, Cowen's departure from politics.

The reshuffle came about in unprecedented circumstances and demonstrated a critical aspect of the ways in which Fianna Fáil had parted company with the constitutional requirements of office, even down to collective Cabinet responsibility. According to one of Cowen's closest allies, during the consultation process before the vote of confidence, he was repeatedly told by his backbenchers that those Ministers not running in the impending general election 'should not be allowed to stay' in Cabinet.

'They were pressurising him to put these guys aside and make changes. He took notice of that and felt that coming into an election we would have new faces rather than tired old faces going out the door. That's the background [to] why Cowen changed the Cabinet,' he states.

Cowen received a mixed reaction when he broached the idea of reshuffling the Cabinet with those outgoing Ministers themselves. Even though it was rumoured that Dermot Ahern was annoyed at being forced to resign and that 'it wasn't a pretty scene' when he was given his marching orders, those close to Cowen rubbish this story and insist that the outgoing Justice Minister thought 'it was a good idea'. Noel Dempsey immediately agreed to offer his resignation, because he saw the value in pushing new faces forward for the election. 'But Mary Harney felt it would be the wrong thing to do. Absolutely opposed. She said the public and media wouldn't wear it,' recalls one former Minister.

Cowen was told by advisers that the Greens would probably pull out of Government if he attempted a reshuffle now. 'That's my fucking prerogative!' he snapped. Twice, according to sources, even his loyal lieutenant Batt O'Keeffe had forewarned him that the Greens would not accept the reshuffle.

After the debacle, it was rumoured that the Cabinet reshuffle idea had emerged on the night of the parliamentary party vote of confidence, as Cowen celebrated in the Dáil bar over a few drinks. Understandably, the victory had boosted his confidence and 'he got carried away'. 'He made the fundamental mistake and just didn't listen to people.' He was still being warned against the idea of a reshuffle. Why he did not listen to such advice is bizarre, but what is inexplicable is that he had not listened to the Greens, who later pointed out that they had previously warned Cowen not to go ahead with any new appointments. They said they could not have been clearer about the consequences of such action. But Cowen believed that he had 'answered any concerns' the Greens had about a reshuffle at a meeting the previous Monday morning.

States Mary O'Rourke:

I know someone who was in the bar, separately like, and I think somebody gave him the idea. 'You have the right now to make new Cabinet Ministers and to make new Junior Ministers and let's do this.' And that evolved in the Dáil bar—nowhere else. 'Ah, you know now, Taoiseach, you have the right, the prerogative, and you can appoint A, B, C, D.'

However, members of the Bar Lobby said it was 'very unfair' to Cowen to suggest that he was so riled up on the night that he had made the decision on 'the hoof', as had been claimed by many other TDs, because they maintain the Cabinet reshuffle idea had come from speaking to the backbenchers during the consultation period the previous weekend. 'But when the fucking thing went pear-shaped, the backbenchers were saying, "Fuck it, what a stupid idea!"' claims one of Cowen's allies.

The dramatic resignations took other members of the Cabinet by surprise. One former Minister recalls 'first having an inkling' when he heard the noisy sounds of shredders working overtime down the corridor. He asked: 'Is there something I should be told around here?' It was all happening so fast, he recalls, 'it was a blur'.

Another former Minister of State had heard whisperings earlier that morning about the planned reshuffle and instantly knew there was going to be a major backlash from the Greens. 'I thought it was a joke. The Bar Lobby getting a bit of a bolt. I thought it was a joke almost. It turned out to be true.'

After accepting the Ministers' resignations, Cowen then started to ring up some of the younger TDs and Junior Ministers to offer them senior Cabinet positions. As rumours started to spread that he had offered a dumbfounded Barry Andrews the Health portfolio, some of the young turks who didn't want to be associated with Cowen switched off their mobile phones, so they couldn't be offered ministerial portfolios. They feared an appointment at this late stage would be the kiss of death and didn't want to be propelled front and centre as the 'new face' of Fianna Fáil before an irate electorate. It would have been political suicide to be perceived as being one of Cowen's men.

Meanwhile, behind this crumbling façade and Cowen's uncertainty, members of the Green Party were trying to work out the truth in the conflicting versions of Cowen's involvement in Anglo as further details came out of the FitzPatrick side of the story, as opposed to the Drumm side. *The FitzPatrick Tapes* had been the story of 'Cowen Light', the answers it gave easy for him to contest. The full Drumm version appeared in the *Irish Daily Mail* on 14 January, raising all over again the unanswered deadly questions about his involvement in the bank's growing crisis when Cowen had been Minister for Finance.

There was no trust between the two coalition partners. Cowen would become annoyed as he watched Eamon Ryan taking copious notes during the Cabinet meetings. 'Sometimes Eamon was taking notes to help his own memory, but there were times when we felt the notes were too detailed and were used by the background group that the Greens had for very detailed and intimate analysis. I wouldn't be surprised if he isn't writing a book,' states a former member of the Cabinet.

By this stage, they thought Gormley looked 'deflated' and had appeared to lose virtually all interest in the Cabinet discussions, according to one ex-Minister:

> There were times when John Gormley would switch off completely. The only time he'd perk up [was] if there was something about the Poolbeg incinerator or some environmental issue; in a whole range of issues he seemed to be completely disengaged. Eamon Ryan made up for that. He was very good, very engaged, determined to hang in there, take the tough decisions no matter how hard it hits [sic]. Eamon Ryan, if you didn't know better, you'd think he was a Fianna Fáil member of the Cabinet. He was always very engaged.

In fact, according to Mary O'Rourke, Brian Lenihan had found Ryan to be 'very steadfast' and 'was used quite a lot on economic debates', going on radio and TV. However, the Greens 'very rarely came into the Dáil for major debates when you'd expect your partners to be there. The PDS used to be there until their demise. But they [the Greens] wouldn't come into the Dáil. They just wanted to semi-distance themselves.'

Cowen was shocked when John Gormley, who had learned about the first resignation from his wife only after she had heard it on the news, informed him that the Greens would not support the reshuffle. The Greens were fuming that Cowen was attempting one last pre-election stunt to appoint new faces, which was clearly designed to help Fianna Fáil in the impending election.

'We did not think this was a good idea. If it went to a vote in the Dáil, we would not have been in a position to support this,' Gormley stated at a press conference, describing the reshuffle attempt as a *fait accompli*.

Cowen also was fuming. He felt it was the Taoiseach's fundamental right to decide who sat in 'his' Cabinet. He felt the Greens were now pulling the plug because they had 'concerns about perception'. 'I'd say he was shocked because he had the right but it just wasn't the right thing to do,' says Mary O'Rourke.

The Greens' refusal to endorse the six replacements at Cabinet meant that an embarrassed Cowen had to announce that the portfolios would be reassigned to existing Ministers. In what can only be described as farcical at best, the Taoiseach reassigned the Department of Health and Children to Mary Coughlan. The Justice portfolio was given to Minister for Agriculture, Fisheries and Food, Brendan Smith, while the Transport portfolio went to Minister for Community, Equality and Gaeltacht Affairs, Pat Carey. The Defence portfolio was given to the Minister for Social Protection, Eamon Ó Cuív, and the Enterprise, Trade and Innovation portfolio was handed to the Minister for Tourism, Sport and Culture, Mary Hanafin.

Never before in the history of the State had so many Ministers double-jobbed at Cabinet level. That looked bad. What was far worse was that the Greens also forced an incensed Cowen to announce in the Dáil the actual date of the general election.

As the fiasco unfolded, those close to Cowen sensed that they were looking at another leadership challenge emerging as Fianna Fáil TDs were coming out of the woodwork calling for him to go, and their message was for him to dissolve the Dáil. This was constitutionally correct. 'That was the advice he was getting from a certain section at that stage,' one former Minister recalls.

Cowen had lost all authority; there was open revolt and Minister of State Conor Lenihan went on radio calling for him to resign. States one TD:

> He had to go. He had no credibility left. He couldn't even sack Conor Lenihan, who for two days running was on the radio saying he had to retire. It was ridiculous. He hadn't a scrap of credibility at that stage and he couldn't even sack a Minister of State. He had no authority at that stage even to sack people who were indicating he should go.

Cowen's reign was over. With his back to the wall, he went home to reflect and discuss his final move with his family. When he rejected the recommendation of sacking the Greens because 'he didn't like sacking people', the 'advice he was then getting from a certain section at that stage', according to one former member of his Cabinet, was to consider going to the Phoenix Park immediately to dissolve the Government. But Cowen explained to his colleagues that he believed in the 'necessity to have a Government to bring in the Budget and bring in the Finance bill. He felt it would be disastrous for the country if we failed to do that,' recalls O'Keeffe.

At this point, as Cowen puts it, he was given 'the time and space' by Cabinet colleagues to make up his own mind. He discussed the crisis with his wife Mary on the night of Friday, 21 January. 'We confide and talk things over. I get her view on things. She has a very common sense point of view,' he once revealed about his wife, who had played a major role in his election campaigns.

Backtracking on something he had vowed never to do, the decision was made for him to step down as leader of the party but remain on as Taoiseach until all the appropriate legislation had been pushed through. It was the only option open to him. Such a move wasn't unusual either; when Albert Reynolds stepped down as leader of Fianna Fáil, he had remained on as Taoiseach as the party's new leader, Bertie Ahern, attempted to put together a new coalition deal, which ultimately failed.

Cowen knew that he would not stand in Laois-Offaly in the next general election, but he decided not to reveal this at the press conference being planned for the next day. He had learned his lesson from Reynolds who, at Ahern's pleading, had decided to run again. 'He didn't want to rot on the backbenches for five years. It was the only decision for him,' explains one of his former colleagues. He also felt it wouldn't be fair not to give his younger brother Barry the opportunity to test himself in the Dáil. Barry had already proved himself to be a formidable councillor and went on in the general election to win a seat.

Another reason for Cowen's decision to go was the media's constant attacks on him, not because he felt personally affronted but because of how it was upsetting his family. 'I know Mary finds it very hurtful and his daughters find it very hurtful. But the media has changed terribly over the last ten years and it's open season,' stated Senator Geraldine Feeney, a cousin of Mary Cowen.

Shortly before 1pm on the Saturday, news started to break that Cowen was going to give a press conference. Mary O'Rourke, who remembers watching the news conference feeling Cowen was stepping down 'with great grace', says:

> I got a text from HQ to watch TV at 2pm. I don't know what triggered it like that. I would say his wife and family would have talked to him. I think in the end it was family advice. He had had enough of it; he had put up with a lot. Tuesday he wins the vote of confidence two to one. Thursday there is the abortive attempt to appoint Ministers. Saturday he resigns. That was a very swift week, wasn't it?

'I'm concerned that renewed internal criticism of Fianna Fáil is deflecting attention from this important debate,' Cowen stated in his resignation speech at the Merrion Hotel in Dublin. 'Therefore, taking everything into account after discussing the matter with my family, I have taken, on my own counsel, the decision to step down.'

During his resignation speech, he stood over his farcical attempt to reshuffle the Cabinet. 'I believe that it was my duty to put in place the best possible team we could to fight this election to put them on the front bench and into position. It was not a cynical view by me; it was a political act,' he stated.

Enda Kenny described Cowen's resignation as party leader as a 'complete contradiction of his stated position less than a week ago'. Sensing he finally had the knock-out punch, Kenny declared that he would move a motion of no confidence in Cowen if the Dáil wasn't dissolved by the following Tuesday. He said that Fine Gael would now also vote against the Government in the following week's motion of no confidence that was being put forward by Labour.

Before he made his resignation speech, Cowen informed John Gormley of his decision to step down as party leader. He believed that doing so would not force the Greens to pull out of Government and that they would accept the election date of 11 March. But, shortly after Cowen's resignation, the Greens were starting to draw up their own exit strategy. Perhaps, theoretically, they could have weathered the storm of Cowen resigning as party leader, but they knew the Government was doomed following Kenny's plan to table a motion of no confidence.

It was too messy for the Greens. The next day at a press conference, Gormley announced: 'Our patience has reached an end. Because of these continuing doubts, the lack of communication and the breakdown in trust, we have decided that we can no longer continue in Government.'

The Greens called for the Finance bill legislation to be accelerated and said they would support it from the Opposition benches. The Opposition parties agreed to drop their motion of no confidence after it was agreed that the bill's deadline would be pushed forward to 29 January, thus allowing for an election to be brought forward to 25 February.

In the same week a *Sunday Independent*/Quantum Research poll showed that support for Fianna Fáil had fallen to a record low of 8 per cent. The stage was set for the biggest political catastrophe in Irish history, the wholesale demise of the country's largest party, Fianna Fáil.

Chapter 17

THE 2011 GENERAL ELECTION

B rian Cowen had lost the confidence of the Fianna Fáil party and its organisation throughout the country. This completed the circle of disapproval, making it clear that he had lost the confidence of the country and all its people. Other political parties had long since lost confidence in him. In these circumstances he should have been sent to the Park by the Dáil to ask the President to accept his resignation, dissolve the Dáil and call an immediate general election. In all material and logical ways Article 28.10 of the Constitution became a reality. It states: 'The Taoiseach shall resign from office upon his ceasing to retain the support of a majority in Dáil Eireann.' On his resignation, the other members of the Government, according to Article 28.11.1, would have been deemed also to have resigned their office and from then on would continue to carry on their duties only until successors had been appointed.

Keeping up the pretence of there being any serious distinction between party leader and Taoiseach offended the people outside Fianna Fáil and damaged the Fianna Fáil party before the electorate. Brian Cowen was treated harshly at the end of January but from the time he became Taoiseach, by acclamation, in May 2008, he was favoured. The scrutiny of his mistakes was pursued by only a small group of journalists. RTÉ showed heavy bias in his favour and was outrageously pro a Yes Vote in the Lisbon Treaty referenda.

There were several main contenders for the 'poisoned chalice' of leadership in an election campaign for which quite inadequate preparation had been made. Brian Lenihan was a leading candidate, despite the mistakes he had made and his ill-health. Hopelessly out of his depth in the Department of Finance, he was the main architect of Ireland's economic chaos, and even up to late January was defending the nonsense he had made of the country's financial affairs in arguments with the Opposition about what might be done in Europe to mend the nation's dire level of debt.

Mary Hanafin, a woman who had been damaged so much she resorted to silence when she should have spoken out, also stood. She was popular with backbenchers and had performed well in the ministries she had occupied, but she was a woman in a man's party. A female leader would have been a novel change for Fianna Fáil and the greater role of women—which she says she would have encouraged—might have been her effective basis for widespread and much-needed reform, but Fianna Fáil was not ready to be led by a woman.

Dermot Ahern was senior, able, unpopular and perceived as something of a bully. He lacked economic experience. In due course he accepted that he did not have the necessary support and eventually withdrew from politics altogether.

Eamon Ó Cuív is a man of integrity who came from a tradition within Fianna Fáil that has been largely lost. His antecedents are admirable, since he is Eamon de Valera's grandson, and his views a reflection of the old-style Fianna Fáil that had gone out of the picture with the departure of Jack Lynch from the leadership of the party.

Micheál Martin had experience in Foreign Affairs and in Health but only a limited decision-making record. There were many uncertainties accruing to him. He had the advantage of his high-profile challenge to Brian Cowen. The grim impact of Charles Haughey, Albert Reynolds and Bertie Ahern, and the devastating damage done by Brian Cowen, had rendered the Fianna Fáil party unelectable whatever leadership changes might be made.

After becoming leader, Martin tried to shift the campaign to one-on-one or group debates in order to 'find a new direction for Irish politics'. At the same time he kept in place all the mechanisms for blocking that search. These have been long-enshrined in the unrevised structure of Fianna Fáil. This was woodenly supported by deputy leader Brian Lenihan and the rest of the party. It was fair to hope from him that he would come clean and admit that he had been terribly wrong about his espousal of the worst of the European Union in this country. However, he did not have the courage to challenge Europe, the task on which Enda Kenny and Michael Noonan have embarked, like the Owl and the Pussycat, who went to sea in a beautiful pea-green boat, bringing some money and plenty of honey wrapped up in a five-pound note. That is the level of farce the nation was facing.

The election campaign was punctuated by too many opinion polls. During the first week of February, most of Thursday's chat programmes on RTÉ were in pursuit of the poll published that morning. Details were teased out endlessly and repeatedly. Interspersed were vox pop expansions of the opinion poll questioning on doorsteps. This resulted in a political quagmire of questions and answers about what would happen if the poll were repeated in the election itself. There was not much agreement about what was being discovered on doorsteps by radio and television teams. It became obvious that another opinion poll would have to be held as quickly as possible to clear up the doubt. The following weekend and early the next week one of the appropriate polling organisations, handsomely rewarded by the client, obliged.

Electoral issues included the bailout and the blanket Bank Guarantee and what the parties would do about them. There had been dishonest handling of these issues by the European Central Bank and the Commission; there was the justified rage of Germany at Ireland's misgovernment under Fianna Fáil during the crisis and the absurdly punitive view taken by José Manuel Barroso. Judgment early in the campaign seemed to suggest that Enda Kenny was out of his depth and that Michael Noonan was struggling: to understand what he should do, to cover for his leader and to choose the weakest point in Europe's unfairly wooden approach to Ireland. Much the same may be said of Joan Burton, who was more clued in and less mesmerised by the EU, and Eamon Gilmore, whose resort to soundbites and instant solutions was becoming distressful. What was additionally troubling was the obvious appeal of Sinn Féin, whose position was simplistic and confrontational, paying little heed to the need to negotiate with skill and subtlety, simply declaring that it would reject the bailout and the blanket Bank Guarantee, the latter creating the former which would not otherwise have been necessary. Though this was more likely to undermine any negotiating position, it did fit in with, and play to, the grimness of the country's collective difficulties: sovereign debt, bank debt, private debt, high unemployment, low competitiveness and being in the wrong currency.

The Independents promised some impact but had got off to a very wobbly start. Within their ranks, however, were voices that expressed the general anger of the public at how Fianna Fáil had led the nation into this mess in the most incompetent and foolhardy way. If these voices— notably of people like Shane Ross and David McWilliams, who was providing a back-up service that was logical and well-reasoned—made the impact they had wished for, then the centre of gravity would have shifted towards a less uncritical approach by Ireland towards Europe.

The position of Fianna Fáil was contained in Micheál Martin's apology, given when he was elected leader of Fianna Fáil: 'I am sorry for the mistakes we made as a party and for the mistakes I made.' He never listed them. He was obviously sticking with them, so he should have added to his apology: 'But we are sticking with our mistakes and we stand over them.' That was his precise position. He claimed that the bailout package could not be altered and he mocked the two main parties in particular for their differences over how they would handle a very difficult but central issue facing Ireland.

The central issue was not the bailout as such but the fixing of the banks that had so catastrophically contributed to Ireland's insolvency. The banks are the oxygen of public and private life and the State cannot continue to ask the taxpayer to cough up tens of billions to keep them going. They have to be stabilised. Nationalising them has not achieved this. Deposits are still flowing out and there is a horrendous level of bad debts. Ireland cannot do without Europe in putting this situation right and Europe itself will be put at risk if Ireland defaults.

Enda Kenny was the enigma of the election from the start. Appalled, no doubt, at the poor misguided electorate that went on supporting Fianna Fáil as it calmly wrecked the country, Kenny had worked long hours on the only solutions that matter, the build-up of a team, a party organisation and a set of principles or manifesto ideas. He also constantly garnered the growing support of voters. This was rewarded as it richly deserved, though it was not fully recognised by the media.

Kenny had one other bonus that resulted from the precipitate onset of a general election. His primary target, Brian Cowen, was out of the picture and he was dealing with a new and inexperienced leader in Micheál Martin. Martin had plenty of ministerial experience but none at all of leading a party, even in normal circumstances. On the other hand, he was leading a party in tatters, many of its main figures departed, its electoral strategy not worked out and its popularity on the floor. For Kenny this was a huge advantage. He treated it with the calmness that governed all his actions from the outset of the campaign.

Despite the fact that Fine Gael and Labour have, between them, strong faith in the arguable nature of the deal and the possibility of making changes in it, on most other issues they appeared to be in conflict. Because of this, a view was gaining some momentum; this was that the best Government to succeed would be a Fine Gael Government on its own, possibly with the moderating support of good Independents from outside, among them Shane Ross and Paul Somerville. Elected or not, they, with economists like Constantin Gurdgiev and David McWilliams, would make up a good team.

It was becoming increasingly likely that from the talent pool that Enda Kenny had put together with a skill no one praised him for, the people would choose the team to lead that Brussels task force.

Enda Kenny's struggle for political recognition and power deserved the reward that voters seemed to be offering him. He had pursued these objectives with dogged determination and against a deeply ingrained and deeply prejudiced opposition from the media and many of its leading columnists. He had contended with a potential partner, Eamon Gilmore, in the run-up to the election, knowing that if he did not achieve an overall majority, he would have to make the best of the looming partnership. Gilmore had distinguished himself by overweening arrogance and a campaign that had been governed by an ill-judged, bombastic and divisive style. He had favoured himself as the future Taoiseach and this had become so routine that he had no fall-back position. He, like Micheál Martin, underestimated Kenny and, when they realised that they had done this, they became increasingly critical, often snidely so, in disparaging him. Kenny ignored them. When the public support for Eamon Gilmore's excessive ambition proved not to be there, he made the mistake of seeking to intensify the undermining of his prospective partner in a way that was unsubtle and negative.

The effect of this was to further reduce support for Labour, a process enhanced, absurdly, by trade union interventions, firstly by Jack O'Connor of ICTU. He did so as the living embodiment of the kind of partnership approach to politics that was Fianna Fáil's stock-in-trade with every significant group in the country. It did not occur to Jack O'Connor that transferring his approaches to the Labour Party would do more harm than good. O'Connor's colleague David Begg then joined the chorus, with RTÉ stirring the pot, though he and his morning show interviewer did not seem to have up-to-date knowledge of what they were talking about.

This political claim of privilege was what was now being so firmly rejected by everyone. The public wanted least of all the trade unions muscling in on their greedy wish to take a lion's share in controlling the sustaining of wages—with its built-in loss of competitiveness—and the operation of a secret voice at the Cabinet table. They were not part of Government, a role they attempted with Fianna Fáil. They should never be so again. Nor were they part of the Labour Party. Their enthusiasm had been lukewarm because of the close connections with Fianna Fáil.

The Labour Party had a good working team for the election and a notably proficient and effective Finance spokesperson in Joan Burton. She was later side-tracked in Government appointments, probably at Gilmore's instigation. Gilmore, however, seemed to be seduced at the outset by his own personal high standing in the opinion polls. The personal standings of leaders matter far less than the potential votes for parties shown in the polls. These are what matter.

At the centre of the campaign Gilmore misjudged the line that needed to be drawn, a line linking the two parties, not dividing them. Fine Gael was larger and improved that position during the campaign, implying it would have the top position if the parties were in power together. Neither Gilmore nor anyone else could have seriously envisaged any other outcome, particularly once Gilmore had abjured linkages with Fianna Fáil.

Enda Kenny continued to place emphasis on his own party and on the campaign and left Eamon Gilmore to his own business, which was to expand his and his party's standing with the voters. This did not happen as planned and it led to a measure of quiet panic within the Labour Party.

Enda Kenny, also wisely, left Micheál Martin to his own devices, merely correcting misrepresentations of fact but allowing Martin to do the rest. Martin obliged with a watery, generally weak campaign. He discovered in the process the legitimate and justified rage of voters at his attempt at a new image when he was at the heart of the shambles of the last two years and had been for much longer the architect of Ireland's lickspittle approach to the EU.

Side by side with this was the spectacle of Brian Lenihan becoming the main spokesman on behalf of Europe against Ireland! Even as the situation changed, he said, over and over, that nothing in the gross overburdening of the country by the EU could be changed. He continued to do this even as Europe proceeded towards the first ameliorating treatment of the penal controls on Ireland's fiscal policy. Without being yet in Government, Enda Kenny breached the blank wall of Europe's stolid indifference and began to change things. Hope was high that he would achieve more when his effective team of lieutenants got to work on the terrible mess Fianna Fáil had left behind.

Enda Kenny's approach was laughed at, as was his meeting with Angela Merkel on 14 February, with Martin talking about 'a photo opportunity'. It turned out to be something more than this, as have his other travels. They do not yet add up to much.

Kenny continued to assert that Ireland has a strong case for change in the bailout deal. This eventually transpired in the form of various improvements in Ireland's debt situation including a reduction in the interest rate. In the campaign's last week, he faced serious but not insurmountable problems. He was going to be Taoiseach. That was clear. Whether it would be on his own or in partnership would have to wait for the count. But he was on the brink of defying history. With it, he was defying the built-in antagonism of so many people in the country who were trying to come to terms with the breakthrough of a party stigmatised as right-wing.

There is no Left and Right in Irish politics. There is undoubtedly wealth and poverty, and both need to be tackled. But the true politics of this have been undermined and corrupted by Fianna Fáil. It sought to be all things to all men, ending up being nothing to anyone. It sought to pocket the money of developers and others and to align itself with many concentric golden circles, including the trade union movement, without actually addressing the wealth and the poverty at all. It never tackled reform. How can you reform corruption when you are also responsible for it? So it became all things to all men, with results that are obvious. It doesn't even deserve the 12 per cent support to which it has sunk.

Fine Gael has been plagued by its history. It bears indelible stains from Blue Shirt days, and more recently from the rigid law-and-order stance adopted by Liam Cosgrave, a leader who held together, quite effectively, the traditional relationship in power of Fine Gael and Labour. All that is distant history. Out of the debacle for Fine Gael of Jack Lynch's landslide victory in 1977, the party remade itself under Garret FitzGerald, a process sustained by Alan Dukes and John Bruton. It stumbled, deliberately and unwisely, under Michael Noonan and deputy leader Jim Mitchell, righted itself under Enda Kenny and then discovered that all the old prejudices—some going back almost a century—were still being thrown in its face.

People found it difficult to understand what Kenny delivered. After 2007, when he could have demolished Bertie Ahern, he fumbled and was outsmarted by quite outrageous strokes, such as the involvement of the British Prime Minister, the White House and Europe in campaigning for Ahern and giving him photo opportunities beside which Angela Merkel's modest gesture of friendly understanding towards Enda Kenny falls into insignificance. The media, hugely silent and fixedly looking the other way over Ahern, focused gimlet and prejudiced eyes on Enda.

Since 2007 he has turned in on the party and continued to redress effectively its shortcomings, forging a good team, a wide range of policies and a collective representation of the united strengths of the party he leads. It worked better than he anticipated and brought him to power almost, but not quite, unfettered by Labour.

There had been a growing debate about this possibility of a new political party since the second Lisbon Treaty referendum a year before. Confronted by all the main political parties, together with the Green Party (though not Sinn Féin) being slavishly under the spell of Europe, the very large numbers who had voted No twice were justifiably seen as inclined to support an alternative political grouping, movement or party. They were the main holders in such a belief.

However, getting a new political party started in Ireland had grown more difficult, just as the need for it was becoming more obvious and more urgent, with increasing numbers of people indicating their interest and potential support. Electoral legislation that had been tailored to help the existing structure and to forestall its enlargement hindered the process.

Desmond O'Malley, by now long since out of politics, was still a wise voice on the subject of creating a new political force in Ireland. He had been motivated to break the mould by forming the Progressive Democrats. His move had been successful and the party, established in December 1985, had enjoyed a long innings, terminated by mistakes before the 2007 election. O'Malley's reputation was an established one. He had been widely credited with playing a major role in the economic recovery during the bleak 1980s by pushing through a low taxation and free trade agenda. He believed the crisis facing the country in 2010 was considerably greater.

In his first major political interview—with Jason O'Toole—since retiring from public life, Desmond O'Malley stated that Ireland's fiscal plight today is even worse than the depressed 1980s and that there was a real need for a new political party to emerge and bring a radical shake-up to the system, as the PDs had done.

While recommending a new political party, O'Malley recognised also that current legislation would make it extremely hard. This was because most 'political funding is public and private funding must be below a certain low threshold'. 'It is now very difficult to be able to raise private money for a political party and particularly to start a political party.'

From the democratic point of view the snag is that the public funding is based on the number of votes a party got in the last general election. But if you didn't contest the last general election ,you can't get any funding; therefore you can't start a new party. And surely it is the essence of democracy that new parties should be formed?

It's very unlikely now, given that the way things are, that there is going to be a new party. The reason that I say that is because I've been looking at the situation and see the existing three main parties have come to a sort of consensus between themselves in the last eight or ten years—and the consensus is that they want to retain the status quo. The legislation that is there is to preserve the status quo. It is not worthy of preservation. It certainly is challengeable.

Declan Ganley had been in discussion during the previous two years with a small group of people about the formation of a new political party. He had demonstrated, during the two Lisbon Treaty referenda, considerable political skill and a good deal of energy in leading the No campaign. He was an ideal central figure for the launch of a new party but he had other business preoccupations during the second half of 2010 and, along with the public generally, could not have foreseen a snap general election fast approaching from the catastrophe that would evolve for Ireland as a result of the banking crisis and the intervention of the EU, the ECB and the IMF. According to those close to Ganley, it all happened too quickly for him to consider contesting the election.

Desmond O'Malley's cautious views, also essentially negative, would have further reassured the Fianna Fáil party. Reassurance of another kind came from a different figure in the growing tidal wave of potential candidates for the coming election, Fintan O'Toole, a columnist with the *Irish Times*. He put it thus, in an article in the *Irish Times* on 29 January 2011, explaining why he had withdrawn before even starting out to get elected: 'The enemy, we discovered, is the one that nothing human can ever defeat: Time. All of the discussions on the project were predicated on an election in late March. The descent into political chaos in the last fortnight threw out of kilter all of the most basic calculations.'

What was astonishing about O'Toole's decision to involve himself in the formation of a new political party was its lateness. He was not defeated by time. It was his own slowness to react. Suggestions for a new political party had been aired regularly since the second Lisbon Treaty referendum, identifying the source for its funding, its voters and its participants among close on one million people who had opposed all three main political parties over the Treaty. Yet, as he told his readers in the first few lines of his article, Fintan O'Toole had only begun to consider the idea 'just after New Year' that is, just four weeks earlier.

He named only David McWilliams, with whom Bruce Arnold had held several discussions on the subject up to that point. But blog sites swiftly filled in others. The movement was called 'Democracy Now'. Its possible candidates would include Eamon Dunphy and Shane Ross, with David McWilliams as a 'front man'. Democracy Now had apparently made approaches to a number of high-profile figures, including businessman and former Wexford hurling manager Liam Griffin, Cork goalkeeper Dónal Óg Cusack, cystic fibrosis campaigner Orla Tinsley and Seamus Boland, CEO of Irish Rural Networks.

O'Toole described his belated thinking:

> Having dismissed the two obvious options, McWilliams, myself and others were left with one big, bold idea, an unusual notion for unusual times. What if it were possible to stand, in every single constituency, someone not currently involved in party politics, but with a track record of civic achievement in business, in the arts, in community and voluntary activity, in sport, in single-issue campaigns? What if they could be united on a small core of big questions, while retaining their independence, so they could bring some free thought to the Dáil?

O'Toole reckoned half the electorate deplored the bank bailout and what it had done. He added to this 'the State in political and institutional terms', a more questionable assumption in terms of power politics. Thirdly, there was 'the amorality of so many aspects of our public life, particularly those where politics and business overlap'. This was certainly the subject of great anger, but again not the stuff of manifestos or campaigns. What was missing was the key source of all Ireland's problems: Europe.

> Two things were completely clear to everyone who was interested in this project [establishing a new political party]. One was that we had a moral duty to try to do it. The other was that we had an even more emphatic duty not to screw it up. A national crisis is not a time for enthusiastic amateurism.

Unfortunately, the next thing was that they did screw it up and the overriding impression of their flawed efforts is one of rank amateurism. Worse was to follow. This was Fintan O'Toole's driving desire to put it all into print in the form of an article that was not discussed with all the participants, some of whom were continuing to work for change anyway.

O'Toole had done what he said was worse than doing nothing at all: to 'raise hopes and then dash them'.

Shane Ross went on to win a seat. David McWilliams kept his eye on the ball and published excellent articles on the real issues that needed to be confronted, most of them related to the appalling bailout, details of which were slowly emerging, to the detriment of any shadow of self-respect attaching to the architects of Ireland's economic chaos, Brian Cowen and Brian Lenihan.

Shane Ross's long overdue arrival as a Dáil deputy was the highest profile result for those committed to changing the political landscape and in itself a surprising aspect of the flawed political enterprise. He went into the 2011 general election campaign as an independent candidate after turning down an 'attractive offer' to run as part of Enda Kenny's team. Fine Gael was determined to have a high profile candidate to replace George Lee and approached Ross and offered him €30,000 for his campaign. During the course of several discussions with the Fine Gael party and a meeting with Phil Hogan, Ross was told that he would be offered a 'high-ranking position' in Kenny's first Cabinet. It was a tempting offer.

> Fine Gael offered me 30 grand to use. They said, 'We'll give you 30,000 if you run.' But I turned it down. I thought about it. And it was quite serious. But I thought that it was impossible to achieve real reform within Fine Gael and I'd end up resigning within weeks if I joined them because they'd just say, 'You can't do this; you can't do that; and you can't do the other.' So I actually rejected the trappings of power pretty rapidly.

Another reason for turning down Fine Gael has already been mentioned. Shane Ross had been hoping to run under the Democracy Now banner or under the umbrella of a smaller alliance of 'like-minded' independents: 'I'd considered a new political group, with other people, but there just wasn't time before the election, which took us by surprise and there wasn't time to get everything together.'

Ross had several meetings with his friends Eamon Dunphy and David McWilliams. Both toyed with the idea of running but eventually decided against entering politics.

Ross was 'very disappointed' that he was unable to persuade McWilliams and Dunphy to run in the election. In the event, Dunphy did not get involved in the election at all. McWilliams had other ideas.

Ross says he 'would have been happier if both of them had been running alongside me. It would have been great. They both considered it very closely,' he states. On the hustings, Ross put on a brave face, but underneath the surface there was still much aching in his heart as he faced into the first—and most important—election campaign of his distinguished political career without his 'number one supporter'. The independent candidate's younger brother Connelly, whom he touchingly described as his 'best friend', who had stood by his side during all his previous campaigns, had tragically died from a heart attack, aged just 47, three years before.

After his election Ross said he would 'seriously look at the possibility of trying to form a really radical political movement' in an effort 'to attack tribal politics'. 'We're talking about uprooting the whole system.'

On the political Left there were equally strong candidates with aspirations towards new political parties. They were essentially more successful in delivering them. One of these was Richard Boyd Barrett. He benefited in the Dun Laoghaire constituency from an act of political suicide by Fianna Fáil when neither Mary Hanafin nor Barry Andrews would move out of the constituency and run elsewhere. It was plain to all that the difficulties for the party in holding on to one of its two seats were considerable. Keeping two put both at risk. And so it transpired. The Fianna Fáil vote was split and allowed the so-called 'Poster Boy of the Radical Left Wing Brigade', Boyd Barrett, to scrape home on his third attempt.

Boyd Barrett had failed to win a seat in the 2007 general election, even though he had managed to carve out a national profile after it was conveniently leaked just prior to that election that his biological mother was Sinead Cusack. She then went on to canvass for him. Boyd Barrett did not like the suggestion that his profile had been raised by the leak. He said he did not 'buy that argument' that his profile was improved dramatically—if that was the case, then it was only 'a little bit in some of the tabloids'. He claimed that he had already 'gained a national political profile for my involvement in [the] Anti-War Movement'.

Boyd Barrett insisted that his famous mother and his stepfather, Jeremy Irons, were not an issue on the doorsteps. Voters were concerned only with what he stood for and his 'principles'. But having a famous mother supporting your candidacy certainly does add glamour to an election campaign—an all too unfamiliar sight for left-wing politics in Ireland.

In fairness to Boyd Barrett, he reluctantly spoke to the media during the 2011 general election when the subject of his mother was broached. And what made him stand out this time, apart from his good media performances, was that he was one of the leading 'instigators' behind both the United Left Alliance (ULA), which ran some 18 candidates under its banner in the general election, and the People Before Profit group. The aim of the ULA group, which also included Joe Higgins' Socialist Party, was 'to build an alliance on a national level that can offer a real alternative, rather than have a fragmented left with pockets of support in this or that area'.

The ULA's main aim in the election, it said, was to 'burn the bondholders'. But, as the mainstream parties and political pundits pointed out, such talk was simply populist. The goal was unrealistic. There was scepticism also over the likelihood of the ULA having any real impact in the Dáil. Boyd Barrett's view was that the alliance would use the Dáil 'as a platform to highlight issues and to organise people to campaign against injustices and to campaign for a positive alternative economic and social programme for this country'.

They were a mixed bag of candidates, colourful, eccentric but successful in winning seats and in taking votes away from Labour. In addition to Boyd Barrett, there were the developer Mick Wallis, who owes millions to NAMA, and Luke 'Ming' Flanagan, and they certainly set tongues wagging with their unorthodox pink shirts and casual sports jackets.

Even though the Socialist Party had moderate success at local level, at national level it was a different story. Joe Higgins' party had never resonated with the electorate. By aligning his niche Socialist Party with the ULA, Higgins hoped not only to regain his own seat, which he had lost in the 2007 general election, but to turn his party into something more than a one-man political organisation by getting some more members elected.

His plan was to put up a 'principled opposition' to the 'most likely' Fine Gael-Labour coalition by targeting the working-class electorate with the message that a vote for these two mainstream parties would only help to 'carry on with the same policies as Fianna Fáil, making working-class people pay for the bankers' bad gambling debts'.

Higgins believed that if the United Left Alliance could perform well in the general election (they would in the event capture 5 seats), it would give them scope to work on forming a new left-wing political party 'for working people'. As the first of the United Left Alliance members to be elected, Higgins reiterated plans to form a new political organisation. 'We're all agreed there is a huge vacuum. The intention is to form a party, but I don't want people to think it's going to happen tomorrow morning because there is a process here. We will discuss with supporters and activists about the next step,' he stated.

Joe Higgins achieved one startling and impressive show of public outrage shortly before the general election was called. At the end of January, in a week of mesmerising political confusion, he spoke with a simplicity and directness that was welcome and incisive. It was also in marked contrast to the displays of histrionics and hypocrisy that passed for political logic in the Dáil. He chose a quite different place for protest when he told the European Parliament about what Europe had done to Ireland and he spoke a great deal of truth in his well-timed and well-judged attack on José Manuel Barroso, president of the European Commission. In fact, he did a better job of speaking up for Ireland than the Government. He did so because his courage is at the root of what he says, while that of the relevant Government Ministers carries enough baggage of fear and respect to crush such people, just as Barroso would arrogantly crush them.

Higgins' performance as a politician is powerful and direct. He also belongs to an honourable tradition that has really ceased to be adequately explained by using the old terms of 'Left' and 'Right'. He is instead engaged on behalf of people whose lives of struggle are not endowed with wealth or privilege. Higgins told Barroso that the Irish taxpayers were bailing out French and German banks for their irresponsible lending decisions. The Irish electorate was being beggared by what had been placed on its shoulders. Barroso lost his temper and responded by claiming, quite falsely, that the fault lay with reckless Irish banks and the incompetent Irish authorities. A sizable proportion of voters in the election saw Higgins as speaking the sad truth about what Europe has done to us, and Barroso indulging in sentimental and highly distorted allegations, claiming that Europe was 'trying to support Ireland ... as it had done'—wait for it—'when Europe was financing your farmers after the war to feed your own people'. One wondered who educated this strange fellow who came from what was then a strict dictatorship sympathetic to the Third Reich and the Axis Powers. What did he mean about financing Irish farmers, who were themselves selling food produce to the UK?

The biggest success of all, well signposted from the Donegal South-West by-election, was Sinn Féin. And the highest profile figure in the party in the 2011 general election was Gerry Adams, running for the first time in the Republic after years of leading Republican Nationalism in Northern Ireland politics. This was the most successful general election in Sinn Féin's history. It more than tripled its number of seats, with 14 TDs now in Leinster House. They were at 4 seats before the election.

While the Government and the main Opposition parties floundered around over the bailout catastrophe, Sinn Féin maximised its position, creating a threatening growth in left-wing support. It continued to strengthen its political standing by sticking with this issue. It was bedrock to the party, concerning as it did national sovereignty and independence; on these issues it shamed the other parties.

Old-fashioned political views strengthened the liaison of voters with Sinn Féin, now tricked out as a party of revolutionary dogma on fiscal policy and sovereignty, something like the Fianna Fáil of the de Valera years. Micheál Martin's superficially legitimate attempt at repositioning the party in the light of its recent history was a bit like the kettle calling the pot black. It is understandable since Fianna Fáil and Sinn Féin are fighting for third place, with Sinn Féin having the edge on the larger party.

It was a major surprise when the party announced that Gerry Adams had decided to run in the Republic for the first time. He mentally prepared himself for a 'tsunami of personal abuse and vilification' from what he described as 'the establishment', though in fact it did not materialise. During the election campaign, underneath the brave façade of a cheerful demeanour and beguiling smile for the electorate, Gerry Adams was still struggling to come to terms with all the emotional turmoil he had endured during the previous 15 months. First of all, the Sinn Féin President had to deal publicly with revelations that his father had sexually abused some of his siblings but also the politically damaging allegation that he had actually conspired to cover up accusations that his younger brother Liam had raped his own daughter.

Coping with this, he also had to deal with the 'terrifying experience' of his wife undergoing life-saving surgery for cancer. Security for both himself and his family was increased following a fresh wave of death threats from dissident Republicans.

Finally, he had to face fresh allegations that he was on the IRA's Army Council and that he had directly ordered the brutal murder of Jean McConville back in 1972. In February 2011 he threatened the *Evening Herald* with legal action for printing an article accusing him of being involved in the murder. For a time before the election, and after he had declared his intention to run in Louth, Jean McConville's daughter had considered running against him in an effort to block him from getting into the Dáil.

Adams was annoyed that the media focus was clearly on his past rather than allowing him to focus on getting across Sinn Féin policy. Adams claimed:

> There are people who write things about me which are totally untrue. There's a madness in there. You have to just accept it and try not to take it personally and get on with your business. Crazy stuff. The wonderful thing about it is that the voters are the people who make the decisions, not the journalists who write these pieces.

During the campaign, Adams, once again, had to deny IRA membership —such an admission could effectively see someone facing criminal charges—after being interviewed on RTÉ radio. In what is surely a controversial statement, TD Dessie Ellis—convicted ex-IRA terrorist who hit international headlines after going on hunger strike for

37 days—insisted that there are prominent members of the Labour Party today—politicians who had previously been members of Democratic Left, The Workers' Party and Official Sinn Féin before joining Labour—who were also members of the IRA. 'There are quite a few hypocrites there. I'm well aware of that. I know some of them from my past. So, I know what they were, the positions that they held. Some of them are still there. Nobody gets scrutinised as much as us [in Sinn Féin].'

But even though Adams once again rejected the accusation during the 2011 general election that he was on the IRA's Army Council—a claim nobody will ever believe—he admits that he does 'accept responsibility' for playing a 'leadership' role in the Northern Ireland conflict.

Adams was an obvious target for anti-Sinn Féin smears during the general election. In previous elections, Sinn Féin had reacted angrily to media features attempting to link prominent Sinn Féin candidates with criminality. It was a case of 'third time lucky' for Dessie Ellis when he finally won a Dáil seat in the 2011 general election after almost a decade of agonisingly close failed attempts. But it was also the first time he had fought a general election without having to endure a smear campaign. He claimed that there had been vicious rumours spread by certain members of the gardaí to derail his campaigns.

'I find it absolutely unacceptable to point the finger at any of us in Sinn Féin and accuse us of being criminal or in any way supporting or facilitating criminality. That is absolutely not the case,' stated Sinn Féin deputy leader Mary Lou McDonald.

The Green Party did not know which way to turn but had to salvage its own political position at the expense of every shred of integrity it once enjoyed. It consisted of a group of men and women who politically were stripped naked but preferred that back-to-nature state over the lost, confused and impossible reality of trying to share the job of caring for the country with Fianna Fáil.

The Greens learned too late that there was no advantage in doing the right thing at the wrong time. They were right to bring down Brian Cowen's increasingly discredited administration over the stroke he tried to play concerning ministerial appointments. But Cowen was done for already and the Greens have won no retrospective electoral gratitude for what they did. The Greens drank the poisoned chalice of partnership with Fianna Fáil. The same potion destroyed the Progressive Democrats. It almost destroyed the Labour Party. And now, mercifully, it was at last destroying Fianna Fáil itself.

The result for Fianna Fáil was nemesis. The Goddess of Retribution punished the party to an unprecedented degree, removing all but one representative from Dublin—that one being Brian Lenihan—and scything through the rest of the country leaving very few party candidates standing. The party had thought it would at least hold on to three seats in the city at the very minimum. It was a big step down from only months earlier, however, when, prior to the IMF bailout, it had been generally felt that the party would pick up at least one seat per constituency. During the campaign there were stories floating around newsrooms about Fianna Fáil candidates being chased out of estates and pubs, but such stories appear to be exaggerated. Stupefied by events, they remained in denial about their defeat right up until the result began to emerge. After finishing his canvassing on the Thursday evening, the outgoing Minister for Community, Equality and Gaeltacht Affairs, Pat Carey, had adjourned to the Autobahn Public House in Glasnevin. He was with his canvassers when he took a phone call from Brian Dowling of RTÉ. Dowling informed him that Fianna Fáil was facing a total collapse in Dublin. 'He said, "Pat, you're going to get one or no seat in Dublin!"' Carey replied: 'For fuck's sake!' He later recalled: 'I didn't believe this though I had been sensing all along that we would be trounced in Dublin.'

If Mary Hanafin was the party's biggest casualty in greater Dublin, their most significant loser outside the capital was deputy leader Mary Coughlan. But even the outgoing Tánaiste was not prepared for the embarrassment of being unceremoniously dumped in the political wilderness by a relatively unknown left-wing independent candidate, Thomas Pringle. The newcomer, who had a minuscule budget and didn't even own a good suit prior to the election, thus put an end to her family's political dynasty, which had seen them continuously hold the same seat in the Donegal South-West constituency since 1980.

In a real sense the party was over. It had been annihilated from within, its greatest destroyer Brian Cowen himself, aided by the tragic figure of Brian Lenihan as the public architect of the country's economic collapse.

Nine-tenths of the damage had been done before the Dáil was dissolved and this made the election itself a very watery affair, predictable in its outcome but stripped of real issues since the economy had been decided upon by Europe, put into place with the Budget, the Four-Year Plan and the bailout. Opinion polls governed public understanding. There was mild interest in the performance of Micheál Martin. He had been thrown in at the deep end, taking over Fianna Fáil at the outset of an election that had annihilation built in as the only prospect for him and the party.

The media debates were unexciting and predictably did not change the public view which was governed, above all else, by the desire to punish the party that had so grievously destroyed the economy and handed the Irish nation, in chains, to the EU to manage Ireland's affairs.

Epilogue ❧

| WHAT WENT WRONG?

Brian Cowen brought the Fianna Fáil party to its end. He did so with great deliberation. He had no doubts about himself. He thought he was the best man for the job and to a marked degree his party accepted that preposterous lack of doubt. He made mistakes from the outset, the first being his defeat in the Lisbon referendum, his second being the decision to override this with a second referendum. The mistakes seemed to have been laid out by fate as a pathway that he followed with intrepid self-confidence. It was entirely misplaced.

His flaws are the obvious ones of a relatively simple and straightforward member of Fianna Fáil as it had become when he took over. This is a party that lived and worked for itself and its supporters, ignoring the interests of the country in a way that was inexcusable. This was political corruption and eventually led to the public turning against Fianna Fáil in a rout that spelt the end of the party for the foreseeable future.

Cowen's faults were obvious. 'He drank. He was lazy. Despite his enormous energy, self-confidence and aggression, he failed to do the work necessary in his various appointments and in particular as Minister for Finance and Taoiseach. In most ministries it has always been possible to get by without intense reading, thought and work,' according to a former Minister. Foreign Affairs is the other ministry where close attention, on a daily basis, to the job in hand is necessary. Cowen had occupied that role and knew this was so, though at that stage of his career he was largely Bertie Ahern's understudy because the predominant issue at the time was Northern Ireland. But knowing what he should have been doing, on a daily basis, and doing it were two different things and Cowen chose the wrong route. He covered it by accomplishments such as his debating skills and his quick mind. Cowen's capacity for debating—he was far better than either Ahern or Reynolds—had a huge impact on Fianna Fáil members, who saw the asset as unique within the party. But without the hard work of preparation, he resorted to the cover-up of anger and spleen and a facility with words that was not possessed by his more ponderous opponents, Enda Kenny and Eamon Gilmore. Instead of reading his briefs and discussing them, he drank with his elected party colleagues and relied far too much on his civil servants. Their quality had suffered from the departures of able men and women for private employment. Notably, the Department of Finance did not have adequate economists and other experts to deal with the events that undermined Cowen when the Celtic Tiger failed and the country was plunged into an economic and banking crisis.

His drinking was divisive. He had bar companions who had his ear and the advantages this gave, while the rest of the party held second place. Inevitably, he did not give sufficient time to the essentials of leadership. These include keeping in close touch with his peers in the Cabinet, his opponents outside it, the media, his constituents and older Fianna Fáil figures.

His relationship with Bertie Ahern was a flawed one. Far from Ahern's 'anointing' Cowen as his successor being what it appeared to be, it was in reality the isolation of Cowen as the chosen successor, thus 'neutralising other voices. Ahern had no intention of ending his leadership by appointing an heir. Quite the opposite was the purpose of the choice and it went wrong only when Cowen realised that Ahern would fail to win the first Lisbon Treaty referendum vote and so orchestrated his removal,' according to one former Minister.

Cowen's relationship with Brian Lenihan was also flawed, even more seriously. When Cowen was asked, after Lenihan's death, to talk about him and recall conversations they had had, it became quite clear that there had been nothing between them. They did not have such conversations and Cowen could remember none. He generalised instead. Worse still, having learned from Bertie Ahern the curious technique of isolation by favouring someone who represents a threat, he appointed Brian Lenihan to be Minister for Finance, a move that was to have tragic implications for the country. Two leaders and one potential leader, Lenihan, were not friends. One episode reveals how little Cowen and Lenihan understood each other or communicated effectively. In September 2010, Brian Lenihan had urged his Taoiseach to call a snap general election. Lenihan had driven out to Tullamore one Sunday afternoon to visit Cowen and urged him to go to the country. Lenihan was worried; he felt Ireland was going to be 'bullied' by EU colleagues into accepting a bailout deal. He instinctively felt the appropriate course of action would be to go to the country immediately before they were forced down the bailout route. Lenihan later told those close to him that Cowen had rejected his recommendation and simply told him 'not to worry, we will muddle through somehow'. All three were mutually suspicious of each other, which accounts for Lenihan's slow rise to Cabinet office notwithstanding his brilliant mind, attractive personality and fluency of self-expression. The pity was he did not understand economics and by putting him into the Department of Finance, Cowen did the country a great disservice.

Cowen was obsessed with Fianna Fáil. The party did not deserve this obsession. It needed to be ruled, controlled, reformed and made subservient to the country's needs and objectives, and all its members would have had to subscribe to this. Indeed, it required far greater regulation than any other institution in the State. Cowen gave a brief initial whiff of this recognition of the widespread need for regulation when he became leader, as he did more widely in respect of reform, and his character, which had appealing aspects to it, seemed to equip him to become the agent of change. But then it did not happen. He did nothing at all. He let the party run the country, never putting the country first, though he frequently claimed that this was what he was doing.

There was another significant defect in his capacity to make this important change and indeed to become a new and vital leader of the party and of the country. It was an inability, indeed a firm disinclination, to restore the primacy of the Civil Service and dismember the adjuncts that had been added, the 'agentisation' that had become a needless and reckless part of public policy. These additional administrative burdens not only included the vast expansion of personal advisers to Ministers but also the expensive establishment of quango-style bodies that took over perfectly valid Civil Service responsibilities. As a result, good, well-qualified people left the Civil Service, accounting for a down-grading. This was particularly so with well-trained and experienced economists in the Department of Finance.

The Fianna Fáil party, in as far as it could, took charge of the Civil Service and made it a corporate arm of its governance of the country. By duplicating many of its functions in bodies that were not directly under State control, it created another corporate arm, effectively under party control and often staffed by party supporters, friends or relations. By reducing the powers of the Seanad and making it little more than a talking shop, Fianna Fáil was well on the way to making the chamber a corporate State body instead of the cradle of Irish democracy, as the Constitution meant it to be.

On the morning after the Dáil was dissolved, a devastated Brian Cowen woke up knowing in his heart that he would in all likelihood be remembered as the most unpopular Taoiseach in the history of the State. It's easy to imagine him being in denial about how really inept a leader he was. As well as refusing to accept responsibility for being one of the main architects of Ireland's nightmare recession, he had overseen the collapse of Irish sovereignty following the embarrassing IMF bailout.

But those close to him believed he would be remembered in the long term, when the history of the period had been written, in a far more complimentary way. 'I'm absolutely convinced that history will be a lot kinder to him than the perception of him today. He took the decisions that needed to be taken and I think he saved us from a much more difficult meltdown,' says Batt O'Keeffe. It is hard to recall those decisions, only the needs that were not fulfilled; harder still to imagine a more terrible meltdown. This judgment by Batt O'Keeffe is perceptive and probably correct. Cowen was neither bad nor wicked; he was clumsy, inept and wrong-headed. He was not up to the crisis that defeated him. This makes our final judgment a sad one.

Today it is hard to believe that this was the same man whose appointment only 30 months previously had been met with an overwhelming wave of euphoria not only from the traditional Fianna Fáil supporters but also from a significant percentage of the media and the public at large. They believed Cowen—someone perceived as having no skeletons in his closet before the disclosure of his uncomfortably close connections with the disgraced Seánie FitzPatrick—could start the cleansing process and rid the party of its image of sleaze and corruption brought on by cosy cronyism with developers and bankers.

When he first became Taoiseach, Cowen believed that having 'served that apprenticeship' since his first election to the Dáil at 24 years of age, having risen through the ranks, he had the vital experience to ensure his tenure as leader would be a smooth one without any embarrassing faux pas. 'If you look at politicians who had talent and who got immediate elevation to high office, many of them without experience as backbenchers, they ended up in some political trouble, for whatever reason, and I think part of the reason was not having served their apprenticeship,' Cowen said.

In the wake of his departure, Cowen seemed sure of being recorded in the annals of modern Irish political history as another flawed and compromised Fianna Fáil leader, worse than Charles Haughey or Bertie Ahern. All three men, however, were found guilty of having dubious links with wealthy private citizens. The history books might paint a simplistic picture of Cowen, resigning after coming under insurmountable pressure following his failure to reshuffle his Cabinet, a change that was blocked by the Greens. But his Achilles' heel was his uncomfortably close relationship with bankers involved in questionable practices now the subject of police investigation. It was his misrepresentation of his knowledge about Anglo Irish Bank that brought him down.

In retrospect, there are some close to Cowen who feel that deep down he never saw himself as a two-term Taoiseach. Shortly after the enthusiastic reaction he received from the public during his inaugural homecoming to Offaly as Taoiseach, it was suggested to him that the atmosphere was so positive—not just in Offaly, but generally—that he would win the next election. 'Do you really think so?' he asked, with self-doubt coming through loud and clear in his tone. He then spoke about how he felt the country was going to face hardship. This would clearly suggest that he was acutely aware that there were huge difficulties facing the economy from the moment he took over.

Those close to him sometimes claim that Cowen never really wanted the leadership role, but the truth is that since getting his first taste of political life in the Cabinet under Albert Reynolds, he always aspired to become Taoiseach and leave behind the political legacy of a revered leader. When he was first appointed to this post, those close to him got the distinct impression that he desperately wanted to be remembered as a truly great Irish leader. He came across in those early days as being very concerned about what type of legacy he was going to leave behind. He privately fretted about his disastrous first 100 days in office. He even told friends how he wished a biography of him, which was published shortly after his ascent, had ended when he was appointed Taoiseach rather than charting this nightmare period.

Everything that could possibly go wrong did go wrong for him, but he appeared determined to rectify this and spoke to his advisers during the summer of 2008 about coming out fighting when the Dáil reconvened the following September.

He repeatedly stated that he was placing country before party and talked about being prepared to sacrifice his 'short-term' popularity in an effort to guide the country out of its fiscal back hole. Particularly in the early days of the recession, Cowen was making tough decisions in the sincere hope that the recession would end before the next general election—and ultimately allow him to be perceived as a formidable leader and thus get re-elected.

Cowen was always at his most comfortable when he was debating. He used this skill to its full potential when leading the charge during previous elections. He felt that if he could get to an election campaign, he could turn the tide towards Fianna Fáil and was confident of beating Enda Kenny in debates. This single attribute had an enormous impact on Fianna Fáil members, who saw the asset set against the limited skills of other party members in that sphere of political conflict. He was undoubtedly a strong debater and good on his feet in the Dáil, unlike Kenny, who was old-fashioned, and Gilmore, who was pompous.

He seemed encouraged by the Greens staying with him and by his own dissidents having second thoughts. But this was achieved by an illusory trick with mirrors. The tricks soon came to an end.

His 'Make sure they add up' was the most preposterous war-cry. He spent the greater part of his time as Minister for Finance finding that his own figures did not add up. But in the rough and tumble of the Dáil chamber he was powerful. He presided over a Government in which his appointed replacement, Brian Lenihan, had figures that did not add up at all, so that they set the country on a course towards financial ruin. The figures on the banks did not add up. The markets saw through the Irish Government's trick with mirrors, so that borrowing costs rose. The announcement of the Four-Year Plan did not help. Those were not even the true figures to start with and there was doubt over whether the nation was not still dealing with inbuilt instability. It drained the huge European fund Ireland was forced to take.

Brian Cowen put this behind him, mainly because the details of it were so appalling. The 10 days of incredibly fast and slick transition were over. First, the State was not going to take the bailout. Then the Government divided into those who knew this and the rest. Ministers were not operating a democratic Government at all. Cowen was doing what he did best, though it always failed in the end: taking the law into his own hands, against the best interests of the Irish people, and implementing that law his way. Despite grave misgivings, he established the inevitability of financial help and moved on to executing the Four-Year Plan.

Brian Cowen looked to Bill Clinton as an inspiration for his own tenure as leader. Cowen read 'a lot about his various policy think tanks' and studied the former American President's dip in popularity and how he somehow managed to turn it around and win a second term in office. Cowen explains:

Bill Clinton is a very interesting case study of how you adapt to the change in circumstances of being in office. This whole idea of triangulation, as they call it, where he took some of his opposition components and adapted himself to his own purposes, thereby sort of cutting out the opposition's attack, particularly after the first Congressional elections when he lost the House and the Senate.... How he recovered his presidency after an uncertain start in his first 12 or 18 months and then grafted onto that a second tenure was very interesting.

But despite everything, after only a year in office, Cowen was starting to look like a neophyte politician rather than a seasoned professional. As time went on, he appeared to be either the most unlucky or, as many of his detractors believed, the least capable political leader since Fine Gael's Michael Noonan, who was ousted within his first year of taking up the mantle.

But Cowen hung on as Fianna Fáil leader until the bitter end in January 2011, which was undoubtedly the most difficult month not only of his political career but also in his personal life. His dramatic resignation occurred only days before the anniversary of his father's death. Ber Cowen, a member of the Dáil at the time, had died suddenly from a brain haemorrhage at the relatively young age of 51 years. Brian Cowen reached that age in January 2011. Cowen no doubt was struggling with the morbid thoughts of how he was the same age as his father when he was tragically cut down in his prime. Many of those close to Cowen believe him to have a death complex; while others close to him have often spoken about him being prone to melancholy.

Hardly anybody perceives Cowen as lacking confidence. Yet those close to him say they found him deep down to be a shy individual in social circumstances, which is in complete contrast to the description of him as the 'Rottweiler of the Dáil'. He certainly possessed a vicious tongue in debates. He managed to hide his innate shyness thanks to his brilliant public speaking skills, which he learned in boarding school. He is also insecure about his looks, which Ian Paisley Snr once cruelly remarked on. He would often admit himself that he wasn't the 'best-looking bloke' or words to that effect. Nor did there ever appear to be any great ego with Cowen; he always came across as down-to-earth. His modesty was evident when Jason O'Toole approached him about a biography.

'Why would you want to do a book on me?'

'Because you're now the Taoiseach and leader of the biggest political party in the country. People want to know about you.' He was genuinely surprised by the notion that he was worthy of a book. Cowen once told a journalist: 'Thankfully, I don't have many enemies—if any. I don't think I have any enemies, actually. Maybe some would think ill of me,' he paused to laugh, before adding, 'but I don't have any enemies.' It's doubtful that he would be of the same opinion today and is probably

of the increasingly paranoid belief that he has many 'enemies' whom he
believes contributed to his downfall. But he is always sanguine about
his fall from grace. After his resignation, he was drinking in the Dáil bar
when one punter approached him and said he was sorry to see him
resign. Cowen shrugged and replied: 'That's politics.' He then added: 'It
was the Greens who brought me down.'

Technically, Cowen was correct—it was the Greens' decision to pull
the plug that ended the coalition—but it was only the final straw in a
series of astonishing events. This book is the account of them.

When once asked about making mistakes in life, Cowen responded:

> Okay, let's look at it straightforward [*sic*]: there are times when we
> don't live up to our best. That happens in life with everyone. It
> happens in all walks of life. Get up and say, 'I'll try to avoid that next
> time.' At the end of the day, we are all human, we are all fallible.
> There are times when we did things that we wouldn't be the
> proudest of. There are times when you should have been a bit bigger
> about things—that will happen—but you've got to be honest with
> yourself in those situations. Acknowledge it when it happens.

Unfortunately, Cowen did not adhere to his own aforementioned
advice.

The end of the party began when a once-great organisation failed to
see the disease growing within itself and was helpless in the face of the
damage that derived from that blindness. The illness took hold when,
after the first major defeat under Brian Cowen, the Lisbon Treaty
referendum, he declared his intention of reversing the people's
decision. This meant telling lies and inventing reasons for the defeat.
The Government wanted answers that would satisfy Europe and
convince them that the vote could be changed. After that it became an
epidemic, as one mistake followed another. There was a period of
remission in the second half of 2008 before the raging fever of the
banking crisis and the Bank Guarantee. In the final stages of the
disease, the opinion polls steadily recorded the decline in Fianna Fáil's
popularity. The party's health deteriorated rapidly, despite the
changeover from a No Vote to a Yes Vote. The emigration of young and
old, the export of deposits, the decline in employment, the

intransigence of vested interests all provided the opportunity for those in power to present themselves as battling to put right the wrongs they had done.

No one believed any longer what the Fianna Fáil party and its leaders said. People watched in horrified disbelief as those they had elected deserted and betrayed them. The introduction of banking legislation and the creation of the organisation called NAMA involved cloak-and-dagger events, secretive legislation, furtive management, covert takeovers that destroyed the lives and properties of the one-time heroes of Ireland's bubble development. They had become the hated human source of empty housing estates, half-finished buildings, gaunt and haunting sites of property dereliction. They had also become the scapegoats in the economic decline and collapse of Ireland. Even greater secrecy surrounded the deal with Europe to sink us into unsustainable debt.

Scapegoating became the final and miserable pursuit of the Fianna Fáil party and the Government in the 2008–10 period. It derived from too close a relationship between an extravagantly expensive property development industry, now largely discredited, and the politicians who had made the whole thing possible.

This approach, unfortunately for Ireland, was not limited to the economy. The Fianna Fáil party, in Government for too long and governing badly for much of the past decade, followed the same principle of bypassing the people in respect of at least the following key issues and there may be more.

Firstly, over the power and misbehaviour of the Church it entirely misjudged the misguided investigation of child sexual abuse in the industrial schools, of diocesan abuse, of the largely inadequate measures taken by the Church. The Government provided inadequate legislation or backing for the investigation of diocesan abuse and prevaricated over wider legislative amendments and on the better protection of children.

Secondly, over Europe, Brian Cowen went immediately against the elective will of the people (in June 2008 in the first Lisbon referendum), using outrageous exaggerations and misrepresentations to reverse that vote.

Thirdly, over Health, it removed too much of its operation from

Oireachtas supervision. It did the same with a multitude of other public responsibilities, setting up administration by directorates not properly answerable to those who pay for them and who used to be able to question their practices and mistakes.

Fourthly, it consistently attempted to construct pay deals with the unions which threatened competitiveness. This was done outside the necessary monitoring by the Houses of the Oireachtas and to the disadvantage of a large part of the population not in membership or represented at such talks. The fourth was of significance in the context of topicality, and it reopened an issue between Government, unions and management which supposedly should have been sorted out in 2009 but came to grief and collapsed.

In due course all else collapsed and the people woke up to the disaster that had governed their lives for far too long. The electorate acted accordingly and a new era dawned. How long it will last and how successful it will be is in the lap of the gods.

Also in the lap of the gods is the future, even the survival, of Fianna Fáil. The party elected a successor to Brian Cowen who had been part of the problem and who has made little reference to what went wrong and how the future for the party will be different. Of the other three candidates for leadership, Brian Lenihan, Mary Hanafin and Eamon Ó Cuív, the first is now dead, the second out of politics and the third committed, as a point of principle, in his loyalty to Micheál Martin.

There is a Brian Lenihan postscript to these dying episodes of Fianna Fáil's life in modern Irish politics. It shows the decency of the man and the way in which people and circumstances betrayed him. Lenihan felt he was 'threatened' into the bailout by Trichet with the withdrawal of emergency liquidity funding. 'There was incredible pressure and he insisted Ireland would need to accept a bailout,' Lenihan's former adviser Dr Alan Ahearne said. 'Two weeks before he died, we sat for coffee, and he told me that on the Friday evening [three days] before Dermot Ahern made his infamous "fiction" remark, the ECB contacted him directly and threatened that if he did not request a bailout, they would cut off funding immediately to Ireland,' former Minister of State Billy Kelleher recalled.

Before his death, Lenihan told those close to him that he had letters from the president of the European Central Bank, Jean-Claude Trichet, that would vindicate him in the mind of the Irish people. The letters explained his role in the bailout and the pressures he was put under. He said he had been reluctant to release them during a period when Michael Noonan was negotiating for a reduction in the interest rate. He explained to those close to him: 'It might affect what they [the present Government] are trying to do in Europe. So I won't let them out.'

The details are simple enough. The night before the Irish Central Bank Governor, Patrick Honohan, went on national radio to announce the news of an offer of a bailout, Brian Lenihan was sitting in the Dáil canteen. It was around nine o'clock. One of his assistants came in and said that the Central Bank Governor wished to speak to him immediately. Lenihan left and was away for half an hour. When he returned he said: 'The Governor of the Central Bank wants me to arrange a Cabinet meeting tonight. I could not possibly do it. I don't have the right to call a Cabinet meeting.' Nor would he have been able to contact all the Cabinet members. He also said he was being 'bullied' into accepting a bailout.

He went on to add that the Governor was in Frankfurt and was planning to go on 'Morning Ireland' to announce the offer of a bailout package. This offer of a bailout weakened Lenihan's hand, preparing the way for the EU intervention in the Irish economy, not for Ireland's sake but to restore confidence in the Eurozone banking system. This was extraordinary: the Governor of the Central Bank pre-empting a non-existent Cabinet decision because the Cabinet could not be called together at nine o'clock at night in order to authorise the arrival of the IMF team alongside members of the European Commission and the ECB. And so, as the news broke, the Central Bank's Governor revealed on RTÉ's breakfast news programme that he anticipated a 'loan will be made available' of tens of billions. Only days before this, Cowen and members of his Government had maintained that there was no question of them being involved in discussions about an ECB/IMF bailout.

One ex-Minister who was sitting with Brian Lenihan that night says that Lenihan pointed out: 'Our Governor was a member of the board of the European Central Bank because he was Governor here of the Central Bank. He was a de facto member. They were doing a pincer job on Ireland because Ireland was slow to go looking for the bailout. We were forced.' The ECB, through Honohan, was forcing the Irish Minister for Finance to accept the bailout. The only fallback position that Brian Lenihan and Brian Cowen had in mind was to get a limited type of loan. Though widely known, and from other sources, this direct explanation from the man whose own Central Bank Governor, acting on behalf of the ECB, had handed over the keys to Irish sovereignty was made only in private.

Honohan put it differently in his 'Morning Ireland' interview, which, according to Lenihan, he had insisted he had to give, whether or not there was a Cabinet meeting.

The Governor of the Central Bank was acting in a dual role quite legally. Under the EU Treaties—and specifically the Maastricht Treaty— the Irish Central Bank is one of what is called the 'European System of Central Banks' (ESCB). Once appointed by their respective national governments, the national Central Bank Governors owe their primary allegiance to the ECB and the ESCB under the EU Treaties, which have the force of constitutional law in Ireland as part of the Irish Constitution. Honohan was in effect telling the Irish Government and Lenihan what to do on the night before the infamous bailout. Lenihan may not have realised this or possibly the full extent of it, though Honohan's radio interview would have brought it home to him. No one sitting with him that night would have known it.

Honohan's broadcast effectively paved the way for the arrival in Ireland of a team from the ECB/IMF/EU. The position of the Government was even more extraordinary. Instead of Brian Lenihan, the man in charge, explaining the situation, Brian Cowen spoke to the press the afternoon of the Honohan interview. He said the Central Bank Governor 'is entitled to give his view of the outcome of talks with European officials and the IMF'. This was inconsistent with what had passed between the Governor and the Minister for Finance the previous evening and did not reflect the fact that Honohan was giving the decision of European officials, the ECB and the IMF, clearly stating that the loan would go ahead.

Cowen said Honohan's responsibility 'is to get the best possible outcome for the country and taxpayers'. This was far from being the case. His main responsibility was to protect the ECB and the Eurozone. Representing Ireland's interests was secondary. In effect this was a denial of what Brian Cowen had said, that 'there was no question of loss of sovereignty for Ireland as a result of the talks'. The question of the people feeling 'ashamed or humiliated' was not one Cowen or anyone else could answer. Only a referendum could do that.

Cowen was right when he said that 'the talks are about stabilising the euro, and dealing with serious market conditions that were [*sic*] affecting all countries'. This, however, cost Ireland dearly over the whole period 2008–11. He denied he was talking in riddles; yet there was denial of transparency about who had made the decision. Two things are certain: it was not Cowen, the Government or the Minister for Finance who made the decision to bring in the IMF and the ECB, and it was done before the required Cabinet meeting that Brian Lenihan could not call. The facts deriving from the details surrounding Brian Lenihan's exchanges with Patrick Honohan the night before the 'Morning Ireland' interview reveal only that the initiative came from Honohan, who insisted on making them public in the way described here. The officials—known as the Triarchy or Troika—had already arrived and began the process of taking over Ireland's economy, which is now controlled, with weekly reporting, from Brussels.

All this, as we have said, was legal. It had the appearance, and in specific terms the reality, of Honohan being more powerful than the Irish Government. His power had been established 18 years earlier, through the Maastricht Treaty. Though Ireland had never faced its implementation in such stark terms, Honohan's primary obligation, in law, is to the ECB. It appears the country was being ordered to cede sovereignty and accept the bailout. The Lisbon Treaty and the Maastricht Treaty embody the powers to do this.

Though the action taken by Honohan may not have been envisaged at the time of the enactment of the provision, in 1992, in the Maastricht Treaty, Ireland had said yes in the Maastricht Treaty referendum. This fiscal regulation was changed only marginally in the Lisbon Treaty, with the term 'European Union' substituted for 'the European Community'. Ireland took no notice of it at the time, in 1992, because it was otherwise concerned with adding an Abortion Protocol to the Maastricht Treaty. Nor was there much concern then about abolishing the Irish currency and adopting the euro.

The unanswerable questions are these: Did Brian Lenihan know how powerful his Central Bank Governor was when he took the phone call? Did he know that calling a Cabinet meeting was irrelevant? A further question, about Patrick Honohan, is, however, answerable: What did he mean when he said on 'Morning Ireland':

> All I'll say is there has been such a need [for a loan to Ireland], but I don't want you to press me on these things, because I'm not allowed to talk about these things. I'd have to make sure, just in case I sound as if I'm exceeding my powers, I would have to make sure that the other members of the ECB, the governors, don't object to making these loans because that's always on a case-by-case basis. Of course if I ask them, they would not object.

But he elected to speak. He was free to speak. What he said clearly indicated that his ECB colleagues had already agreed and their team was already in Ireland. So why this?

Perhaps the worst aspect of Fianna Fáil rule, during the period in which its standing collapsed and its defeat became inevitable, was the savagery with which it turned on those the party had favoured and petted during the Celtic Tiger. Builders, developers, speculators, businessmen, bankers, financiers, the whole crew of wealthy people who had supported the party and in many cases had been favoured by it, became undesirables. Where possible they were made scapegoats, in the case of developers through the draconian NAMA legislation, designed to strip them of all they had and all they had made.

Bankers were more wily. Instead of being the victims, the strong ones were able to victimise those in power, running rings round the Minister for Finance and the Taoiseach and helping to plunder the State's assets.

As Phil Hogan of Fine Gael put it in May 2011:

> It's outrageous what has gone on in the banking system and there certainly needs to be an investigation of all the matters in all the banks to make sure that we don't have these problems again and that we have proper regulatory structures in place, that we're making sure that these policy decisions that are made by Government and by financial institutions won't bring about a

situation where we have to go back to the IMF in the near future .... I can't see any tribunal but I can see a robust and properly resourced Dáil committee investigating these matters.

Among those blamed was David Drumm, which brings us back to where we started. By November 2010, when the authors of this book wrote about Drumm and Anglo Irish Bank, he was already a bankrupt appearing in a Boston courtroom. The Irish State was attempting to become involved in the court proceedings for what Drumm believed was little else than a publicity stunt. 'They would not take repayment when I begged them to. They wanted Optics.'

Drumm fought the case as well as tried to settle. The bank did not want to settle. The thinking—part of the scapegoating policy of the Government—was that the hot pursuit of bankers made for good spin. They would not take repayment when Drumm proposed it. They were prepared to engage in unnecessary public expenditure in order to present the image of the Irish State in pursuit of bankers and developers. Drumm, who knew a bit about the cost of such actions, estimated that the unnecessary pursuit of publicity in the cause of bringing one banker to book had cost the State €6 million. Drumm claims what was done against him was wasteful and cynical, and seems also to have been vindictive. It appears to have involved two very expensive law firms, one in Boston and one in Chicago, and all this came at a high cost to taxpayers in Ireland.

These were days out for the media. The pursuit of Drumm by many newspapers in Ireland and by RTÉ radio and television was squalid and prejudicial. It had become a kind of blood sport. As Drumm said, in the late glow of Fianna Fáil's last enjoyment of this kind of power, 'There should be a portrait of me on the wall of Fianna Fáil headquarters, they've got so much value out of me!' He called it an 'Oppression for Optics' strategy, the same force that inspired and nurtured NAMA. Anglo Irish Bank was behaving in this manner to its customers, thereby causing legal issues and value destruction in every direction.

This was done for, and against, the same people who had, once upon a time, frequented and fraternised in the Galway Tent, their harmony false and shallow. As David Drumm said of all this: 'Poor Ireland'.

INDEX

Fig references refer to the plate section.